The Threshold Level

for Modern Language Learning in Schools

Council of Europe

1976

The Threshold Level

for Modern Language Learning in Schools

Dr. J. A. van Ek

Department of English/University of Groningen

with contributions by L. G. Alexander

Longman

Text © Council of Europe, Strasbourg 1976

Layout © Wolters–Noordhoff–Longman, Groningen, The Netherlands 1977

This edition first published by Longman Group Ltd., 1977

ISBN 0 582 55700 3

Printed in Great Britain by
Butler & Tanner Ltd., Frome and London

Contents

Preface

The present study is based on the author's earlier publication, *The Threshold-Level in a European Unit/Credit System for Modern Language Learning by Adults*, Strasbourg, 1975. For the extent of his indebtedness to contributions by numerous colleagues the reader is referred to the introduction to the earlier document. In preparing the present study the author has again benefited from the encouragement and advice generously provided by a great many government officials, teachers and researchers in several European countries. He would like to express his gratitude to those who organized meetings for him and to all those who participated in them. Without these consultations it would not have been possible to give the "threshold level" the form in which it is now presented. The author can only hope that when reading the present document all those who in any way contributed to it will feel their advice has not been wasted. He also hopes they will forgive him for not referring to them individually. A full list would contain so many names that this preface would have to cover several pages. Special thanks, however, are due to the Austrian Ministry of Education, who, in the best European spirit, have once again taken the lead in initiating practical experimentation. The author would also like to thank the Dutch Minister of Education and his staff for enabling him to carry out his present task. Without the facilities provided by them *The Threshold Level for Schools* would not have been written.

The author is particularly indebted to the Schools Council Modern Languages Project of the University of York, whose draft examination syllabuses, made available to him by Mr. Antony Peck, have provided some of the behavioural specifications used in the present document. He would also like to thank Mr. L. G. Alexander for permission to include the "structural inventory" originally prepared by him for the "threshold level for adults". A further contribution by Mr. Alexander is added as a supplement. It constitutes the first major analysis of various methodological implications of the approach used in *The Threshold Level*, some of which are summarily dealt with in the study itself (1.4). Strictly speaking, a document devoted to the specification of an objective is not the right place to deal with methodology. Yet, if an objective is to be considered for incorporation into educational curricula, insight into the problems involved in enabling learners to reach this objective is obviously required. Mr. Alexander's contribution on the subject should provide at least some of this insight.

Bussum, March 1976   Jan. A. van Ek

0 Introduction

0.1 European background

Although at times it may seem as if the European community is characterized by diversity rather than unity, there are broad areas where an increasing convergence of views and attitudes may be observed. In these areas the same ideas tend to develop simultaneously and in similar fashion in several places in different countries, so that it would seem to be justified to speak of a European development rather than of a multitude of national ones. One of these areas is education. Although emphases may differ from one country to another there is a remarkable degree of agreement as to the roles of education, the rights to education, and the forms in which educational opportunities are to be offered. Educational reforms in several countries tend to follow parallel lines and there is a growing awareness of the benefits to be derived from mutual consultation, exchange of views and experiences, and intensified collaboration. It is not surprising that, in an endeavour to promote European unity and coordination in the field of education, foreign language learning should have been given special attention.

Even as early as 1954, when the European Cultural Convention was signed in Paris by the representatives of the member states of the Council of Europe, it was agreed that foreign language study was to be promoted because "a greater understanding of one another among the peoples of Europe" would further the Council's aim, which was the achievement "of a greater unity between its Members". Since then successive conferences of European Ministers of Education have reaffirmed this decision, stating that knowledge of foreign languages is to be considered "indispensable both for the individual and for Europe as a whole" and emphasizing "that ways and means should be devised of extending the teaching of modern languages to the greatest extent possible to children and adults to whom it is not yet given".

Foreign language teaching, we may conclude, is one of the educational priorities of European governments. At the same time it is the subject *par excellence* for international cooperation in education. Whatever the ulterior aims of foreign language teaching all member states of the Council of Europe recognize at least one common aim, which is the ability to *use* the foreign language in one way or another. Moreover, foreign language teachers are, by virtue of their subject, more apt to look beyond national boundaries for enlightenment, guidance and teaching-materials than teachers of many other subjects.

0.2   Concrētization

What proved to be the most significant concrete step towards the implementation of the decisions made by the European Ministers of Education with regard to foreign language teaching was the constitution in 1971 by the Council for Cultural Cooperation of a small multinational group of experts who were invited to examine the feasibility of the development of a unit/ credit system for foreign language learning by adults as proposed by a Council of Europe symposium held in the same year. The work of this group has meanwhile resulted in a number of fundamental studies and practical applications. Because of the fundamental place of objectives in any learning-system the highest priority was given to the development of a model for the specification of foreign language learning objectives and to the application of this model in the construction of at least one objective. In order to give the work of the group the widest possible relevance it was decided to choose the objective which was likely to appeal to the largest single group of potential adult learners, those who would wish to be able to communicate non-professionally with foreign language speakers in everyday situations on topics of general interest. These learners, it was felt, would not only wish to be able to survive, linguistically speaking, as tourists in a foreign country, or in contacts with foreign visitors to their own country, but they would also require the ability to establish and maintain social relations of however superficial a kind. The attempt to define for this class of learners what they would minimally need to be able to do in the foreign language resulted in the specification of what has since come to be known as the "threshold level", developed by the present author and exemplified for English.

0.3   Application to school-education

After publication of the "threshold level" the Committee for General and Technical Education convened a meeting of experts on foreign language learning and teaching with a view to examining the potential of this objective for school education. This meeting resulted in a request to the present author to undertake the development of an objective for foreign language learning in compulsory education comparable to the threshold level previously developed for adult education. This objective, it was decided, would

1. be such as to enable the great majority of pupils to reach it;
2. correspond to a minimum level of proficiency;
3. make possible communication, especially oral communication, with children or adults in the language studied;
4. be based on the exploitation of everyday real-life situations;
5. include a methodological initiation which would, on the one hand, facilitate continued study of the language and, on the other hand, make it possible to acquire a sufficient understanding of the learning-processes used, so that these may be profitably applied to the study of other languages.

0.4   Relevance

The request was of particular interest because, if it would prove to be possible to define in terms of the model constructed for the unit/credit system for adult education a basic objective acceptable to the various member states of the Council of Europe, this would serve a variety of purposes:

1. it would provide the great majority of pupils in a very large part of Europe with an objective in terms of practical communicative ability;
2. it would give meaningful direction to foreign language teaching and contribute to increased efficiency and motivating power;
3. it would be a basis for the harmonization of foreign language teaching in the member states of the Council of Europe;
4. it would form a foundation for international cooperation in educational innovation, the production of learning-materials, tests, the exchange of experiences, the conduct of experimentation, etc. etc., on a hitherto unprecedented scale;
5. it would fall within the same system as that developed for adult education and thus fulfil an essential condition for the implementation of any scheme of permanent education or recurrent education;
6. as a low-level objective in its own right it would provide a useful learning-aim for pupils unable to receive more than a minimum – say three years – of instruction in a foreign language;
7. it would enable curriculum-planning, particularly the definition of successive terminal objectives, to start at the logical end, i.e. at the lowest objective, rather than starting at the highest – academic – objective and derive lower objectives by means of a process of elimination.

0.5   Feasibility

One question of special importance, and crucial to the whole project, was that of feasibility. Would it be feasible to define one single foreign language learning objective which would be equally relevant to countries as far apart as Norway and Italy, England and Austria? Would it be possible to make a principled selection of situations, topics, etc., which might be acceptable in each of these countries as probably the most useful choice for their learners? An additional complication was that the objective would have to be formulated in such a way that it would apply to a variety of languages, at least the languages most commonly used in the member states of the Council of Europe. Finally, the objective would have to be relevant to children of various age-groups: in some countries foreign language learning begins at a considerably younger age than in others.

The question of multinational relevance of one and the same objective was easily settled by eliciting reactions from groups of language-teaching experts in some ten different countries to one and the same provisional list of selected items. Somewhat surprisingly there were hardly any negative reactions to the selection proposed except for the almost general wish that the flexibility inherent in the model should be made more explicit.

The non-language-specificity of the definition, in the sense that it can be used for a variety of different languages, has meanwhile been demonstrated for the parallel version for adults, where on the basis of the master specification and the English exemplification, draft versions for various other languages have been successfully developed.

A more difficult requirement is that the objective should be relevant to children of different age-groups. It has been attempted to satisfy this requirement by introducing the possibilities of strictly controlled adaptation of the objective, so that it may be adapted to the needs and interests of different age-groups without affecting the general communicative ability which is the essential aim of the specification.

0.6   Presentation

In this volume we present the full specification of the "threshold level for schools" as a basic foreign language learning objective for compulsory education. Chapter 1 describes the model used in the specification, the choices made in the selection of items, the place the objective may be given in a curriculum, and methodological implications of the principles underlying the objective. Chapter 2 presents the objective itself, with exemplification for English. Chapter 4 contains a lexical index, a structural inventory and a grammatical survey of the language-forms used in the English exemplification.

1 The development of the objective

1.1 The model

1.1.1 Behavioural objectives

The basic characteristic of the model used in our definition is that it tries to specify foreign language ability as *skill* rather than *knowledge*. It analyses what the learner will have to be able to *do* in the foreign language and determines only in the second place what *language-forms* (words, structures, etc.) the learners will have to be able to handle in order to *do* all that has been specified. In accordance with the nature of verbal communication as a form of *behaviour* the objectives defined by means of this model are therefore basically *behavioural* objectives. To preclude misunderstanding it should perhaps be pointed out right at the beginning of our presentation that a behavioural specification of an objective by no means implies the need for a behaviouristic teaching-method. The way in which the objective has been defined does not impose any particular methodology – behaviouristic or otherwise – on the teacher.

1.1.2 Explicitness

Objectives defined by means of the present model have a high degree of *explicitness*. Yet, they are not explicit in an absolute sense. Language learning objectives can never be defined with absolute explicitness because language-use is neither fully predictable (except perhaps in the most restricted situations) nor fully describable. Nevertheless, definitions based on our model are more explicit than most definitions of language learning objectives. This has obvious advantages in that it gives all those involved in the teaching/learning process, including the learner himself, a clear view of just what is expected of them. The result of this should be a considerable increase of efficiency.

1.1.3 Functions and notions

In essence, the model is a very simple one, in that it analyses verbal behaviour into only two components: the performance of *language-functions* and the expression of, or reference to, *notions*. What people do by means of language can be described as verbally performing certain *functions*. By means of language people assert, question, command, expostulate, persuade, apologize, etc. etc. In performing such functions people express, refer to or – to use a more general term – "handle" certain notions. They will, for instance, apologize for *being late*, for being late for a *party*, for being late for a party *yesterday*, etc. etc. Other *notions* are less directly correlated with lexical items, e.g. the notion of "possession", which may be expressed by means of a verb (*have*, *possess*, etc.), but also by means of a prepositional construction (*of* + nominal group), a genitive case or a possessive pronoun.

Our task, then, in defining a language learning objective, is to determine what language-functions the learners will have to be able to perform and what notions they will have to be able to handle.

1.1.4 Determining factors

It will be obvious that we can only perform our task if we have some insight into what may be expected to be the communication needs of the learner. This, in turn, would seem to depend very much on the learner himself, on the type of contacts he may be expected to have which necessitate the use of a foreign language. The first step towards the specification of an objective is, therefore, the selection of a target-group and a general characterization of the type of foreign language contacts its members may be expected to engage in. Subsequently we attempt to describe the nature of these contacts more precisely. We may determine whether the learners will be expected to have mainly (or even exclusively) *oral* contacts or *written* contacts, whether they will use the foreign language mainly (or exclusively) *receptively*, as listeners or readers, or also *productively*, as speakers or writers. In other words, we determine the *language-activities* the learners are expected to engage in. We may also determine *where* they may be expected to use the foreign language. Especially for target-groups with restricted (e.g. professional) needs this may be highly relevant. If a telephone operator is expected to use a foreign language almost exclusively in front of a switchboard, this *setting* is obviously an important factor in determining what language-functions she will have to fulfil and what notions she will have to handle. Another factor is the *roles* the learner may have to play. Will he have to be able to play mainly subordinate roles or will he have to command, to instruct? Apart from these *social roles* we may distinguish *psychological roles*. A "gentle persuader's" language-needs will, to a certain extent, differ from those of a "bully", to mention two extremes. Then, of course, the *topics* the learner may be expected to deal with will have an important influence on, particularly, the notions he will have to be able to handle. It will make a lot of difference whether a learner will deal mainly with the topic of public transport, as a railway employee may do, or with the topic of health, ailments, accidents, as may be the case with a nurse. To a certain extent we can integrate the various factors mentioned above by specifying for each topic just what the learner may be expected to *do* with regard to it. This relates language-activities, settings and roles directly to the topics.

To sum up: we determine what language-functions the learner will have to be able to fulfil and what notions he will have to be able to handle on the basis of:

-   a general characterization of the type of language-contacts which, as a member of a certain target-group, he will engage in;
-   the language-activities he will engage in;
-   the settings in which he will use the foreign language;
-   the roles (social and psychological) he will play;
-   the topics he will deal with;
-   what he will be expected to do with regard to each topic.

It goes without saying that, except in extreme cases, our decisions with regard to each component will only be based on estimates. We cannot possibly predict with certainty exactly what a learner is going to do with a foreign language once he has mastered it to a certain degree. We can, however, make useful estimates and prepare the learner for those foreign language contacts he is most likely to engage in. Moreover, such is the transfer-potential of linguistic ability, once the learner has been successfully prepared for certain foreign language contacts he will find that he can also cope more or less adequately in numerous other foreign language situations.

If the above components play an important role in determining our choice of language-functions and of notions for a certain objective, they also influence – in many cases even decisively – our choice of *exponents* for the various functions and notions. By exponents we mean the actual language-forms by means of which the learner will fulfil each function and express each notion. It will be obvious that, for instance, the actual *language-forms* the learner will be taught to use in order to fulfil the function "asking others to do something" will depend to a large extent on the social and psychological roles he will be playing. In this respect, too, the specification is learner-oriented in that, in each decision we make, we ask ourselves what is most appropriate to a particular class of learners, what will most adequately satisfy their individual foreign language communication needs.

1.1.5 Common core and specific notions

It cannot be said that each of the above components is equally influential in each choice we make. This applies particularly to the component which we called "topics". Some parts of the specification will be more directly affected by our selection of particular topics than others. The linguistic needs for asking, inviting, apologizing – in short, for the functions – will be less stringently determined by the choice of a particular topic than those for expressing certain concrete notions. Whether the learner will need to be able to express the notion "peanut-butter" or the notion "airport" will depend more directly on the situations he will find himself in, particularly the topics he will deal with, than the need to refer to past, future, present or to say whether something is located before, behind, under or above something else. This is a reason for making another subdivision in our specification. We subdivide the notions into general notions and specific notions. The specific notions are those that are directly determined by our choice of individual topics, whereas the general notions are appropriate to a large variety of topics, to a large variety of situations. This generality with respect to the topics also characterizes the language-functions. We can therefore group the language-functions and the general notions together and refer to them as the "common core", to distinguish them from the strictly topic-related specific notions.

We have now successively made the following subdivisions in our intended specification:

a	language-functions	notions	

b	language-functions	general notions	specific notions

c	common core		specific notions
	language-functions	general notions	

1.1.6   Variability

The last subdivision offers the clue to the reconciliation of the need for comprehensive learning-systems and the individual requirements of a variety of sub-groups within a target population. The organization of large-scale learning systems is, on the whole, only practically viable if (potential) learners can be grouped together into large target-groups. All the members of such target-groups will show the same general characteristics and will have the same overall language needs. Yet, the larger the target-group, the greater the differences in specific needs and interests will be. In other words, a large target-group will inevitably consist of a number of sub-groups whose needs and interests are largely identical but at the same time in some respects significantly different.

The distinction within the specification of an objective between a common core and a category of specific notions makes it possible to adapt an objective for a large target-group to the requirements of each individual sub-group within this target-group without changing its identity in any essential way. It simply means that, with perhaps certain minor reservations, the common core will be the same for all members of the overall target-group but that the category of specific notions will be adapted to the needs and interests of each individual sub-group by replacing certain topics from which they have been derived by other topics and making the corresponding changes in the specific notions. Thus the overall communicative ability as specified in the objective will be common to all learners, both in level and in range, but certain sub-groups will be more competent in dealing with certain topics than other sub-groups, and the reverse. We shall make use of this feature of our model in the development of one single objective for our target-population, pupils in compulsory education, exploiting those needs they have in common and simultaneously making full allowance for the heterogeneity of various sub-groups within our target-population.

1.2 The application

1.2.1 Task

The application of the model in the construction of an objective involves making a number of successive choices. As described in 1.1 these choices have to be made with regard to:

- target-group
- language-activities
- settings
- roles
- topics
- language-functions
- general notions
- specific notions
- exponents

The choices to be made in the specification of the present objective were partly dictated by the brief the author was given.

The target-group was to be "the great majority of pupils in compulsory education". The language-activities were to be "especially oral communication". The specification was to be "based on the exploitation of everyday real-life situations", which places constraints on the selection of topics. The level of the objective was to be "a minimum level of proficiency". Finally, the objective was to be "comparable to the threshold level previously developed for adult education".

1.2.2 Procedure

In view of the last condition the obvious way to set about the construction of the required objective was to examine the threshold-level specification for adults and to determine to what extent it could simply be copied in the

specification of the new objective and where the two objectives would have
to differ from each other. In the following sections we shall deal with each of
the items mentioned in 1.2.1. successively.

1.2.3   Target-group

It was clear from the start that, in spite of obvious differences in age and,
probably, interests, the target-group for which the original threshold level
had been developed and "the great majority of pupils in compulsory education" had very much in common. In the "threshold level for adults" the
members of the target-group were characterized as follows:

1. they would be temporary visitors to the foreign country (especially tourists); or:
2. they would have temporary contacts with foreigners in their own
   country;
3. their contacts with foreign language speakers would, on the whole, be
   of a superficial, non-professional type;
4. they would primarily need only a basic level of command of the foreign
   language.

This characterization seemed to fit the new target-group as well as the one
for which it was first set up. Perhaps the parenthetic addition to the first
characteristic could be omitted, but apart from this it seemed to apply to
the large majority of school-children and adolescents as well as to adults.
This conclusion was hardly surprising since in both cases we were dealing
with beginners needing a minimum general proficiency in a foreign language
with strong emphasis on oral communication.

The main difference between the two target-groups is probably that the
school-pupils are in the process of receiving a general education and that,
hence, foreign language learning would function in a wider educational context. We shall return to this in 1.3, but right now it can be said that this
difference does not necessarily affect the content of the objective as such.
The threshold level is a level of *communicative ability*. The definition of this
objective specifies what the learner can *do* at this level and what *language-
forms* he will be able to handle. Whatever the ulterior aims of foreign language
teaching, communicative ability remains an essential condition. So whether
the learner only learns in order to communicate or also in order to achieve
more comprehensive aims, a specification of what is needed in order to communicate is equally required in both cases.

If the characterization appears to fit both target-groups, there is one
characteristic which, according to several consultants, should be added to
those of the school-population. They pointed out that although in a minimum
objective for the first foreign language the ability to use the language orally
was of primary importance there was no denying that, especially in more
isolated areas of Europe, the possibilities for establishing foreign language
contacts orally were very much smaller than those for establishing contacts

in writing. We accordingly added one further characterstic to the description of our target-group:

5. their contacts with foreign language speakers will not only be oral contacts but, to a greater or lesser extent, also contacts in writing.

The consequence of this additional characteristic is the extension of the requirements for reading and writing to include the ability to communicate in informal writing in very much the same way as when speaking and listening. This differentiation between the threshold level for adults and the corresponding objective for the school-population may be regrettable from one point of view, but it would be unrealistic not to recognize the very obvious need of many school-children to communicate with "pen-friends" in other countries. Indeed, it is not unlikely that even for the majority of European school-children the chances of establishing early contacts with foreign language speakers by means of correspondence are much greater than those of communicating orally. Since the ability to establish and maintain social contacts in the foreign language is an essential part of the threshold-level objective, the ability to read and to write at least that which the pupils learn for purposes of oral communication must be included even in our minimum objective. Whether this actually involves an increase in the total learning-load is doubtful. Language learning in schools is very rarely, if ever, an exclusively oral activity, and what the pupils learn orally is almost invariably reinforced by written work. Of course, even the writing of an informal letter requires some further ability than just the ability to spell what one would normally speak. A letter-writer lacks immediate feedback from his communication-partner. He has to produce a continuous text and to aim at immediate comprehensibility. This means that he must pay special attention to orderly presentation, paragraphing, etc. However, in the school-situation this particular ability is not primarily acquired during foreign language classes but in native language lessons, and, at least in the culturally fairly homogeneous European community, it has a high transfer potential from one language to another. Where the inclusion of informal letter-writing may cause a somewhat more noticeable increase of the learning-load is in those languages (notably French) where, even at an elementary level, spoken language and written language may favour different language-forms. Even in this case, however, the extra investment of learning-efforts which may be needed seems to be fully justified in view of the obvious needs of the pupils.

It may be asked whether, in view of what is generally current all over Europe, more extensive reading should not also be included in a minimum objective. There are excellent reasons for encouraging this practice right from the beginning of the foreign language learning process. Yet, it does not fall within the general aim of the threshold level, which is "to enable learners to survive, linguistically speaking, in temporary contacts with foreign language speakers in everyday situations, whether as visitors to the foreign country or with visitors to their own country, and to establish and maintain social contacts". That the great majority of schools would wish to place this objective into a richer context does not affect the validity of the objective as such. We shall return to this point in 1.3.

1.2.4   Language-activities

Because the present target-population differs only in characteristic 5 (see 1.2.3) from the target-group for the threshold level for adults there will be no further major difference in the specification of language-activities than what may be derived from this additional characteristic. There may be some minor differences as a result of a slightly less heavy emphasis on the adult tourist's needs. "The ability to read road-sign texts", to give one example, which is explicitly required for the threshold level for adults, will therefore be marked as optional in the corresponding objective for schools.

In spite of the addition of informal letter writing and the reading of such letters, the objective remains essentially an objective for oral communicative ability. This ability, then, will be the fundamental part of the specification of our objective. Reading and writing will be more summarily dealt with and related to the specifications for oral ability.

What the objective is primarily designed for is the ability to carry on a conversation. This involves two skills: speaking and understanding. It will be obvious that the pupils will have to be able to understand much more than what they can say themselves. They can try to express themselves within the limitations of their linguistic command, but they have no such control over what is said to them by others. We can specify with some confidence the ability they will need in order to initiate a conversation on the topics which will be listed, to get things done for them, or to fulfil other language functions. We can only guess at the ability they will need in order to react adequately when others initiate a conversation or respond to their own language-acts. Even if we take into account – as we must – the efforts a native speaker will make in order to make himself understood by a foreigner with only a basic level of command of his language, we shall have to provide the learner with a fairly great receptive ability if he is to maintain himself in a conversation at all. In our specification of language-forms which the learner should be able to handle we shall distinguish between what is considered indispensable for the learner in order to express himself adequately and what is considered essential for understanding only. For a further specification of language-activities the reader is referred to section 2.4.

1.2.5   Settings

The members of our target-group will learn the foreign language for general purposes. This means that the specification of what they will have to learn will not be particularly geared to any special setting or type of setting (as might be the case in specifications for professional purposes). The learner will be expected to use his foreign language ability in such a variety of settings, ranging from a family living-room to an open-air swimming pool, from a post-office to a friend's bed-sitter, that an attempt to enumerate them more or less exhaustively can neither be very successful nor particularly useful.

Those readers who would nevertheless prefer to have some guidance on this point are referred to chapter 5 of the threshold-level specification for adults,[1] where some 90 settings are listed.

1.2.6 Roles

It would be both unrealistic and unnecessary to require that at a minimum level the learner should be able to play any other than the more neutral roles. Although we might like the learner to have the ability to play also more strongly marked roles and to use the highly informal, typically formal, condescending or self-effacing kind of language that might go with them, this is obviously something to be aimed at at higher levels than the minimum level. On the whole, the inclusion of any typically marked language-forms in our specification will be avoided. Although the pupils' language may consequently sound somewhat colourless it will at least save them from committing social blunders through an inappropriate use of strongly marked language-forms.

The roles which, at this level, the learner may be expected to play are the same as those selected for the adult target-group. The principal social roles he should be prepared for are those of *stranger/stranger* and *friend/friend*; the psychological roles those of *neutrality, equality, sympathy, antipathy.*[2]

1.2.7 Topics

It may be expected that the main difference between the threshold level for adults and the corresponding objective for the school-population will be found in the selection of topics and the specification of what the learners will have to be able to do with regard to each topic. It will also be clear that in the choices to be made for this component there will be a stronger element of subjectivity than in the choices for the other components. On the face of it, it may even seem to be an impossible task to determine which topics general learners will be most likely to deal with in a foreign language. Yet, teaching would not be possible unless such a selection were made. Moreover, it appears that where efforts have been made to draw up lists of topics for general learners the results have, on the whole, been very similar in each case. Such lists have been made on the basis of common sense, intuition, introspection, experience. It would appear that on this basis a high degree of consensus might be reached, which would counterbalance the subjectivity of the selection. Such consensus was actually reached with respect to the topic-specification in the threshold level for adults. It consequently seemed to be an appropriate procedure to examine the topic-specification for adults, to retain what was felt to be equally relevant to all general beginners, to modify, replace or eliminate what might be irrelevant to younger learners,

1. J. A. van Ek, *Systems Development in Adult Language Learning, the Threshold Level,* Council for Cultural Cooperation, Council of Europe, Strasbourg 1975.
2. The roles have been selected from a study by R. Richterich: *A Model for the Definition of Language Needs of Adults Learning a Modern Language,* Council of Europe document CCC/EES (72), Strasbourg 1972.

and to add any further elements which might be particularly useful to them. In this adaptation the author was greatly helped by the availability of draft examination syllabuses composed by the Schools Council Modern Languages Project of the University of York. The topic-specifications in these syllabuses provided most of what was needed to adapt the specification for adults to the interests and estimated needs of younger learners. The first results of the adaptation were submitted to foreign language teaching experts in some ten European countries and discussed with them. On the basis of these discussions the specifications were further modified and the flexibility of the objective was made more explicit by marking certain elements as optional (cf. 1.1.5). The final result of this procedure is presented in Chapter 2. If the possibilities for adaptation which it allows are fully exploited it should now be suitable for a wide variety of sub-groups within the overall target-population.

It will be found that certain topics have been retained which would seem to be much more directly relevant to adult learners than to school-children. This is not only the case in the present specification, it is typical of all comparable selections which have previously been made elsewhere. One reason is, of course, that school-education is typically a process which leads to a change of roles. Much of the educational effort aims to prepare the school-child for assuming the role of an adult in an adult society. Another reason is that these topics are of particular importance when visiting the foreign country. If a major aim of foreign language teaching is to enable learners to establish direct contacts with foreign language communities, visits to the foreign country should be encouraged and the pupils should be as well prepared for them as possible. This means that the topics in question may be considered indispensable even in school-education.

1.2.8   Language-functions

The specification of language-functions forms the first part of what is referred to in 1.1.4 as the "common core". The distinction between the common core and the category of topic-derived specific notions was implicitly present in the threshold-level specification for adults but had not been worked out with full consistency. Before developing the present specification, therefore, it was decided first to rearrange the elements of the original threshold level in such a way that a greater consistency in the categorization would be achieved. The list of language-functions resulting from this procedure was then examined for its relevance to younger learners. It appeared that no changes were required apart from the marking of one or two elements as optional. The full list is presented in Chapter 2.

1.2.9   General notions

What was said in 1.2.8 with regard to language-functions applies equally to the second part of the common core, the general notions. Again the reader may be referred to Chapter 2 for the full specification.

1.2.10 Specific notions

The specific notions are derived from the topic-specifications. Consequently, what was said in 1.2.7. forms the basis for the adaptation of the lists of specific notions to the estimated needs and interests of the school-population.

The variability of the objective is especially apparent in this component. It contains a considerable number of replaceable elements, marked O (= optional), and is, to this extent, open-ended. This open-endedness is an essential condition for making the specification fit the needs and interests of a wide variety of sub-groups within the target-population. Particularly the interests may be expected to differ considerably with age and social or regional background. Some sub-groups may not be older than 14 when reaching the objective whereas others may be virtually adults. Some groups may be passionately interested in cattle-raising whereas others may hardly know the difference between a sheep and a goat. Some will live in an urban environment with strong cultural interests whereas others may never have been inside a museum or a theatre. All these differences make it necessary to allow teachers and pupils a certain amount of freedom to vary the content of the objective to suit their own interests. At the same time it must be recognized that foreign language teaching, like other subjects, has a role in contributing to the pupils' conceptual and cultural enrichment and that, consequently, there can be no objection to including certain elements that some pupils may be unfamiliar with but which may, nevertheless, be considered to be of importance in the framework of a general education.

Having built the possibilities for replacing certain elements by others into the objective, the author has refrained from giving further suggestions as to what they might be replaced by. One reason is that such suggestions might be misinterpreted as recommended priorities, another that where there are clearly discernible special interest areas individual teachers should find it easy enough to supplement the corresponding topic-specification and set of specific notions themselves.

1.2.11 Exponents

The major part of the present specification (not in bulk but in importance) is non-language-specific. It specifies what the learner may be expected to be able to do in a foreign language, what language-functions he will be able to fulfil and what notions he will be able to handle. Up to this point the specification should apply equally to at least all the languages of the member states of the Council of Europe. In order to make the specification sufficiently explicit, however, we have to determine what is required in each individual language to fulfil the various functions and to handle the various notions. In other words, we have to determine which exponents, or language-forms, are commonly used for each function and for each notion and then select those which we consider to be the most appropriate forms for our target-population. In the present document this selection is made for English. The development of other language versions will be undertaken in the near future.

In selecting the English exponents the following criteria have been used.

1. The total learning-load must be kept as small as possible. This means that preferably those forms are to be chosen which can serve more than one purpose, which can be used in more than one language-function, or for more than one notion. It should be particularly attempted to exclude forms which combine a very narrow range of applicability with a high degree of difficulty to foreign learners.
2. The total set of exponents selected should be as coherent and as well balanced as possible. This applies to the coverage of semantic fields by lexical items as well as to the consistency of the total grammatical content.
3. The learner will, at this level, be expected only to play the more neutral social and psychological roles. This means that the exponents selected are to be, on the whole, socially and psychologically "unmarked". Extremes of informality, formality, etc. etc., must be avoided.
4. The learner will have to be able to understand more than he can produce himself. It is obviously impossible, at this level, to prepare the learner for the full range of language he may be confronted with, but it should be attempted to prepare him at least for what he is most likely to be confronted with. In addition to exponents marked P, which the learner would be expected to be able to produce himself, further exponents marked R (receptive use only) may be included in cases where they are very likely to be used by foreign language speakers.

The exponents selected on the basis of these criteria, it should be superfluous to say, are no more than *recommended* language-forms. A pupil who has reached this objective will be expected to be able to do what has been specified, but it is comparatively unimportant whether he uses one particular language-form in fulfilling a certain language-function or a different one, always assuming that they are equally adequate. A different attitude might be taken with regard to receptive ability. If it is accepted that the language-forms listed in the specification have a high degree of communicative usefulness it would seem to be reasonable to expect that all learners would have at least a recognition knowledge of these forms. The exponents are listed in Chapter 2. Inventories of the total lexical and structural content are presented in Chapter 4.

1.2.12   The adaptation and the original compared
The procedure described in 1.2.1–1.2.11 has resulted in an objective which is strictly comparable to the threshold level for adults. This strict comparability is a consequence of using the same model for the development of both objectives but also of the extent to which the two respective target-populations share the same characteristics. In fact, it has appeared that, as far as the content-specifications are concerned, the objectives are identical with respect to the language-functions and general notions and only differ in the choice of specific notions. In terms of what was discussed in 1.1.5 and 1.1.6 this means that the two objectives have the same common core and that, consequently, they are not really two different objectives but two versions

of one and the same objective. We may consequently regard the threshold level as a master-objective for oral communication designed for the overall target-population of general beginners, with versions for various sub-groups. It may be assumed that this will have considerable advantages for the planning of comprehensive systems of education, especially those including provisions for permanent or recurrent education, as well as for the production of educational materials.

1.3   Place in a curriculum

1.3.1   In a wider context
It has been attempted in this document to define as explicitly as possible what a learner will have to be able to do in a foreign language if he is to satisfy certain minimal communication needs. In most, if not all, countries the ability to communicate orally is recognized as an essential objective of foreign language teaching. Very rarely, however, is it regarded as the only objective of this kind of instruction. Almost invariably the ability to read more or less independently a wide variety of foreign language publications is included in the objective, often the ability to write is given much more weight than in the present specification, and in many cases foreign language teaching is expected to contribute to the more general educational aim of providing insight into and understanding of foreign cultures. It is obvious, then, that the present objective cannot be offered as *the* objective of foreign language teaching. It is merely offered as *the minimum objective for the teaching of (mainly oral) foreign language communication.* As such it can, in most cases, only be one part of a more comprehensive foreign language curriculum. Yet, it is an essential part, and an indispensable step towards reaching further educational aims. It is also the one part where early agreement of the various interested parties may be anticipated and consequently the obvious starting-point for any endeavours to achieve some sort of international coordination in foreign language teaching. It is therefore offered for incorporation into any richer curriculum which individual countries may favour.

1.3.2   In its own right
The objective is also offered as a worthwhile objective in its own right. If those pupils – and in several countries they form the majority – who, for whatever reason, will not follow more than, say, three years of foreign language instruction can be induced to master what is required for the present objective they will have achieved something of immense value: they will be able to cross the threshold into a foreign language community. They will also, one would expect, experience the satisfaction of successful learning, of learning something which makes sense to them. Such an experience is often a sufficient inducement to undertake further efforts and to widen the scope of their

ability. If, on the other hand, for these pupils too, more ambitious objectives are set from the beginning, the usual result seems to be that nothing is learnt well enough to serve any practical purpose and that the learner is left at the end of his studies with a sense of frustration.

1.3.3   Incorporation

For more privileged pupils – and fortunately their numbers are increasing – the present objective, as it was said above, can be incorporated into more comprehensive curricula. If this is done it would seem to be desirable to place it in a richer context right from the start, particularly by adding opportunities for extensive reading-practice. This would seem to be preferable to a sequential order, in which first the present objective would be reached in its entirety and then further extensions would be added. Perhaps a warning should be added here that, also in courses of longer duration, the present objective should never be lost sight of. It is a far from uncommon experience that after the first few years of foreign language learning secondary school pupils can cope reasonably well with all sorts of practical situations, but that after continued learning they seem to have lost much of their practical ability and are only capable of performing more specialized or academic tasks. Of course, one can hardly expect a teacher and his class to go on for five or six years practising "buying railway tickets" and "talking about the weather". However, one might expect them to spend at least part of the learning time on a recycling of what was learnt earlier, especially if this would include a well-planned expansion of the pupils' practical ability. Such planning may be undertaken on the basis of the present objective. It would involve an increase of the number of exponents of various language-functions and general notions, so as to enable the pupils to handle the language with more subtlety. It would also involve an addition of further topics, an enrichment of the vocabulary for a number of topics and greater behavioural ability with regard to each of them. In this way it might be possible to define a second level of practical communicative ability, thus ensuring that when the pupils leave school they are fully prepared not only for further studies or vocational work but also for contacts with foreign language speakers in everyday situations.

1.3.4   Height

The present objective, it was stipulated in the author's brief, was to "correspond to a minimum level of proficiency". It would also have to be attainable by "the great majority of pupils". The trouble is, of course, that we do not know what constitutes a minimum level of proficiency nor what is attainable by the great majority of pupils. However, such is the state of our knowledge, we have to use – and accept – such terms or we could give no indications at all. As it is, one can only go by experience, suppositions and assumptions. At the same time one can try to reach agreement on what kind of ability is felt to be minimally required and then try to analyse this ability and construct an objective accordingly. This, of course, is what has been done in the present case. It was generally agreed by all the people involved and consulted that in order to function satisfactorily in our modern society one should at least be able "to survive, linguistically speaking, in temporary contacts with foreign-language speakers in everyday situations, whether as visitors to the foreign country or with visitors to one's own country, and to establish and maintain social relations". Once this was agreed upon it could be determined what this involved and what foreign language equipment was needed in order to function in the way described. The result of this procedure is the present objective. Whether for some learners it may be more than what they really need and for others less, it is impossible to say. Individuals differ widely in their capacity to exploit limited resources. One can only hope that the present specification will be adequate for that legendary *homo sapiens*, the average learner. Whether he can reach it or not, provided he is given adequate facilities, is another open matter. To this question the author can only say that he certainly assumes that the objective is not beyond the intellectual capacities of "the great majority of learners" and that most of the people he has consulted fully share this view. Whether or not he is right can only be determined by experimentation. The objective would certainly seem to be attainable for the great majority of European children who are at present in secondary education. In fact, it is below what is minimally required in several countries for official recognition in the form of certification.

Some sort of indication of the height of an objective – although one wonders how reliable this is – is provided by counting all the different lexical items in the content-specification. In the present objective their total number amounts to *ca.* 1100 for productive and receptive use and another 480 for receptive use alone. This seems to correspond to what is often aimed at in courses of two years (four weekly periods) for more gifted children and in three-year courses for slower learners.

An important factor in estimating the time required to reach the objective is the degree of skill that is expected of a successful learner, in other words *how well* the learners are expected to do all that is specified in the objective. More will be said about this in section 2.6, but right now it may be useful to point out that the threshold level is a level of communicative ability and not a level of foreign language perfection. This means that the main criterion in assessing the learner's success is whether communication takes place with some degree of efficiency. If it is accepted that formal correctness comes only secondarily – in the case of more gifted pupils one might perhaps demand a little more in this respect – the chances of also the less gifted learners reaching the objective may be considerably greater than one might traditionally expect.

The consistent application of the above criterion of assessment might be particularly important in estimating the attainability of the threshold level in more "difficult" languages, i.e. difficult in view of the learner's native language. Although as a language teacher one may often be appalled by the way many learners tend to abuse a foreign language one cannot help being impressed from time to time by the ease with which the less inhibited "under-achievers" do succeed in communicating with foreign language speakers.

If the objective is communicative ability and if "the great majority" is to be given a chance to reach it, we should perhaps be prepared to introduce the same sort of flexibility into our assessment procedures that most of us so eagerly desire to find in syllabus-contents.

1.4   Methodological implications

1.4.1   Disposition to further learning

In the brief given to the author it was stipulated that the objective should

"include a methodological initiation which would, on the one hand, facilitate continued study of the language and, on the other hand, make it possible to acquire a sufficient understanding of the learning-processes used, so that these may be profitably applied to the study of other languages".

It will be clear that this condition is different in kind from the other stipulations (cf. 0.3), which refer to the communicative ability of the target-population. This condition does not so much refer to linguistic skill as to a disposition for further study. As such, it cannot be fulfilled directly in the same framework (the behavioural objective) as the other conditions. Moreover, one does not see very well how it may be ascertained whether or not the disposition referred to has been acquired by the learners. This does not mean that we should only teach what we can test, but there does not seem to be much point in setting as an objective something which there is no way to describe in operational terms, consequently something of which neither teachers nor pupils can determine whether it has been achieved or not.

In spite of all this there can be no doubt that foreign language teaching can and should in some way or another prepare the student for continued study of the same foreign language and facilitate the acquisition of other foreign languages. So without including this disposition directly into our behavioural objective, where there is no place for it, we should examine the objective itself and determine to what extent it may be assumed to induce the disposition referred to and in what ways the nature of learning-processes the pupils have to undergo in order to reach the objective may contribute to it.

1.4.2   No privileged method

It should be stated right away that there can be no question of proposing a certain methodology. There is no royal road to foreign language ability, and methodological choices will have to vary in accordance with the characteristics of the learners and those of the teachers and also in accordance with the circumstances under which the learning/teaching process has to take place. The present objective is meant for learners of different age-groups, from a large variety of social and regional backgrounds, with many different educational backgrounds and learning-habits, showing great differences in learning-ability, taught by teachers who are, at least in some ways, as diverse as their pupils, in circumstances which vary from almost ideal to, by comparison, desperate. Laying down one single methodology, or even suggesting one, for all these diverse conditions would be unjustifiable and irresponsible.

All this does not mean, however, that the objective as described in Chapter 2 would not have certain implications, methodologically or otherwise, which may be expected to satisfy the condition quoted at the beginning of this chapter.

1.4.3 Motivation through success

One consequence of reaching the objective will be the satisfaction provided by successful learning. This satisfaction may be induced by any kind of educational success and by any recognition of this success in the form of a diploma, a certificate, or the teacher's praise. It may be expected to be stronger, however, and more lasting, and consequently more apt to lead to another sustained effort in learning, as the results of the learning-process make more sense to the pupils, as they appear to be more adequate in meeting their most urgent personal needs. In this sense the present objective should have the desired consequences because it is directly derived from the learners' estimated needs and, aiming at maximum ability with minimum means, it is calculated to meet the learners' needs in the most efficient way possible.

1.4.4 Orientation

Other consequences of reaching the objective are relatable to the learning-experiences the learner must have undergone in order to reach it, in other words to the methodological implications. As it was stated above, the objective cannot – and must not – impose a method, but it does have certain broad methodological implications, supposing all the time that it is attempted to make the teaching as effective and efficient as circumstances permit.

In the first place, if the teaching reflects the emphases in the objective, it will be strongly functional and situational. The *learning-syllabus* will be functional in the sense that, right from the first lesson, the pupils will acquire the ability to *function* in the foreign language, to *do* something practical with it, and the *learning-process* will have a clearly situational character in the sense that practice will to a large extent take place in simulated real-life situations. If at the same time it is recognized that learning with insight into the learning-process is more effective than learning without it, the pupils will be made aware of this functional and situational emphasis and thereby get a better understanding of what it is to use a foreign language and of what is the essence of foreign language learning. This understanding will not only be a powerful support for their motivation, it will also improve their chances of further success in foreign language learning, whether in the same language or in a different one.

1.4.5   Receptive range
Another implication of the objective is that the learners will not only be
trained to understand more than what they can produce themselves but that
they will be trained to understand language which contains unfamiliar elements. In other words they will have to be given intensive practice in deducing
the meaning of unknown elements from context. The ability to do this, "not
being put off by unknown elements", is perhaps one of the most powerful
factors in foreign language learning.

1.4.6   Listening-practice
A further methodological implication on the receptive side is the need for
intensive listening-practice with a wide variety of foreign language speakers.
The objective cannot be reached unless the learner is confronted with many
more voices than that of his teacher; in other words, intensive practice with
recorded material will be essential.

1.4.7   Productive ability
On the productive side the principle of maximum effect with minimum means
will have significant implications. It is a well-known fact that beginning
foreign language learners may have strong inhibitions when required to
express themselves within a range of language which is very much smaller
than they have available in their native language. They should be made aware,
therefore, of the possibilities of functioning adequately in many situations
with a highly restricted language code. In other words, the ability they had
as very young children in their own language should be as much as possible
revitalized. Through the principled selection of exponents, so that a comparatively small number of language-forms suffices for a large variety of language-
functions, the present objective should contribute to this revitalization.

1.4.8   Course-construction
After dealing with the methodological implications of the objective in so far
as they would seem to be relevant to the condition quoted at the beginning
of this chapter, we should perhaps say a few words about possible consequences of the objective for course-construction. Some of these consequences, such as functional and situational emphasis, the need for extensive
listening-material, etc. etc., have been dealt with above and will not be
repeated here. An adequate course will have to be based, to a certain extent,
on a functional/notional syllabus, i.e. the learner will have to be systematic-
ally trained to fulfil the various language-functions and to handle the various
notions. Lesson one, to give an extreme but significant example, will not deal
with "the simple present of *to be*" but with "introducing oneself", "identifying
objects", or some such communicative activity. Of course, this does not
exclude in any way at all that the *language-forms* which the learner is made
familiar with in lesson one might be especially the present tense forms of
to be. In other words, a functional/notional emphasis does not preclude
the possibility of well-considered structural grading! Certain functions will

naturally appear to favour certain structures and it would seem to be possible to gradually introduce the structural framework of a language into a basically functional/notional syllabus as well as to gradually increase the pupils' ability to function in the language on the basis of a structurally graded syllabus. The fact that for various functions and notions (especially general notions) several exponents are given in the specifications reinforces this possibility of combining a functional/notional orientation with structural grading. It enables the course-constructor to select those exponents which, at a certain stage of the pupils' progress, fit in with their structural command of the language and will lead to a recycling of certain functions and notions at those stages of a course where further, structurally more demanding, exponents can be added.

The distinction between a common core and a category of topic-related specific notions would also seem to have implications for the construction of course-materials. The common core provides the pupil with the essential and indispensable components of his linguistic ability – the topics and the specific notions derived from them may be important but they are by comparison incidental. They are to a certain extent interchangeable or replaceable. They may be selected, reduced or expanded, to fit the needs and interests of individual groups of learners. The general foreign language ability of the learners rests on the common core, their specific ability derives from the topics. This would necessarily seem to have an influence on the procedures by which a course-constructor composes his material. The first step in his selection of items would be a choice from the common core, with an obvious priority for language-functions, and only then would he go to the topics and select from the topic-specifications and the specific notions those elements which he considers best suited for situationalizing the selected common-core elements and simultaneously for sustaining the interests of his target-group. It would seem likely that the last-mentioned condition would carry more weight than the first because there is no *a priori* reason why almost any topic-area could not be exploited as a context for practising most of the common-core elements.

2 The description of the objective

2.1 Introduction

In this part of the study we present the objective which results from the application of the model as described in chapter 1.

In 2.2 the objective is described in the most general terms. This is not part of the definition proper, but a characterization which will serve the practical purpose of making the objective easily identifiable.

In 2.3 we describe the objective analytically, but only in the most general categories, again to facilitate rapid identification.

Section 2.4 is the first part of the definition itself. It describes the language-activities, in terms of the traditional four skills, which the learner will be expected to be able to engage in.

In 2.5 we specify what the learner will be able to do with respect to each topic, and in 2.6 we indicate how well he will be expected to be able to do all this.

Sections 2.7 and 2.8 are indexes of those language-functions and general notions which are distinguished in this objective. They are presented for easy reference and as surveys of the categorization which has been used.

Chapter 3 is the content-specification of the objective. It presents both the non-language-specific specification and the exemplification for English. In its three divisions, respectively specifying the language-functions, the general notions and the specific notions, the non-language-specific items are listed in the left-hand column and the English exponents in the right-hand column. Optional elements are marked O, and exponents which are recommended for both productive and receptive use and those for receptive use alone are marked P and R respectively.

2.2 General description

The learners will be able to survive (linguistically speaking) in temporary contacts with foreign language speakers in everyday situations, whether as visitors to the foreign country or with visitors to their own country, and to establish and maintain social contacts.

2.3   Language-functions and topic-areas

The learners will be able to use the foreign language to fulfil the following (general) functions:

1. imparting and seeking factual information
2. expressing and finding out intellectual attitudes
3. expressing and finding out emotional attitudes
4. expressing and finding out moral attitudes
5. getting things done (suasion)
6. socializing

They should be able to function particularly in respect of the following topic-areas:

1. personal identification
2. house and home
3. life at home
4. education and future career
5. free time, entertainment
6. travel
7. relations with other people
8. health and welfare
9. shopping
10. food and drink
11. services
12. places
13. foreign language
14. weather

2.4   Language-activities

Speaking: The learners will be able to fulfil the language-functions specified in division I of the content-specification (Chapter 3) and to deal with the topics listed in 2.5 in the way described there. In doing so they will be able to express the general and specific notions listed in divisions II and III of the content-specification (Chapter 3) and they will be able to use the exponents marked P in the content-specification or equally appropriate exponents.

Listening: The learners will be able to understand:
- The most likely answers to questions asked by themselves.
- The most likely responses to matters raised by themselves or to answers given by themselves.
- Questions asked by others within the topics listed in 2.5.
- Information given by others within the topics listed in 2.5.
- (Optionally: the texts of the commonest announcements via public address systems in airports, at railway-stations, etc.)
- Warnings such as "look out", "be careful", "stop!", "hurry!"

The learners will be expected to understand only those utterances which
- can be easily understood on the basis of a command of vocabulary and structure not exceeding that specified in the exponents of language-functions and of general and specific notions (Chapter 3),
- are spoken in the standard dialect with either the standard accent or accents which have a slight regional, foreign and/or socio-economic colouring,
- are produced at a speech-rate which lies in the lower range of what is considered normal.

Writing: The learners will be able to write both formal and informal letters in accordance with the following specifications:

1	*Formal letters.*
1.1	*accommodation* – inquiring about availability of accommodation (hotel, youth-hostel, camping-site, etc.); – inquiring about prices and conditions of accommodation; – inquiring about situation of room or camping-site, amenities, view, arrangement (whether meals are included); booking accommodation.
1.2	*recreation* – inquiring about tourist attractions, sights, etc.
1.3	*employment* – inquiring about temporary employment (vacation jobs) and conditions of work.
1.4	*courses* – inquiring about vacation-courses, terms and conditions.
2	*Informal letters.* Letters to friends and relatives within the topics specified in 2.5.

Reading: The learners will be able to read:
- Letters and simple brochures sent in return for formal letters written by the learners themselves (see "Writing").
- Informal letters from friends and relatives within the topics specified in 2.5.
- (Optionally: generally used texts on road-signs.)
- (Optionally: generally used public notices and announcements.)
  The learners will be expected to understand only those texts which
- can be easily understood on the basis of a command of vocabulary and structure not exceeding that specified in the exponents of lan-

guage-functions and of general and specific notions (Chapter 3);
– have the general legibility of typescript or print.

2.5 Topic-related behaviour

1   **Personal identification**
Learners should be able to give information about themselves, and, if applicable, others, and to seek information from others, with regard to:

1.1   *name:* first name, initials, surname, spelling them out if required.
1.2   *address:* home address, spelling it out if required.
1.3   *telephone-number.*
1.4   *date and place of birth:* spelling out the place-name if required.
1.5   *age.*
1.6   *sex.*
1.7   *marital status.*
1.8   *nationality.*
1.9   *origin.*
1.10   *education:* what sort of education they have had, at what type of educational institution (general, vocational, primary, secondary, higher), how long; whether formal education has been completed or is continued, if continued for how long and at what type of educational institution.
1.11   *intended profession or occupation:* what they intend to do for a living after completing their formal education.
1.12   *family:* composition of family; family relations.
1.13   *religion:* name of religion, if any.
1.14   *likes and dislikes:* especially with regard to people, hobbies and interests, food and drink.
1.15   *character, temperament, disposition:* general characterization of other people.

2   **House and home**
Learners should be able to discuss where and under what conditions they and others live, specifically:

2.1   *types of accommodation:* describe the type of house, flat, etc., in which they live themselves, as well as those in the neighbourhood; seek similar information from others.
2.2   *accommodation, rooms:* describe their own accommodation, house, flat, etc., and the rooms in it; seek similar information from others.

2.3   *furniture, bedclothes:* mention and inquire about the availability of the most essential pieces of furniture and bedclothes.

2.4   *room:* say whether they have a room of their own or share one with others; describe their room or the room where they sleep; seek similar information from others.

2.5   *services:* say whether they have gas and electricity at home, how their house is heated, whether they are on the telephone; seek similar information from others.

2.6   *amenities:* say whether they have bath, shower, fridge, radio, TV, garage at home, and whether they have a garden.

2.7   *region:* characterize and inquire about the nature of their own region and that of others: agricultural, industrial, scenery, whether it is attractive or not, etc.

2.8   *flora and fauna:* characterize and inquire about flora and fauna of their own region and that of others.

3   Life at home
Learners should be able to exchange information about life at home specifically with regard to:

3.1   *family:* composition of their family.

3.2   *occupation of parents:* the nature of their parents' jobs.

3.3   *daily routines:* state at what times they usually get up and go to bed, at what times they have their meals, how they spend their evenings and weekends, how much homework they have; seek similar information from others.

3.4   *money:* say whether they have a spare-time job, if so what job, what working-hours, and how much they earn; how much pocket-money they have and what they do with it; seek similar information from others.

3.5   *pets:* say whether they have any pets, if not whether they would like to have them, what pets; seek similar information from others.

4   Education and future career
Learners should be able to exchange information about:

4.1   *schooling:* see 1.10 above.

4.2   *daily routines:* when school begins and ends; how many lessons and how long they last; break-times; when and where they have lunch; how much homework they get.

4.3   *school-year:* approximate dates and lengths of school-holidays.

4.4   *subjects:* which subjects they study; which subjects they like or dislike and why; which subjects they would like to study further; which subjects are compulsory and which are optional.

4.5   *recreation:* possibilities at school for taking part in games, sports or school clubs, their own preferences; other organized recreational activities such as school parties, celebrations, excursions, etc.

4.6   *examinations, diplomas:* which examinations they have taken or will take; whether they have ever passed or failed; what diplomas or certificates they intend to have.

4.7   *future career:* what they intend to be after completing their formal education; where they would like to work; what further training, if any, they will need; prospects of employment and income.

5   Free time, entertainment
Learners should be able to exchange information about:

5.1   *hobbies:* say what their hobbies are and inquire about those of others.

5.2   *interests:* say what their special interests are and inquire about those of others.

5.3   *radio, TV:* say whether they like watching TV, listening to the radio, which programmes they like particularly, which they dislike, and inquire about the preferences of others.

5.4   *cinema, theatre, opera, concert, etc.:* state own preferences and inquire about those of others, inquire about programmes and booking facilities, buy tickets, ask for the cloakroom, find their way.

5.5   *sport:* state own preferences and inquire about those of others, inquire about sporting events, buy tickets for stadium, etc., discuss result of a match.

5.6   *intellectual pursuits:* say whether they like reading and studying, whether they actually read or study in their spare time, if so, what; seek similar information from others.

5.7   *artistic pursuits:* say what forms of art they are interested in, if any; inquire about the preferences of others; give and seek information on the availability of public facilities: cinemas, theatres, museums, etc.

5.8   *museums, galleries, exhibitions:* say whether they are interested in museums, galleries, exhibitions, inquire about the interests of others; give and seek information on availability, price of tickets, opening-hours, etc.

5.9   *press:* say what they read regularly: newspapers, magazines, etc.; inquire about the preferences of others; inquire about the press in the foreign country.

6   Travel
Learners should be able to deal with various aspects of travelling:

6.1   *travel to school:* say how they get to school, what means of transport (if any), duration of journey; seek similar information from others.

6.2   *holidays:* say and inquire about where they and others normally spend their holidays and how long they last, how they spend them (camping, in youth-hostels, hotels, etc.), with whom (friends, relatives, etc.); describe a previous holiday, where they went, how, with whom, for how long, where they stayed, what the weather was like, what they saw, what they did, give their general impressions and say whether they enjoyed the holiday and would go again, describe their plans for a future holiday and seek similar information from others; say whether they have been in the foreign language country, seek similar information from foreigners with respect to their own country; say which foreign country (countries) they would particularly like to visit and why, seek similar information from others.

6.3   *countries and places:* characterize countries, places and regions: say something about their size, where they are situated and in what surroundings; mention possibilities for sight-seeing in their own neighbourhood; seek similar information from others, what to visit and how.

6.4   *public transport:* ask how to get to a place by public transport, give information on this to others; buy tickets; inquire about lost property; discuss times of arrival and departure; discuss routes; discuss restaurant/refreshment facilities; (optional: understand the commonest public announcements).

6.5   *private transport:* obtain and give information about routes, types of roads, traffic-rules, parking facilities, car-maintenance facilities, (optional: documents, road-sign texts).

6.6   *entering and leaving a country:* (optional: state whether they wish to declare anything at the customs; inquire about documents needed; ask about import-regulations); state reasons for visiting foreign country, duration of stay; fill in forms if required when entering or leaving the foreign language country; give personal information (cf. 1); change money.

6.7   *nationalities:* state own nationality and inquire about that of others.

6.8   *languages:* say which foreign languages they speak, understand, read, write; say something about their level of proficiency; say what experiences they had, how they have learned them, how easy/difficult they think they are, whether they intend to continue learning foreign languages, whether they need or expect to need them much; seek similar information from others.

6.9   *hotel, youth-hostel, camping-site, etc.:* inquire about availability and nature of accommodation (single room, double room, dormitory), situation of rooms or camping-site, amenities, view; discuss terms and prices; fill in registration-forms; ask about meal-times, closing-time; ask for key; inquire about laundry facilities.

6.10 (O)   *travel-documents:* (optional: ask what documents are needed; inquire about how to obtain visa, insurance, tickets).

6.11	*fares:* inquire about fares, price reductions, single and return, children and adults.
6.12	*tickets:* obtain tickets and pay for them.
6.13	*luggage:* ask for one's luggage by identifying it; inquire about lost property office.
6.14	*traffic:* ask about traffic-rules, especially one-way streets, parking, speed limits; give information on same subjects; (optional: understand commonly used texts on traffic-signs).

7.   Relations with other people

Learners should be able to deal with various aspects of social life:

7.1	*friendship, aversion:* say what people they like or dislike; seek similar information from others.
7.2 (O)	*invitations and appointments:* (optional: invite others for a visit, a meal, a drink, private or public entertainment; accept and decline such invitations; make an appointment, fix a time and place to meet, make arrangements to call for someone).
7.3	*correspondence:* say whether they correspond with foreign language speakers, with whom, about what, how frequently; seek similar information from others; ask for writing materials, notepaper, postcards.
7.4	*club-membership:* say whether they are members of any clubs, if so what clubs and what activities; seek information from others about the same subject.
7.5	*politics (and optional: social security):* (optional: say something about their political views, whether they support a political party); say what sort of government their own country has; (optional: say something about social security in their own country, especially old-age pensions and medical care); seek similar information from others.

8.   Health and welfare

Learners should be able to deal with various aspects of health and welfare:

8.1	*parts of the body:* refer to some parts of the body where simple gesture does not suffice to locate the source of pain, disorders, etc.
8.2	*ailments, accidents:* report illness, injury, accident; say whether they have been ill before and whether they have been operated upon; say whether they have to take medicine regularly, if so, what medicine.
8.3	*personal comfort:* say whether they are comfortable or the reverse, whether they are hungry, tired, ill or well, want to rest; inquire about the same subjects.
8.4	*hygiene:* inquire about bathing, washing, hairdressing facilities; ask for articles of personal hygiene.

8.5 (O)	*insurance:* (optional: say whether they are insured or not, against what risks, if so where; inquire about the same subjects).
8.6	*medical services:* inquire about medical facilities, surgery-hours, conditions of treatment; make an appointment with a doctor, a dentist, at a hospital; buy medicine at a chemist's; answer a doctor's questions; make clear to a doctor what is wrong.
8.7	*emergency services:* ask for the police or the fire department; ask for an ambulance, a doctor; (optional: ask for the consul).

9.   Shopping

Learners should be able to deal with various aspects of shopping:

9.1	*shopping facilities:* ask for and give information about supermarkets, shopping-centres, markets, shops (baker, butcher, etc.); ask in a shop whether particular goods are available, ask to see them, find out how much they cost, ask to be shown something cheaper, better, different, pay for goods bought, be familiar with expressions of quantity, weight, and with the money in the foreign country.
9.2	*foodstuffs:* ask for the more common foodstuffs.
9.3	*clothes, fashion:* ask for the more common articles of clothing and articles of personal use; ask for specific colours and materials.
9.4 (O)	*smoking:* (optional: ask for smokers' requisites).
9.5	*household articles:* ask for the more common household-articles, particularly those most likely to be needed by a visitor to a foreign country.
9.6	*medicine:* ask for chemist's; buy medicines against common physical disorders.
9.7	*prices:* inquire about prices, discounts, method of payment; say whether price is convenient, (too) high or (too) low.
9.8	*weights and measures:* discuss size and weight in general terms (big, small, heavy, light, etc.) and in terms of the commonest standard weights and measures in the foreign language community and in their own.

10.   Food and drink

Learners should be able to deal with some aspects of eating and drinking:

10.1	*types of food and drink:* ask for the more common foodstuffs in a shop; order a meal in a restaurant, cafeteria, snack-bar, canteen, etc., refer to the menu, say what meal they want, what they want to eat, (optional: how it should be prepared: boiled, fried, etc.); express likes and dislikes when enjoying private hospitality; seek similar information from others.
10.2	*places where you eat and drink:* ask about places where one can

eat and drink; give information to others about same subject; order food and drink (see 10.1 above); ask for the bill; paying and tipping.

11. **Services**

Learners should be able to make use of a number of important services and help others to use them:

11.1 *post:* give and seek information about where the post-office is, where a letter box is; inquire about postage for letters and parcels; buy stamps; inquire about poste restante.

11.2 *telephone:* give and seek information about where phone-calls can be made; ask someone to ring them up; tell others they will ring them up; ask if they can make a call; ask for a telephone-number and give their own number; ask for coins.

11.3 *telegraph:* send a telegram; ask when it will arrive; inquire about the price.

11.4 *bank:* give and seek information about where the nearest bank is, where foreign money can be changed; change money at a bank, (optional: cash a cheque; say whether and, if so, where they have an account).

11.5 *police:* give and seek information about where the nearest police-station is; report a loss or a theft; pay a fine.

11.6 *hospital surgery:* (see "Health and welfare" – medical services, above).

11.7 *repairs:* give and seek information about where things can be repaired; ask for things to be repaired.

11.8 *garage:* give and seek information about where the nearest garage is; report a breakdown; ask for technical help.

11.9 *petrol-station:* give and seek information about where the nearest petrol-station is; (optional: buy petrol, have oil, water and tyres checked).

12. **Places**

Learners should be able to ask the way and to give strangers directions; they should be able to refer to a map, and to state and inquire about distances.

13. **Foreign language**

Learners should be able to discuss the use of a foreign language:

13.1 *ability:* say how well they speak, understand, read, write, a foreign language, whether they consider it easy or difficult; seek similar information from others.

13.2 *understanding:* ask what things are called; ask what phrases, words, etc., mean; ask someone to speak slowly, clearly, to repeat something, to explain what he means.

13.3   *correctness:* ask whether something is correct; ask someone to
            correct mistakes; ask how something is pronounced.

14.   **Weather**
            Learners should be able to discuss the weather:

14.1   *climate:* characterize the climate in their own country and in the
            foreign country (if they know it); inquire about the climate in
            the foreign country.
14.2   *weather-conditions:* describe weather-conditions in the four sea-
            sons in their own country, and, as far as known, in the foreign
            country; inquire about weather conditions in the foreign country.

2.6   Degree of skill

An objective is not complete unless we include an indication as to the degree
of skill that will be expected of the learner. In other words, we have to specify
how well the learner will be required to do all that has been described if he
is to be considered as having reached the objective. Unfortunately, this component cannot be specified with anything like the degree of exactness, of explicitness, with which we deal with the other components, unless we were to
specify it in terms of a minimum score on a particular objective test. However,
the provision of a test is not part of the definition of an objective. A test
is simply an instrument for measuring in how far an objective has been
reached. Moreover, even if we did include a sample test, it would be no more
than what it is called here: a sample. Other tests constructed in the same
way might require an adjustment of the minimum score; consequently we
would not have defined the required degree of skill with sufficient generality.
In addition, although it is possible to construct objective tests of high validity
for receptive skills, oral understanding and reading, there is no such possibility for the skills of speaking and writing. For productive skills we still have
to be satisfied with either global tests of reduced reliability or tests of high
reliability and somewhat doubtful validity. These limitations must be borne
in mind, even though sample tests for threshold level will become available
in the near future.

In the present study, of which the aim is primarily to define the threshold
level in non-language-specific terms, and where consequently it is impossible
to have recourse to a particular test, which would necessarily be language-
specific, we shall have to content ourselves with an attempt to characterize,
rather than define, the degree of skill required in fairly general terms. This
characterization can serve as a guideline to those who will construct tests
and to those who will evaluate the scores.

In whatever way we evaluate a learner's ability the main criterion will have to be whether communication takes place. If a speaker does not succeed in making himself understood, he has not reached the objective, nor has a listener who cannot make sense of what is said to him.

A second requirement must be that communication takes place with some degree of efficiency. A speaker who, when giving information about something, has to pause after every second word in order to find a way to continue, who makes numerous grammatical and/or lexical mistakes even in short utterances, whose pronunciation does not conform to any standard his partner in the conversation may be familiar with, etc., cannot be said to communicate efficiently because he puts a great strain on those listening to him and runs the risk of losing his audience altogether. There is a similar lack of efficiency when a listener, in order to understand what is said to him, needs constant repetition or obliges a speaker to speak with unnatural slowness or to rephrase his sentences all the time so as to express himself within an inadequately narrow range of vocabulary and grammar.

Our criteria for efficiency of communication will be:

a. that as a speaker the learner can make himself easily understood by a listener with native or near-native command of the language;
b. that as a listener the learner can understand the essence of what is said to him by a speaker with native or near-native command of the language without obliging the speaker to exert himself unduly.

Both criteria apply, of course, exclusively within the behavioural specification and the content specification of the objective.

At least two key-words in the formulation of the above criteria are subjective and vague: "easily" in criterion a, and "unduly" in criterion b. We cannot make them fully explicit, but we can at least attempt to characterize them somewhat more closely.

A speaker may be considered to make himself "easily" understood if he expresses himself:

a. at a reasonable speed,
b. with sufficient precision,
c. with reasonable correctness (grammatically, lexically, phonetically).

A listener may be considered to save a speaker "undue" exertion if he understands the essence of the speaker's utterances:

a. without frequent repetition,
b. at a speech-rate which is not below the lower range of what is "normal",
c. with an accent which is either the standard accent or a variant close to the standard accent.

These characterizations are still far from explicit, containing such terms as "reasonable", "sufficient", "frequent", "close to", etc. Nevertheless they will serve to indicate which aspects of a learner's behaviour when using the foreign language should be given special attention to in an evaluation of his degree of skill. At present, they could be made more explicit only with reference to particular tests.

The degree of skill which will be needed in reading and writing is similar to that in speaking and oral understanding:

a. what the learners are expected to be able to write must be easy to read;
b. of what the learners are expected to be able to read they must understand the essence.

There are various techniques which may be used for determining in how far learners have reached the objective. We may roughly divide these techniques into two categories:

a. those which require the learners to do just what is specified in the objective;
b. those which require the learners to perform certain operations which are not specified in the objective but which, singly or collectively, can be shown to predict the learners' ability to do what has been specified in the objective.

Techniques of type a are used in lifelike, overall tests, those of type b in batteries of tests of sub-skills (such as vocabulary, grammar, etc.) or in tests which require the learners to perform operations which are less obviously related to the overall skill.

Overall, lifelike tests have a high validity, i.e. they test just that which they are designed to test. Objective tests of this kind can be constructed for receptive skills, listening and reading. When speaking and writing are to be tested in this way reliable scoring presents a problem. It is true that an acceptable degree of reliability can be achieved by a team of highly competent and well-trained judges, but, unfortunately, judges of such a high standard are not always available. Consequently, evaluation usually relies heavily on techniques of the second category. Unfortunately, these techniques, too, have more or less serious disadvantages. If exclusively batteries of tests of sub-skills are used the validity of the resulting measurements is open to doubt since neither the nature of the various components of an overall language skill nor their relative importance (weighting) is sufficiently well known to us. If tests of less obviously related abilities are used – some of which, e.g. closing-tests in which testees are required to complete blanks in a text, may correlate very highly with overall language-ability – the most obvious risk is that language-teaching practice may be adversely affected. If learners wish to take a test at the end of a course the techniques used in the test will almost certainly influence the nature of the instruction they get. It is therefore very important that testing-procedures should be selected which correspond very closely to what are considered to be the most useful teaching techniques. Consequently, tests of abilities which are less directly related to the objective should be used sparingly. Ideally, only lifelike, overall tests should be used. However, practical circumstances may, and usually do, preclude this. In such cases a combination of an overall test with a battery of sub-skill tests may be an acceptable compromise.

2.7 Index of language-functions for threshold level

1   *Imparting and seeking factual information*
1.1   identifying
1.2   reporting (including describing and narrating)
1.3   correcting
1.4   asking

2   *Expressing and finding out intellectual attitudes*
2.1   expressing agreement and disagreement
2.2   inquiring about agreement or disagreement
2.3   denying something
2.4   accepting an offer or invitation
2.5   declining an offer or invitation
2.6   inquiring whether offer or invitation is accepted or declined
2.7   offering to do something
2.8   stating whether one knows or does not know something or someone
2.9   inquiring whether someone knows or does not know something or someone
2.10   stating whether one remembers or has forgotten something or someone
2.11   inquiring whether someone remembers or has forgotten something or someone
2.12   expressing whether something is considered possible or impossible
2.13   inquiring whether something is considered possible or impossible
2.14   expressing capability and incapability
2.15   inquiring about capability or incapability
2.16   expressing whether something is considered a logical conclusion (deduction)
2.17   inquiring whether something is considered a logical conclusion (deduction)
2.18   expressing how certain/uncertain one is of something
2.19   inquiring how certain/uncertain others are of something
2.20   expressing one is/is not obliged to do something
2.21   inquiring whether one is obliged to do something
2.22   expressing others are/are not obliged to do something
2.23   inquiring whether others are obliged to do something
2.24   giving and seeking permission to do something
2.25   inquiring whether others have permission to do something
2.26   stating that permission is withheld

3	*Expressing and finding out emotional attitudes*
3.1	expressing pleasure, liking
3.2	expressing displeasure, dislike
3.3	inquiring about pleasure, liking, displeasure, dislike
3.4	expressing interest or lack of interest
3.5	inquiring about interest or lack of interest
3.6	expressing surprise
3.7	expressing hope
3.8	expressing satisfaction
3.9	expressing dissatisfaction
3.10	inquiring about satisfaction or dissatisfaction
3.11	expressing disappointment
3.12	expressing fear or worry
3.13	inquiring about fear or worry
3.14	expressing preference
3.15	inquiring about preference
3.16	expressing gratitude
3.17	expressing sympathy
3.18	expressing intention
3.19	inquiring about intention
3.20	expressing want, desire
3.21	inquiring about want, desire

4	*Expressing and finding out moral attitudes*
4.1	apologizing
4.2	granting forgiveness
4.3	expressing approval
4.4	expressing disapproval
4.5	inquiring about approval or disapproval
4.6	expressing appreciation
4.7	expressing regret
4.8	expressing indifference

5	*Getting things done (suasion)*
5.1	suggesting a course of action (including the speaker)
5.2	requesting others to do something
5.3	inviting others to do something
5.4	advising others to do something
5.5	warning others to take care or to refrain from doing something
5.6	instructing or directing others to do something
5.7	offering assistance
5.8	requesting assistance

6	*Socializing*
6.1	to greet people
6.2	when meeting people

6.3	when introducing people and when being introduced
6.4	when taking leave
6.5	to attract attention
6.6	to propose a toast (O)
6.7	to congratulate
6.8	when beginning a meal

2.8   Index of general notions

The general notions are listed under the following categories:

1	existential
2	spatial
3	temporal
4	quantitative
5	qualitative
5.1	physical
5.2	evaluative
6	mental
7	relational
7.1	spatial relations
7.2	temporal relations
7.3	action/event relations
7.4	contrastive relations
7.5	possessive relations
7.6	logical relations
8	deixis

Under the above categories the following notions have been listed:

1	*Existential*
1.1	existence/non-existence
1.2	presence/absence
1.3	availability/non-availability
1.4	possibility/impossibility (objective)
1.5	occurrence/non-occurrence
1.6	demonstration
2	*Spatial*
2.1	location
2.2	relative position
2.3	distance
2.4	motion
2.5	direction

2.6	origin
2.7	arrangement
2.8	dimension
2.8.1	size
2.8.2	length
2.8.3	pressure
2.8.4	weight
2.8.5	volume
2.8.6	space
2.8.7	temperature

3	*Temporal*
3.1	point of time/period
3.2	priority
3.3	posteriority
3.4	sequence
3.5	simultaneousness
3.6	future reference
3.7	present reference
3.8	past reference
3.9	reference without time-focus
3.10	delay
3.11	earliness
3.12	lateness
3.13	length of time (duration)
3.14	speed
3.15	frequency
3.16	continuity
3.17	intermittence
3.18	permanence
3.19	temporariness
3.20	repetitiousness
3.21	uniqueness
3.22	commencement
3.23	cessation
3.24	stability
3.25	change/transition

4	*Quantitative*
4.1	number
4.2	quantity
4.3	degree

5	*Qualitative*
5.1	physical
5.1.1	shape

3 Content-specifications with exponents for English

The following lists contain the full specification of language-functions, general notions and specific notions with, for each item, the English exponents selected for the present objective.

Each list is composed in **bold** type and normal type. The text in bold type gives the functions and notions themselves and is non-language-specific. The text in normal type lists the English exponents, partly with examples in *italics*. Where the symbol $\sim$ is used, it replaces the immediately preceding exponent, excepting any elements preceded by $+$.

The exponents are marked either P or R. If marked P, they are recommended for productive *and* receptive use, if marked R for receptive use alone.

Both in the entries and in the exponents for English certain items are marked O. This indicates that these items are optional items, that they may be retained, eliminated or replaced by others in accordance with the estimated needs and interests of each target-group.

For easy reference three inventories have been added to this study in chapter 4. The first inventory is an alphabetical list of all the words used in the English exponents of the three divisions, the complete lexicon for the present objective; the second is a structural inventory derived from the exponents by Mr. L. G. Alexander; the third is a short grammatical summary.

The total number of different words (including so-called grammatical words) occurring in the English exponents is *ca.* 1100 for productive and receptive use and a further 480 for receptive use alone. Of the words marked P, 545 occur in divisions I or II, so belong to the "common core"; of the words marked R, 151 belong to the common core.

Forty-five words for productive and receptive use are marked as optional items, of which 6 belong to the common core. The corresponding figures for words for receptive use alone are 94 and 7 respectively.

Where, in the following lists, grammatical categories are referred to, it has been attempted to use those terms which have the widest currency or, at least, are widely understood. It has been found convenient to use some common abbreviations:

NP	Noun-phrase, i.e. something which, in a sentence, has a nominal function.
VP	Verb-phrase, i.e. a verb or verbal group with objects, if any.
N	Noun.
V_{inf}	Infinitive without *to*.
V_{to}	Infinitive with *to*.
V_{ing}	Verbal form in *-ing*.
V_{ed}	Past participle.

I Language functions

1 Imparting and seeking factual information

1.1 identifying: demonstrative pronouns: this, that, these, those + BE + NP(P); demonstrative adjectives: this, that, these, those + N + BE + NP (P); personal pronouns (subject form) + BE + NP(P); declarative sentences (P); short answers: *Yes, he is*, etc. (P).

1.2 reporting (including describing and narrating): declarative sentences (P); head-clause containing verb of saying (to say), thinking, etc. + complement clause (indirect speech) (P).

1.3 correcting: same exponents as above; in addition: no (adverb) (P); negative sentences with not (P); sentences containing the negation-words never, no (adjective), nobody, nothing (P).

1.4 asking: interrogative sentences (yes/no questions) (P); declarative sentences + question intonation (R); question-word sentences with: when, where, why, what (pronoun), which (pronoun), who, what (adjective), which (adjective), how far/much/long/etc. (P); whose(pronoun and adjective)(R); question-tags, type: *You aren't afraid, are you?* (R); tell me + sub-clause (P); about + NP (P).

2 Expressing and finding out intellectual attitudes

2.1 expressing agreement and disagreement

agreement: I agree (P); that's right (P); all right (P); of course (not) (P); yes (P); (yes +) affirmative short answers: it is, I am, I can, he may, etc. (P); certainly (R).

disagreement: I don't agree (P); I don't think so (P); no (P); (no +) negative short answers (P); that's incorrect (R).

2.2 inquiring about agreement or disagreement: do(n't) you agree? (P); do you think so, too? (P); don't you think so? (P); short questions (P).

2.3 denying something: no (adverb) (P); negative sentences with not (P); sentences containing the negation-words never, no (adjective), nobody, nothing (P); (no +) negative short answers (P).

2.4 accepting an offer or invitation: thank you (P); yes, please (P); I shall be very glad + V$_{to}$ ... (P); that will be very nice (P); all right (P); with pleasure! (R).

2.5 declining an offer or invitation: no, thank you (P); I'm afraid I cannot ... (P); unfortunately I cannot ... (R).

2.6 inquiring whether offer or invitation is accepted or declined: will you + VP (*do it, come*, etc.) (P).

2.7 offering to do something: can I + VP (P); shall I + VP (P).

2.8 stating whether one knows or does not know something or someone: I (don't) know (P); ~ + noun (-group) or pronoun (P).

2.9 inquiring whether someone knows or does not know something or someone: do(n't) you know? (P); ~ + noun(-group) or pronoun (P).

2.10 stating whether one remembers or has forgotten something or some-

one: I (don't) remember + noun
(-group) or pronoun (P); ∼ +
gerund (P); ∼ + that-clause (P); I
have forgotten to (*bring my
glasses*, etc.) (P).

**2.11 inquiring whether someone re-
members or has forgotten something or someone:** do(n't) you remember + noun(-group) or pronoun (P); ∼ + gerund (P); ∼ +
that-clause (P); have you forgotten to (*bring your glasses*, etc.) (P);
I have forgotten (*my passport*) (P).

**2.12 expressing whether something is
considered possible or impossible**

possibility: it is possible (P); ∼ + that-
clause (P); NP + can + VP (P).

impossibility: it is impossible (P); it is
not possible + that-clause (P);
NP + cannot + VP (P).

**2.13 inquiring whether something is
considered possible or impossible:** is
it possible? (P); ∼ + that-clause
(P); can + NP + VP (P).

**2.14 expressing capability and incap-
ability:** NP + can(not) + VP (P);
NP + BE (not) able to + VP (P);
NP + BE unable to + VP (R).

**2.15 inquiring about capability, or in-
capability:** can(not) + NP + VP(P);
BE (not) + NP + able to + VP (P);
BE + NP + unable to + VP (R).

**2.16 expressing whether something is
considered a logical conclusion (deduction):** so + declarative sentence
(P); therefore + declarative sentence (R); NP + must + VP (P);
necessarily (in declarative sentence) (R); NP + cannot + VP (P).

**2.17 inquiring whether something is
considered a logical conclusion (deduction):** necessarily (in interrogative sentence) (R).

**2.18 expressing how certain or un-
certain one is of something**

strong positive: I am sure (P); ∼ +

that-clause (P); I am certain (R);
∼ + that-clause (R); no doubt +
declarative sentence (R); I certainly think/believe + that-clause
(R).

positive: declarative sentence (P); I
know + that-clause (P).

intermediate: I think + so (P); ∼ +
that-clause (P); I suppose so (R);
∼ + that-clause (R); I believe +
that-clause (R).

weak: NP + may + VP (P); perhaps
... (P); I am not sure (P); ∼ +
that-clause (P); I wonder (R);
∼ + if-clause (R).

negative: NP + cannot + VP (P); I
don't think + so (P); ∼ + that-
clause (P); I don't believe + noun
(-group) or pronoun (R); ∼ + that-
clause (R).

**2.19 inquiring about how certain or
uncertain others are of something:**
are you (quite) sure (P); ∼ + that-
clause (P); do you think + so (P);
∼ + that-clause (P); do you
believe/suppose + that-clause (R).

**2.20 expressing one is or is not obliged
to do something:** I/we (don't) have
to + VP(P); I/we must + VP (R).

**2.21 inquiring whether one is obliged
to do something:** do I/we have to +
VP(P); must I/we + VP(R).

**2.22 expressing others are or are not
obliged to do something:** NP +
(don't/doesn't) have to + VP (P);
you must + VP (P); NP + must +
VP (other persons) (R); you need
not + VP (R); it is (not) necessary
(P).

**2.23 inquiring whether others are
obliged to do something:** do/does +
NP + have to + VP (P).

**2.24 giving and seeking permission to
do something**

giving permission: you may + VP (P);
you can + VP (R); answering a re-

quest: of course (P); ∼ you may (R); (that's) all right (P).

seeking permission: may I + VP (P); can I + VP (R); let me + VP (R); do you mind + if-clause (R).

2.25 inquiring whether others have permission to do something: are you allowed to + VP (P); are you supposed to + VP (R).

2.26 stating that permission is withheld: NP + BE not allowed to + VP (P); don't + VP (P); NP + BE not supposed to + VP (R); NP + must not + VP (R); forbid (R).

3 Expressing and finding out emotional attitudes

3.1 expressing pleasure, liking: this is very nice/pleasant (P); I like + noun(-group) or pronoun (very much) (P); ∼ + V$_{ing}$ ... (very much) (P); I enjoy + noun(-group) or pronoun (R); ∼ + V$_{ing}$ ... (R); I love + noun(-group) or pronoun (P); it's a very good + noun (P).

3.2 expressing displeasure, dislike: this is not very nice/pleasant (P); I don't like + noun(-group) or pronoun (very much/at all) (P); ∼ + V$_{ing}$ ... (very much/at all) (P); I don't enjoy + noun(-group) or pronoun (R); ∼ + V$_{ing}$ ... (R); I hate + noun(-group) or pronoun (R); ∼ + V$_{ing}$ ... (R); ∼ + V$_{to}$ ... (R).

3.3 inquiring about pleasure, liking, displeasure, dislike: do(n't) you like + noun(-group) or pronoun (P); ∼ + V$_{ing}$ ... (P); ∼ + V$_{to}$ ... (R); would you like + noun (-group) or pronoun (P); ∼ + V$_{to}$ ... (P); do(n't) you enjoy + noun (-group) or pronoun (R); ∼ + V$_{ing}$ ... (R).

3.4 expressing interest or lack of interest: that's (very) interesting (P); I am (not) interested (P); ∼ + in + noun(-group) or pronoun (P).

3.5 inquiring about interest or lack of interest: are(n't) you interested (P); ∼ + in + noun(-group) or pronoun (P).

3.6 expressing surprise: this is a surprise! (P); what a surprise! (R); it's surprising! (R); I'm surprised (R); ∼ + that-clause (R); how nice + V$_{to}$ ...! (P); fancy + V$_{ing}$ ...! (R).

3.7 expressing hope: I hope + so (P); ∼ + that-clause (P); I do hope + that-clause (P).

3.8 expressing satisfaction: this is very good/nice (P); it's (quite) all right now (P); this is just what I want(ed)/need/meant (P)/had in mind (R).

3.9 expressing dissatisfaction: I don't like this (P); I don't like it like this (R); this is not right yet (P); this is not what I want(ed)/need/meant (P)/had in mind (R).

3.10 inquiring about satisfaction or dissatisfaction: do you like this? (P); do you like it like this? (R); is it all right now? (P); is this what you want(ed)/need/meant (P)/had in mind? (R).

3.11 expressing disappointment: that's a (great) pity (P); I'm very sorry + V$_{to}$ ... (P).

3.12 expressing fear or worry: I'm afraid (P); I'm worried (P); ∼ + about NP (P).

3.13 inquiring about fear or worry: you aren't afraid, are you? (P); are you afraid? (P); are you worried? (P).

3.14 expressing preference: I prefer + noun (-group) or pronoun (P); ∼ + V$_{ing}$ ... (R); I'd rather + V$_{inf}$ ... (than ...) (P); I'd rather not (P); ∼ + V$_{inf}$ (P).

3.15 inquiring about preference: which do you prefer? (P); would you prefer + V_{ing} ...? (R); would you rather + V_{inf} ... (than ...)? (P).

3.16 expressing gratitude: thank you (P); $\sim$ + very much (indeed) (P); it is/was (very) nice of you (P); $\sim$ + V_{to} ... (P); it is/was (very) kind of you (P); $\sim$ + V_{to} ... (P); I am very grateful to you (R).

3.17 expressing sympathy: I am (so) sorry (+ V_{to} ...) (P); I am very glad + V_{to} ... (P); I am delighted + V_{to} ... (R).

3.18 expressing intention: I'm going + V_{to} ... (P); I'll + V_{inf} ... (P); I intend + V_{to} ... (P); I'm thinking of + V_{ing} ... (R).

3.19 inquiring about intention: are you going + V_{to} ...? (P); will you + V_{inf} ...? (P); do you intend + V_{to} ...? (P); are you thinking of + V_{ing} ...? (R).

3.20 expressing want, desire: I'd like + noun(-group) or pronoun (P); $\sim$ + V_{to} ... (P); I want + noun(-group) or pronoun (P); $\sim$ + V_{to} ... (P); may I have + noun(-group) or pronoun (please)? (P).

3.21 inquiring about want, desire: would you like + noun(-group) or pronoun (P); $\sim$ + V_{to} ... (P); do you want + noun(-group) or pronoun (P); $\sim$ + V_{to} ... (P).

4 Expressing and finding out moral attitudes

4.1 apologizing: I am very sorry (P); sorry! (P); please forgive me (R); I do apologize (O, R); excuse me, please (P).

4.2 granting forgiveness: that's all right (P); it's all right now (P); it doesn't matter (at all) (P).

4.3 expressing approval: good! (P); that's fine! (P); excellent! (R).

4.4 expressing disapproval: you shouldn't + V_{inf} ... (P); $\sim$ + have + V_{ed} ... (P); it's not very nice (P).

4.5 inquiring about approval or disapproval: is this all right? (P); do you think this is all right? (P).

4.6 expressing appreciation: (it's) very good/nice (P).

4.7 expressing regret: I am so/very sorry + that-clause (P); $\sim$ + if-clause (P); that's a (great) pity (P).

4.8 expressing indifference: it doesn't matter (P); I don't mind (R); $\sim$ + if-clause (R); I don't care (R).

5 Getting things done (suasion)

5.1 suggesting a course of action (including the speaker): let's + VP (P); shall we + VP (P); we could + VP (P); what about + V_{ing} ... (P); we might + VP (R).

5.2 requesting others to do something: please + VP (P); would/could you (please) + VP (P); would you be + so kind as to ... (R); $\sim$ + kind enough to ... (R); would you mind + V_{ing} ... (R); can I have + NP + V_{ed} (, please)? (P).

5.3 inviting others to do something: would you like + V_{to} ... (P); what about + V_{ing} ... (P); $\sim$ + a drink, a nice walk, etc. (P); how about + V_{ing} ... (R); $\sim$ + a drink, a nice walk, etc. (R).

5.4 advising others to do something: you should + VP (P); you ought to + VP (R); why don't you + VP (P); I can recommend ... (O, R).

5.5 warning others to take care or to refrain from doing something: be careful! (P); look out! (P); don't +

VP (P); mind + NP! (e.g. *Mind your head*) (R).

5.6 instructing or directing others to do something: declarative sentences with you as subject (P); imperative sentences (P).

5.7 offering assistance: can I help you? (P).

5.8 requesting assistance: can you help me, please? (P).

6 Socializing

6.1 to greet people: hallo (P); good morning/afternoon/evening (P).

6.2 when meeting people: hallo (P); how are you? (P); (I'm fine, thank you) how are you? (P); I'm very well, thank you, and how are you? (R).

6.3 when introducing people and when being introduced: this is ... (P); I'd like you to meet ... (R); may I introduce you to ... (R); response: how do you do (P); hallo (P).

6.4 when taking leave: good-bye (P); good night (P); I'll see you *tomorrow/next week*/etc. (P); bye-bye (R); cheerio (R).

6.5 to attract attention: excuse me ... (P); I say ... (R).

6.6 (O) to propose a toast: here's to ... (P); cheers (P).

6.7 to congratulate: congratulations! (P).

6.8 when beginning a meal: no exponents.

II   General notions

1 Existential

1.1 existence, non-existence: there is ... (P); there's no ... (P); is there ...? (P); exist (P); make (P) *We ~ bicycles here.*

1.2 presence, absence: here (P); not here (P); away (P).

1.3 availability, non-availability: have/have got (P), used in affirmative and in negative contexts; there is ... (P); there's no ... (P); is there ...? (P).

1.4 possibility, impossibility (objective): possible, impossible, can, cannot (P) (see I.2.12).

1.5 occurrence, non-occurrence: happen (P).

1.6 demonstration: show (P) *Please, ~ me another one.*

2 Spatial

2.1 location: here (P); there (P); somewhere (P); (not ...) anywhere (P); nowhere (P); where? (P); everywhere (P); inside (P) *Put the car ~*; outside (P) *The children are playing ~*; the north (P); in ~ (P) *He lives ~*; the south (P); in ~ (P) *Bournemouth is ~*; the east (P); in ~ (P) *Norfolk is ~*; the west (P); in ~ (P) *There are beautiful beaches ~*; demonstrative adjectives and pronouns: this, that, these, those (P).

2.2 relative position: against + NP (P) *He stood ~ the wall*; at + NP (P) *We'll wait ~ the station/I bought this book ~ Colchester*; behind + NP (P) *There's a tree ~ the house*; between + NP (P) *He walked ~ two policemen*; in + NP (P) *I live ~ London/The letter was ~ the envel-ope*; in front of + NP (P) *There's a tree ~ the house*; next to + NP (P) *Please, sit ~ me at dinner*; on + NP (P) *The meat was ~ the table*; opposite + NP (P); outside + NP (P) *He spends most of his time ~ the house*; over + NP (P) *We flew ~ the city*; round + NP (P) *There's a wall ~ our garden*; under + NP (P) *The dog slept ~ the table*; with + NP (P) *I shall be ~ you in five minutes*; above + NP (R) *We were flying ~ the clouds*; among + NP (R) *We found a ring ~ the flowers*; before + NP (R) *There was a tree ~ the house*; below + NP (R) *We were flying ~ the clouds*; beside + NP (R) *Come and sit ~ me*; in + NP (R) *He's ~ the room above*; inside + NP (R) *I have never been ~ this museum*; at the end (P); ~ of + NP (P) *Turn left ~ the street*; at the side (P); ~ of + NP (P) *Put your car ~ the road*; in the centre (P) *I'd like to sit somewhere ~*; in the centre of (P) *The best shops are ~ the town*; where + sub-clause (R).

2.3 distance: distance (P) *The ~ from A to B is 5 miles*; near (P) *The village is quite ~*; near + NP (P) *We live ~ the cathedral*; far (away) (P) *The museum is not ~*; far (away) from + NP (P) *We live ~ the town*; in the neighbourhood (of + NP) (R).

2.4 motion: to move (P) *The car did not ~*; stand still (R); stop (P) *The car ~ped suddenly*; go (P) *The car would not ~/Why did you ~?*; get up (P) *I got up at six*; lie down (P) *I would like to ~ for an hour*; sit

down (P) *Would you like to* ~?;
fall (P) *Be careful or you will* ~ *on
the ice*; walk (P) *Try to* ~ *to the
car*; hurry (P) ~, *or you will
miss the train*; go + prepositional
adjuncts of place (P) (see also
II.2.5) *He went to London/He went
into the house*; go home/away/out
(P); leave (P) *We left the station at
10*; arrive (P) *The train* ~*d at 11*;
reach (P) *We shall* ~ *Amsterdam
at 5 p.m.*; pass (P) *You* ~ *a big
building on your right*; come (P) *He
came very late*; come to + NP (P)
He came to our house; come along
(R) *Why don't you* ~?

2.5 direction: direction (P) *In which* ~
is Slough?; north (P) *From this
point you go* ~; south (P) *Turn* ~
when you come to the river; east (P)
We are going to travel ~; west (P)
If you drive ~ *you cannot miss it*;
(to the) left (P) *Turn* ~ *at the crossing*; (to the) right (P) *Turn* ~ *for
Liverpool*; straight on (P); to + NP
(P) *Let's go* ~ *London*; towards +
NP (P); for + NP (R) *He's leaving*
~ *Rome*; from + NP (P) *The
wind is* ~ *the east*; into + NP (P)
Let's go ~ *the museum*; past + NP
(P) *We drove* ~ *the castle*;
across + NP (R) *We walked* ~ *the
street*; along + NP (R) *Walk* ~
this street, then turn left; up + NP
(R) *We walked* ~ *the hill*; down +
NP (R) *We walked* ~ *the hill*;
through + NP (P) *We drove* ~ *the
centre of the town*; away (P) *He
walked* ~; away from + NP (P) *Go*
~ *that car!*; up (R) *He looked* ~;
down (R) *Shall we walk* ~?; in (P)
Shall we go ~?; out (P) *We walked*
~; back (P) *Finally we went* ~;
follow (P) *Just* ~ *me till we get to
the station*; turn (P) ~ *left at the
river*; bring (P) ~ *me some water*;

send (P) *I sent the letter to your
office*; carry (P) *Can you* ~ *this
heavy suitcase for me?*; take (P) *I'll*
~ *you to your room*; take away (R)
Can I take this away?; put (P)
Where shall I ~ *your coat?*; pull
(R) ~ *to open the door*; push (R)
~ *to open the door*.

2.6 origin: from + NP (P) *We came* ~
London; out of + NP (P).

2.7 arrangement: after + NP (P) *John
came* ~ *Peter*; before + NP (P)
John came ~ *Peter*; between + NP
(P) *We have a holiday* ~ *Christmas
and Easter*; first (P) *John came* ~;
last (P) *Peter came* ~/*The* ~
guest arrived at 10.

2.8 dimension

2.8.1 size: size (P) *What* ~ *shoes do
you take?*; big (P), large (R), small
(P), wide (R), narrow (R), high (P),
low (P), deep (P), tall (P), short (P),
thick (P), thin (P): these and other
items belonging to the grammatical category of adjectives, to be
used both attributively and predicatively and also in the comparative and the superlative degree
where applicable.

2.8.2 length: mile (P); yard (P); foot
(P) *The road is 20 ft. wide*; inch (P);
kilometre (P); metre (P); centimetre (P); long (P) *This road is
very* ~; short (P) *It is only a* ~ *distance*.

2.8.3 pressure: heavy (P) *This blanket
is too* ~; light (P) *I want a very* ~
blanket.

2.8.4 weight: weight (P) *This is not the
right* ~; weigh (R) *This will* ~ *5
lbs.*; kilo (P); lb. (P); oz. (P); see
further 2.8.3. above.

2.8.5 volume (O): gallon (P); pint (P).

2.8.6 space: big (P); small (P); room
(P) *You have plenty of* ~ *here*.

2.8.7 temperature: temperature (P)

The ~ *is too high for me*; degree (P) *It is 10* ~*s below zero*; hot (P); warm (P); cold (P); cool (P).

3 Temporal

3.1 point of time, period: time (P) *What* ~ *is it?*; it's/at ... o'clock (P); it's/at a quarter to/past ... (P); it's/at half past ... (P); it's/at ... minutes to/past ... (P); it's/at ... a.m./p.m. (R); yesterday (P); today (P); tomorrow (P); this morning/afternoon/evening/week/ month/year (P); last/next week/ month/year (P); last night (P); tonight (P); the day before yester- day (P); the day after tomorrow (P); on (*Monday*) (P); in (*four days*) (P); (*four days*) ago (P); names of the days of the week (P); names of the months (P); dates: e.g. *4 February 1974* (P); century (R); spring (P); summer (P); autumn (P); winter (P); Easter (P); Christmas (P); weekdays (R); weekend (R); then (P); now (P); when? (P); during + NP (R) *We met him* ~ *the holidays*; by + NP (point of time) (R) *He'll be here* ~ *6 o'clock*; not ... till/until + NP (point of time) (R) *He won't be here till/until 6 o'clock.*

3.2 priority: perfect tense (P) *I have not yet seen John*; pluperfect tense (P) *I had not done it*; before + NP (P); ~ + sub-clause (P); earlier than ... (P); before (P) *I have never done it* ~; already (P) *I have* ~ *done it*; yet (P) *Has he come* ~?/ *He hasn't* ~ *come.*

3.3 posteriority: after + NP (P); ~ + sub-clause (P); afterwards (R) *I'll do it* ~; later (P); ~ + on (P) *I'll do it* ~; later than ... (P).

3.4 sequence: first (P) ~ *we went to Madrid*; then (P) *First we went to Madrid,* ~ *we travelled to Gibraltar*; next (R) *What did you do* ~?; finally (P) ~ *we went back*; later on (P); in the end (R); after- wards (R).

3.5 simultaneousness: when + sub- clause (P); while + sub-clause (R); as soon as + sub-clause (R); at the same time (P).

3.6 future reference: NP + be going to + VP (P); NP + will + VP (P); present continuous of verbs of motion (R); soon (P); next week/ month/year (P); in (*four days*) (P); tonight (P); tomorrow (P); the day after tomorrow (P).

3.7 present reference: present con- tinuous (P); simple present (P); now (P); at present (P); today (P); this *morning/afternoon/year*/etc. (P); still (P) *Are you* ~ *here?*

3.8 past reference: past continuous (P); simple past (P); last week/ month/etc. (P); yesterday (P); the day before yesterday (P); formerly (P); just (P); recently (R); lately (R).

3.9 reference without time-focus: simple present (P) *Edinburgh is in Scotland.*

3.10 delay: later (P) *The train will come* ~; delay (R) *There will be a* ~ *of two hours*; be delayed (R) *The train has been delayed.*

3.11 earliness: early (P) *You are* ~/ *There is an* ~ *flight on Sundays/ You came too* ~.

3.12 lateness: late (P) *We'll have to hurry, we are* ~/*We came* ~ *for the show*; too late (P) *We were* ~, *the train had left.*

3.13 length of time (duration): for + NP (durational nouns) (P); since + NP (point of time) (P); till + NP (point of time) (P); ~ +

sub-clause (P); take (P) *The journey* ~*s two hours*; long (P) *We had to wait (a)* ~ *(time)*; short (P) *We waited only a* ~ *time*; quick (P) *We'll have a* ~ *meal*; year (P); month (P); week (P); day (P); hour (P); minute (P); moment (P).

3.14 speed: fast (P) *We went very* ~/ *This is a very* ~ *car*; slow (P) *We went very* ~*ly/We have a* ~ *car*; ... *miles/kilometres per hour* (P).

3.15 frequency: never (P); sometimes (P); often (P); always (P); ever (P); ... *times a/per (week)* (P); on *weekdays/Sundays/etc.* (P); *every Sunday/week/etc.* (P); *once every (day)* (R); daily (R) *There is a* ~ *flight to Montreal*; weekly (R) *There is a* ~ *flight to Kuala Lumpur*; monthly (R) *We have* ~ *meetings*; rarely (P); seldom (R); hardly ever (P); usually (P).

3.16 continuity: go on (P) *It will* ~ *for five years*; present continuous tense (P); past continuous tense (P); perfect tense (P) *I've lived here for two years*.

3.17 intermittence: not always (P).

3.18 permanence: always (P).

3.19 temporariness: for + NP (durational nouns) (P); not always (P).

3.20 repetitiousness: many times (P); again (P); twice (P); several times (R); again and again (R).

3.21 uniqueness: once (P); only ~ (P); simple present tense (P); simple past tense (P).

3.22 commencement: start (P) *The game* ~*ed at 7/He* ~*ed to speak*; begin (R); from + NP (point of time) (P); since + NP (point of time) (P); go + V$_{ing}$ (P) *Let's go sailing*.

3.23 cessation: stop (P) *The game will* ~ *at 9/He* ~*ped talking*; end (R); finish (R) *When will he* ~?; be ready (P) *When will you* ~?; till + NP (point of time) (P); until + NP (point of time) (R); to + NP (point of time) (P) *I work from 9* ~ *12 every morning*.

3.24 stability: stay (P) *I will* ~ *here for a week/It won't* ~ *dry for long*; remain (R) *How long will you* ~ *here?/Will it* ~ *dry today?*; lie (P) *He has been lying here for half an hour*; sit (P) *Don't* ~ *on that table!*; stand (P) *I cannot* ~ *any longer, I am too tired*; wait (P) *We had to* ~ *only five minutes*.

3.25 change, transition: change (P) *The country has* ~*ed since the war*; become (P) *Sugar has* ~ *very expensive*; get (R) *He's* ~*ting old*; suddenly ... (P).

4 Quantitative

4.1 number: singular or plural (grammatical category) (P); cardinal numerals up to four digits (P); ordinal numerals up to two digits (P); other numerals up to nine digits (R); another (P) *Give me* ~ *cup of tea*; about (P) *I have* ~ *£10*.

4.2 quantity: all + NP, a lot of + NP, any + NP, hardly any + NP, not any + NP, both + NP, each + NP, enough + NP, few + NP, little + NP, a little + NP, many + NP, much + NP, more + NP, most + NP, no + NP (P); half (P) *Give me* ~ *of it/Give me the other* ~/*Give me* ~ *a bottle*; see further II.2.8; at least (P) *I need* ~ *£5*.

4.3 degree: very ... (P); too ... (P); enough (P) *This is good* ~; much + adjective or adverb (P) *He's* ~ *better now*; a little + adjective or adverb (P) *He's* ~ *worried*; a bit + adjective or adverb (R) *He's*

~ tired; a lot + adjective or adverb (R) *He's ~ better now*; the + superlative degree of adjective (P); almost (P); hardly (R); rather (P) *He is ~ old*; quite (P) *He is ~ old*; such (R) *It was ~ fun!/He's ~ a nice boy!*; so (P) *I'm ~ sorry*; even (P) *I've ~ paid £5.*

5 Qualitative

5.1 Physical

5.1.1 shape: round (P) *I saw a ~ thing on the road*; square (P) *I received a ~ box.*

5.1.2 dimension: see II.2.8.

5.1.3 moisture, humidity: dry (P) *My shirt is not quite ~*; wet (P); dry (P) *where can I ~ my clothes?*; make wet (P).

5.1.4 visibility, sight: NP + can(not) see + NP (P); NP + can(not) be seen (R); dark (P) *It is too ~ to work in the garden*; light (P) *We'll go for a walk as soon as it gets ~*; look (P) *Don't ~ now, this is not very nice*; look at + NP (P) *~ his new car!*; watch (P) *I like ~ing a game of cricket.*

5.1.5 opaqueness: NP + can(not) see through + NP (P).

5.1.6 audibility, hearing: NP + can (not) hear + NP (P); NP + can (not) be heard (R); loud (P) *The music is too ~*; soft (P) *I like ~ music when I wake up*; listen (P) *~, the train is coming*; listen to + NP (P) *~ me, please*; sound (P) *We could not hear a ~*; noise (P) *There's too much ~ here*; silence (R).

5.1.7 taste: taste (P) *How does your soup ~?/Would you like to ~ this cheese?*; taste (P) *I don't like this ~*; sweet (P) *The coffee is not ~*

enough; bitter (P); nice (P) *It's a very ~ taste*; bad (P) *This soup has a very ~ taste.*

5.1.8 smell: smell (P) *The food ~s good/Can you ~ gas?*; smell (P) *This flower has a very pleasant ~*; nice (P) *The flower has a ~ smell*; pleasant (P) *The flower has a very ~ smell*; unpleasant (P) *These flowers have an ~ smell*; bad (P) *This meat has a ~ smell.*

5.1.9 texture: soft (P) *I want a ~ pillow*; hard (P) *This leather has become ~*; rough (P) *I want a coat of ~ wool*; smooth (R) *This material is very ~*; strong (P) *This is a very ~ material*; weak (R) *This material looks rather ~.*

5.1.10 colour: colour (P); blue (P); black (P); brown (P); green (P); grey (P); orange (P); red (P); white (P); yellow (P); light (P) *I want a ~ colour*; dark (P) *I want a ~ blue skirt.*

5.1.11 age: I am ... (years old) (P); how old are you (*is he, she*, etc.)? (P); age (R) *What's her ~?*; old (P) *I am too ~ for this*; young (P) *This is a party for ~ people*; year (P) *I am ... ~s old*; month (P) *Our baby is six ~s old*; adult (P) *We are two ~s and three children*; child (P) *We are two adults and three ~ren*; new (P) *I want to buy a ~ car.*

5.1.12 physical condition: ill (P) *I have been ~ for a week now*; well (P) *I feel very ~*; look (P) *You ~ very well*; dead (P); alive (P); break (P) *He has broken his leg*; cut (P) *I've ~ my finger*; repair (P) *Can you ~ this watch?*; fasten (P); all right (P) *Your car is ~ now*; out of order (R) *The telephone is ~.*

5.1.13 accessibility: open (P) *The museum is ~ now*; open (P) *The museum ~s at nine*; closed (P) *The*

museum is ～ *on Sundays*; close (P)
The shop ～*s at six.*

5.1.14 cleanness: clean (P) *This shirt is not* ～; clean (P) *My rooms are* ～*ed twice a week*; dirty; wash (P) *Can you* ～ *these clothes for me?*

5.1.15 material: gold, leather, metal, nylon, plastic, silver (P); cotton (R): used attributively (*a silver coin*) and as head of NP (*This is made of nylon*); wood, wool (P): used as head of NP; wooden (R); woollen (R).

5.1.16 genuineness: real (P) *Is this* ～ *leather?*

5.1.17 fullness: full (P) *The train is quite* ～; full of + NP (P) *The bus is* ～ *children*; empty (P) *The bus was* ～; fill (P) *Please* ～ *this bottle with water.*

5.2 Evaluative

5.2.1 value, price: price (P); expensive (P); cheap (P); high (P) *Prices are very* ～ *in this country*; low (P) *Prices are rather* ～ *in this shop*; how much? (P) ～ *are these shoes?*; be (P) *These shoes are £23*; cost (R) *These shoes* ～ *£23.*

5.2.2 quality: good (P) *This is a very* ～ *book*; better (P) *This book is much* ～ *than that*; best (P) *This is the* ～ *book I've ever read*; bad (P) *The weather is very* ～; worse (P) *The weather is much* ～ *now*; worst (P) *This is the* ～ *weather I've ever seen*; fine (P) *The weather will be* ～ *tomorrow*; well (P) *He cannot write English very* ～; quality (P) *I don't like the* ～ *of this material.*

5.2.3 rightness, wrongness: right (P) *This is the* ～ *thing to do*; wrong (P) *What's* ～*?/It is* ～ *to be lazy*; what's the matter? (P); NP + should (not) + VP (P); NP + ought (not) + VP (R).

5.2.4 acceptability, inacceptability: I cannot accept (*this*) (P); that's all right (P); that's fine/nice (P); I'm against + noun(-group) or pronoun (R).

5.2.5 adequacy, inadequacy: NP + be + all right (P); NP + be + (not) enough (P); that will do (R).

5.2.6 desirability, undesirability: I (don't) like + noun(-group) or pronoun very much (P); ～ + V$_{ing}$ ... very much (P); I would (not) like + noun(-group) or pronoun (P); ～ + V$_{to}$ ... (P).

5.2.7 correctness, incorrectness: right (P) *The answer is* ～; better (P) *Your English is much* ～ *now*; wrong (P) *The answer is* ～; worse (P) *The answer is* ～ *now*; be right (P); be wrong (P); true (P); correct (R); incorrect (R); false (R).

5.2.8 successfulness, unsuccessfulness: succeed (P) *He tried but did not* ～; fail (P); success (P); successful (R); try (P).

5.2.9 utility, inutility: (not) useful (P); NP + can(not) use + NP (P).

5.2.10 capacity, incapacity: NP + can(not) + VP (P); NP + will/won't + VP (P).

5.2.11 importance, unimportance: important (P); not important (P); unimportant (R).

5.2.12 normality, abnormality: normal (P); strange (P); ordinary (R).

5.2.13 facility, difficulty: easy (P); difficult (P); difficulty (R); hard (R) *His English is* ～ *to understand.*

6 Mental

6.1 reflection: see also I; be sure (P) *I'm sure that he will come*; hope (P) *I* ～ *that you'll win*; know (P) *I don't* ～ *that word*; remember (P) *I* ～ *my first visit to your country/*

$I \sim$ *seeing him last year*/$I \sim$ *that he went there last year*/I *don't* $\sim$ *that*; think (P) $I \sim$ *so*/$I \sim$ *that you are right*/*I'll have to* $\sim$ *about that*; be certain (R) *I am not certain*/*I am certain that this is wrong*; believe (R) *I (don't)* $\sim$ *that this is wrong*; suppose (R) $I \sim$ *so*/$I \sim$ *that you are right*; wonder (R) $I \sim$ *if you could help me*; no doubt (R) $\sim$ *this is right.*

6.2 expression: see also I; answer (P) *Have you received an* $\sim$ *to your letter?*; ask (P) *Why don't you* $\sim$ *him?*/*May I* $\sim$ *a question?*; laugh (P) *I had to* $\sim$; question (P) *May I ask a* $\sim$?; say (P) *He said that he was ill*/*How do you* $\sim$ *that in English?*; speak (P) *Can you* $\sim$ *French?*; talk (P) *We* $\sim$ *ed for a long time*; tell (P) $\sim$ *me what you've done*/$\sim$ *me about your work*; thank (P); write (P) *We* $\sim$ *to each other every month*/*We have not learned to* $\sim$ *English*; answer (R) *Has he* $\sim$ *ed your letter?*; apologize (O, R); forbid (R); invite (R) *They have* $\sim$ *ed us for dinner tonight*; recommend (O, R) *I can* $\sim$ *a trip to Rome*; request (R) *Guests are* $\sim$ *ed to leave their keys at the desk.*

7 Relational

7.1 Spatial relations: See II.2.2, II.2.3, II.2.5, II.2.6, II.2.7.

7.2 Temporal relations: See II.3.2–3.12.

7.3 Action, event relations
7.3.1 agency: agent as subject (P); agent in *by*-adjunct (passive) (R); agent in emphatic "It was X who ..." (R).

7.3.2 objective, incl. factitive: objective as object (P) *John opened the door*; objective as subject (P) *The door is open*; objective as subject of passive (R) *The door was opened by John*; factitive as object (P) *They're building a house here*; factitive as subject of passive (R) *This cathedral was built in the thirteenth century.*

7.3.3 dative: dative as indirect object (P) *I'll give you your own ticket*; dative in *to*-adjunct (P) *I'll give the ticket to your brother*; dative as subject (P) *I am ill*; dative as subject of passive (R) *He was given a book.*

7.3.4 instrumental: instrumental as object (P) *He used the key to open the door*; instrumental in *with*-adjunct (P) *You can open the door with this key.*

7.3.5 benefactive: benefactive as subject (P) *Joan received a nice present*; benefactive in *for*-adjunct (P) *I want to buy a present for my wife.*

7.3.6 causative: have (P) *Can I* $\sim$ *my skirt washed, please?*

7.3.7 place: see II.2.

7.3.8 time: see II.3.

7.3.9 manner, means: adverbial phrases: in this way (P) *You do it* $\sim$; like this (R) *You do it* $\sim$; adverbial derivatives in *-ly* (P): *You do it slowly*; adverbs without *-ly* listed elsewhere: fast (P) *You walk too* $\sim$; hard (P) *We have to work very* $\sim$ *in December*; how (P) $\sim$ *can I do it?*; by means of + NP (R); as + noun(-group) (R).

7.4 Contrastive relations
7.4.1 equality, inequality: (not) the same (thing) (P); different (P); $\sim$ from ... (P); differ (R); difference

(R); other (P) *Give me the ～ book*; another (P) *Give me ～ (=different) book*; else (P) *Anything ～?*

7.4.2 correspondence, contrast: (not) the same thing/book/etc. (P); different (P); quite ～ (P); differ (R); difference (R); like (P) *It's ～ an orange/It's ～ tea*; comparative degree of adjective + than ... (P) *John is bigger than his brother*; as ... as (R) *He is as big as his brother*; not so ... as (R) *He is not so big as his brother*.

7.5 Possessive relations

7.5.1 ownership, possession: possessive adjectives: my, your, etc. (P); possessive pronouns: mine, yours, etc., as complement (P) *This is mine*; possessive pronouns as subject (R) *Mine is better*; genitive singular of personal nouns (P); of-adjuncts (P); with-adjuncts (P) *Did you see a man ～ a big suitcase?*; without-adjuncts (P) *You cannot travel here ～ a passport*; have (got) (P) *I ～ a small caravan*; own (R); belong to ... (R) *This book belongs to me*; get (=receive) (P) *I got a nice present from him*; give (P) *I gave him a nice present*; keep (P) *May I ～ this?*; own (P) *This is my ～ book*.

7.6 Logical relations

7.6.1 conjunction: and (P); as well as ... (R) *I have bought a car ～ a motor-cycle*; but (P) *I want a new car, ～ I have no money*; also (P) *John will ～ come*; too (P) *John is coming ～*; not ... either (P) *I cannot swim either*; together (P) *We all went ～*; pair (P) *I want to buy a ～ of shoes*; group (P) *We went to Scotland with a ～ of friends*.

7.6.2 disjunction: or (P).

7.6.3 inclusion, exclusion: with + NP (P) *We'll take John ～ us*; without + NP (P) *We'll go ～ John*; except + NP (R) *We all went, ～ John*; also (P) *John will ～ come*; too (P) *John is coming ～*.

7.6.4 cause: why ...? (P); because + sub-clause (P); as + sub-clause (R).

7.6.5 effect: then ... (P); so ... (P) *He ate too much ～ he didn't feel well*; so ... that (R) *He ate so much that he fell ill*; the result is ... (R).

7.6.6 reason: why ...? (P); because + sub-clause (P); the reason is ... (R).

7.6.7 purpose: to + V_{inf} ... (P) *He came ～ help me*; in order to + V_{inf} ... (R) *He came ～ help me*; the purpose is ... (R).

7.6.8 condition: if + sub-clause (P).

7.6.9 focussing: about (P) *I don't want to talk ～ the war/What ～ me?*; on (R) *I cannot give you any information ～ train-services*; only (P) *I ～ wanted to help you/He came ～ once*.

8 Deixis

Deixis is the grammatical system used for referring or identifying by means of linguistic items belonging to closed sets. Deixis may be definite or indefinite (*he* vs. *someone*), non-anaphoric or anaphoric (*Why don't you come?* vs. *I'll buy those books because I need them*), independent or attributive (*I want that* vs. *I want that book*).

A. Definite:

a. non-anaphoric: personal pronouns (subject forms and object forms) (P); possessive adjectives: *my*, *your*, *their*, etc. (P); possessive pronouns: *mine*, *yours*, *theirs*, etc., as complement (P) *This is mine*; possessive pronouns as subject (R) *Mine is better*; demonstrative adjectives (attributive): *this*, *these*, *that*, *those*, *such* (P); independent relative pronoun *what* (P); definite article *the* (P); interrogative pronouns (independent): *who* (P), *whom* (R), *whose* (R), *what* (P), *which* (P); interrogative adjectives (attributive): *whose* (R), *what* (P), *which* (P).

b. **anaphoric**: personal pronouns (subject forms and object forms) (P); possessive adjectives (P); possessive pronouns as complement (P) *You take it; it's yours*; demonstrative adjectives (P); demonstrative pronouns (P); relative pronouns: *who* (P), *whose* (R), *whom* (R), *which* (P), *that* (R), omission of rel. pr. (R); emphatic pronouns: *myself*, *yourself*, etc. (R) *I've done it myself*; definite article *the* (P); adverbs: here, there, now, then, so (P) *He wanted to leave, but he didn't say* ∼; prop-word *one* (P) *I like the red* ∼ *better*; substitute-verb *do* (P) *He asked me to help him and I did* (P).

B. **Indefinite**:

indefinite article *a* (P).
indefinite pronouns: someone, somebody, no one, (not . . .) anybody, (not ...) anyone, nobody, each, everybody, everyone, something, (not ...) anything, nothing, everything, all (P) *They* ∼ *went home/I want* ∼ *of it*; both (P) *They* ∼ *went home/I want* ∼ *of them*; some (P) ∼ *of them went home*; it (P) ∼ *'s raining*; you (P) *It is a nice record if* ∼ *like modern music*.
adverbs: somewhere, nowhere, everywhere, (not ...) anywhere, sometimes, never, always (P).
indefinite semi-deictics: person (R) *There are five* ∼*s present*; man (human beings) (R) *There were animals here before* ∼ *came*; people (P) *What do* ∼ *think about the government?/There are five* ∼ *present*; thing (P) *What do you call that* ∼*?*; do (P) *What are you going to* ∼ *tonight?*

III Specific notions

1 Personal identification

1.1 Name

name: name (P) *What's your ~?*

forename: first name (P) *His ~ is Charles*; forename (P); Christian name (R).

surname: surname (P) *His ~ is Robinson*; family name (R).

initials: initials (R) *Are your ~ G.B.S.?*

Mr. (+proper name): Mr. (P) *This is ~ Jones.*

Mrs. (+proper name): Mrs. (P) *This is ~ Jones.*

Miss (+proper name): Miss (P) *This is ~ Jones.*

terms of address: if no proper name is used (Fr.: *monsieur, madame, mademoiselle*, as in: *merci beaucoup, monsieur*): no English exponents at threshold level.

to spell: spell (P) *Can you ~ your name, please?*

names of letters of the alphabet: a, b, c, etc. (P); z: [zed] or [zi:] (P), the other pronunciation (R) *My name is spelled b-l-a-c-k.*

to call (=to refer to by the name of ...): call (P) *We ~ him Pete.*

to be called (=be referred to by the name of ...): (*his*) name is ... (P); be (P) *I am Pete Robinson*; be called (R) *He is called Pete.*

to sign (=to write one's signature): sign (R) *Have you ~ed your cheque?*

signature: signature (R) *Before we can pay this cheque we must have your ~.*

letter (Ger. *Buchstabe*): letter (P) *What is the last ~ of your name?*

1.2 Address

address (=place of residence): address (P) *What is your ~?/My ~ is 15 Church Road, Cricklewood.*

to live (=to be domiciled): live (P) *Where do you ~?/I ~ in France.*

road: road (P).

street: street (P).

park: park (P) *My house is near Hyde Park.*

square: square (P) *I live in Portman Square.*

house-number: number (P) *I live at ~ 15*; cardinal numerals up to four digits (P).

countries: country (P); names of own country, country (major countries) of foreign language, neighbouring countries of own country (P); neighbouring countries of foreign language country (R).

1.3 Telephone number
(See also 11.2)

telephone: telephone (P) *Have you got a ~?*; phone (R).

to telephone: telephone (P); call (R) *I'll ~ you at 5 o'clock*; ring up (R); make a (phone-)call (R).

telephone number: telephone number (P); cardinal numerals of one digit, including 0 (P).

1.4 Date and place of birth

to be born: be born (P) *I was born in 1925.*

place (Ger. *Ort*, Fr. *lieu*): place (P).

birth: birth (R).

date (=indication of day, month, year): date (P); names of the months (P); cardinal or ordinal numerals up to 31 (P); cardinal numerals used to indicate years, e.g. 1974 (P).

birthday: birthday (R) *When is your* ∼?

1.5 Age

age (=length of time a person has lived): I am . . . (years old) (P); *How old are you (is he, she, etc.)?*; age (R) *What's her* ∼?

old: old (P) *I am too* ∼ *for this.*

young: young (P) *This is a party for* ∼ *people.*

year: year (P) *I am . . .* ∼*s old.*

month: month (P) *Our baby is six* ∼*s old.*

1.6 Sex

sex (=being male or female): sex (R).

male: man (P); boy (P); m. (writing only) (P); gentlemen (as on lavatory doors) (R); male (R).

female: woman (P); girl (P); f. (writing only) (P); ladies (as on lavatory doors) (R); female (R).

1.7 Marital status

married: married (P).

single (=not married): not married (P); single (R).

family (=children): children (P); family (R).

husband: husband (P).

wife: wife (P).

child: child (P).

1.8 Nationality

nationality: nationality (R); names of one's own nationality, of

nationality of native speakers of the foreign language, of inhabitants of countries neighbouring one's own country (P); names of nationality of inhabitants of countries neighbouring the foreign language country (countries) (R).

foreign: foreign (P).

foreigner: foreigner (P).

1.9 Origin

place of origin (O): place of origin (R).

country of origin: Where are you (is he, she, etc.) from? (P); I am from . . . (P); country of origin (O, R).

port of embarkation: (O) port of embarkation (R).

1.10 Education

school: school (P).

primary school: primary school (P).

secondary school: secondary school (P).

university: university (P).

college (=school for higher or professional education): college (R) *I'll go to a* ∼ *for business studies.*

vocational school: if the learner goes to or intends to go to a vocational school: name of this type of school (P).

institute: institute (R).

education: education (P).

form (=class in school): form (P) *I'm in the fifth* ∼.

course (=series of lessons): course (P) *At this institute there are* ∼*s in several foreign languages.*

lesson: lesson (P).

to train (=to give instruction): train (P) *She was* ∼*ed to be a nurse.*

to teach: teach (P).

to learn: learn (P).

to take lessons, a course, etc.: take lessons, a course, etc. (P).

to go to (school): go to (school) (P).

to leave (school): leave (school) (P) *I shall ~ school in two years.*

pupil: pupil (P).

student: student (P).

teacher: teacher (P); master (R) *Mr. Jones is our English ~.*

year: year (P).

month: month (P).

1.11 Intended profession or occupation

occupation (=what one does for a living): job (P); profession (O, R); occupation (O, R); What do you do (for a living)? (R); name of one's own intended occupation (P).

factory: factory (P) *I'm going to work in a ~.*

labourer (O): labourer (O, R).

office: office (P) *I want to work in an ~.*

office-worker: office-worker (R); clerk (R); typist (R).

farm: farm (P) *I am going to work on a ~.*

farmer: farmer (R).

business: business (P) *I am in ~.*

business-man/woman: business-man/woman (R).

shop: shop (P) *I work in a ~.*

shop-assistant: shop-assistant (R).

baker: baker (P).

butcher: butcher (P).

grocer: grocer (P).

greengrocer: greengrocer (P).

to sell: sell (P).

to buy: buy (P).

hospital: hospital (P) *I want to work in a ~.*

doctor: doctor (P); physician (R).

nurse: nurse (R).

school: school (P) *I am going to work in a ~.*

teacher: teacher (P).

army: army (P) *I am in the ~.*

soldier: soldier (P).

to work: work (P); be (P) *I'm going to ~ a teacher.*

1.12 Family

family (=parents and children): family (P).

parents: father and mother (P); parents (R).

father: father (P).

mother: mother (P).

child: child (P).

son: son (P).

daughter: daughter (P).

brother: brother (P).

sister: sister (P).

husband: husband (P).

wife: wife (P).

baby: baby (P).

grandfather: grandfather (R).

grandmother: grandmother (R).

grandchild: grandchild (R).

1.13 Religion

religion: religion (R); name of one's own religion, if any (P).

to believe in (O): believe in (P) *Do you ~ God?*

God: God (P).

church: church (P).

cathedral: cathedral (R).

service (O): service (R) *There are three ~s in this church on Sundays.*

1.14 Likes and dislikes

to like: like (P); be fond of (R).

to dislike: I don't like ... (P); hate (R).

1.15 Character, temperament, disposition

character: What sort of man/ woman/boy/etc. is he/she? (P).
kind: (adj.) kind (P).
nice: nice (P) *He is a very ~ man.*
bad: bad (P).
unpleasant: unpleasant (O, P); not (very) nice (P).
quiet (adj.) (O): quiet (O, R) *He is a very ~ boy.*
active (O): active (O, R) *He is a very ~ person.*
lazy: lazy (R).

2 House and home

2.1 Types of accommodation

to live (= to be domiciled): live (P).
house: house (P).
flat: flat (P).
apartment: apartment (R).
building (Fr. *bâtiment*): building (P) *I have an apartment in a big ~.*
furnished (O): furnished (R) *We have rented a ~ apartment.*
to buy: buy (P).
to rent: rent (O, P) *We shall ~ an apartment.*

2.2 Accommodation, rooms

room (Ger. *Zimmer*, Fr. *pièce*): room (P) *We have two ~s on the ground-floor.*
room (= space): room (P) *You have plenty of ~ here.*
kitchen: kitchen (P).
bathroom: bathroom (P).
bedroom: bedroom (P).
living-room: living-room (P).
lavatory: toilet (P); lavatory (R); w.c. (R).
garden: garden (P).

floor (Fr. *étage*): floor (P) *The bedrooms are on the first ~.*
ground-floor: ground-floor (P).
basement: basement (R).
cellar: cellar (P).
downstairs (= on a lower floor): downstairs (R) *The kitchen is ~.*
downstairs (= to a lower floor): downstairs (R) *Let's go ~ and watch television.*
upstairs (= on a higher floor): upstairs (R) *The bathroom is ~.*
upstairs (= to a higher floor): upstairs (R) *Let's go ~ and go to bed.*
stairs: stairs (P).
lift: lift (P).
door: door (P).
wall: wall (R).
window: window (P).
cupboard: cupboard (R).

2.3 Furniture, bedclothes

furniture: furniture (R).
chair: chair (P).
lamp: lamp (P).
table: table (P).
bed: bed (P).
blanket: blanket (P).
pillow: pillow (P).
sheet: sheet (P).

2.4 Room

(See 2.2 and 2.3; in addition:)

bookcase: bookcase (P).
desk: desk (P) *I have a big ~ in my room.*
picture: picture (P) *I have a nice ~ on the wall.*
plant: plant (P) *I have many ~s in my room.*
poster: poster (P) *I have a ~ on the wall.*
shelf: shelf (P) *I have a ~ for my books.*

2.5 Services

electricity: electricity (P).

gas: gas (P).

water: water (P).

heating: heating (P) *We have no ~ in this room.*

central heating: central heating (P).

oil: oil (P).

telephone: telephone (P) *We have no ~ in our apartment.*

to clean: clean (P) *The apartments are ~ed twice a week.*

to turn on (*gas*, etc.): turn on (P) *How do you ~ the gas?*

to turn off (*gas*, etc.): turn off (P) *How do you ~ the gas?*

on (=turned/switched on): on (P) *The heating is ~.*

off (=turned/switched off): off (P) *The heating is ~.*

2.6 Amenities

bath: bath (P) *The ~ is upstairs.*

shower: shower (P).

refrigerator: fridge (P).

radio: radio (P).

television: television (P); TV (R).

washing-machine: washing-machine (R).

garage (=place in which to keep a car): garage (P) *There's a ~ behind the house.*

garden: garden (P).

washing-machine: washing-machine (R).

to wash (clothes): wash (P) *You can ~ your clothes downstairs.*

to clean: clean (P) *My rooms are ~ed twice a week.*

2.7 Region

region: part of the country (P) *In our ~ there are many farms.*

agriculture: farmland (R); farms (P)

In our part of the country there are many ~.

industry (=manufacturing): factories (P) *In our part of the country there are many ~*; industry (R).

lake: lake (P).

hill: hill (P).

mountain: mountain (P).

mountains (Fr. *montagne*): mountains (P) *I like to spend my holidays in the ~.*

forest: forest (P); wood (R).

seaside: near the sea (P) *We live ~*; seaside (R).

coast: beach (P) *We walked on the ~*; near the sea (P); coast (R).

island: island (P).

water: water (P).

canal: canal (R).

river: river (P).

land: land (P).

valley: valley (P).

field: field (P) *He is working in the ~s.*

countryside: country (P) *I'd like to live in the ~, but I have not got the money for a second house.*

flat (= not hilly): flat (P) *Our part of the country is quite ~.*

beautiful: beautiful (P) *The mountains are very ~.*

top: top (P) *We could see the ~s of the mountains.*

bottom: bottom (P) *We could see the ~ of the lake.*

high: high (P).

deep: deep (P) *This is a very ~ river.*

2.8 Flora and fauna

plant: plant (P) *There are many beautiful ~s in the wood.*

flower: flower (P).

tree: (tree (P).

grass: grass (P).

animal: animal (P).

bird: bird (P).
insect: insect (P).
fly: fly (P).
dog: dog (P).
cat: cat (P).
cattle: cattle (P).
cow: cow (P).
pig: pig (P).
sheep: sheep (P).
horse: horse (P).

3 Life at home

3.1 Family
(See 1.12)

3.2 Occupation of parents
(See 1.11)

3.3 Daily routines

to wake up: wake up (P) *I ∼ at six.*
to get up: get up (P) *I ∼ at six.*
to go to (bed, school): go to (bed, school) (P).
to go home: go home (P).
to have breakfast: have breakfast (P).
to have lunch: have lunch (P).
to have dinner: have dinner (P).
meal: meal (P).
homework: homework (P).
(to be) busy: busy (P); be ∼ (P) *We are very ∼ in the morning.*
(to work) hard: hard (P) *We have to work very ∼ at school.*
after school: after school (P) *∼ I first do my homework.*
(to be) free: free (P); be ∼ (P) *I'm ∼ on Wednesday afternoons.*
spare time: spare time (R) *What do you do in your ∼?*
to read: read (P).
book: book (P) *I like to read a ∼ in the evening.*
to listen (to): listen (P); listen to (P) *I like to ∼ the radio in the evening.*

radio: radio (P).
gramophone record: record (P) *I like listening to good ∼s.*
record player: record player (P).
to watch (TV): watch (TV) (P).
to go out: go out (P) *I often ∼ in the evenings.*
to visit (friends): visit (P) *I hope you'll ∼ us when you are in Holland.*
friend: friend (P).
present (=gift): present (P) *I've brought you a ∼.*
to go for a walk: go for a walk (P).
(to go) into the country: into the country (P).
to play games: play games (P).
See also 5 Free time, entertainment.

3.4 Money

job: job (P).
working-hours: working-hours (R).
to earn (money): earn (P) *I ∼ £75 a week now.*
money: money (P).
pocket-money: pocket-money (P).
monetary system: £, pound (P); penny-pence (P); any foreign language equivalents of the names of the principal units of the learners' own monetary system (e.g. *guilder* for Dutch *gulden*) (P).
to spend (on): spend (P); ∼ on (P) *I spend my money on clothes.*
to save (money): save (P) *I ∼ money for the holidays.*
to buy: buy (P).
to put in the bank (money): put in the bank (P) *I put some money in the bank.*

3.5 Pets

pet (animal): pet (R) *Have you any ∼s?;* the foreign language words

for the learner's own pets, if any (P).
cat: cat (P).
dog: dog (P).
bird: bird (P).
fish: fish (P).
birdcage: birdcage (R).
aquarium: aquarium (R).

4 Education and future career

4.1 Schooling
(See 1.10)

4.2 Daily routines

school (=school-time): school (P) ~ *begins at 8.30.*
to begin: begin (P).
to end: end (P) *School ~s at 4.*
lesson: lesson (P).
break (=interval): break (P) *We have a ~ at 10.30.*
See also 3.3.

4.3 School-year

term (=periods into which the school-year is divided): term (P) *During the first ~ we often play football.*
holidays (=period of rest from work): holidays (P).
summer-holidays: summer-holidays (P).
Christmas: Christmas (P).
Easter: Easter (P).

4.4 Subjects

subject (=school-subject): subject (P) *What ~s do you take at school?*
reading: reading (P) *~ is taught in primary schools.*
writing: writing (P) *~ is taught in primary schools.*

mathematics: mathematics (P); arithmetic (R).
geography: geography (P).
history: history (P) *I like ~ lessons very much.*
school subjects: names of the learner's own subjects (P).
to do (a subject): do (P) *I ~ French at school.*
to study: study (P).
to choose: choose (P) *We have to ~ one foreign language.*

4.5 Recreation

club: club (P) *We have several school-~s.*
party (=celebration): party (P) *We have a nice Christmas-~.*
excursion: excursion (P) *We made an ~ to the mountains last year.*
dance (=social gathering for dancing): dance (R) *We have a ~ in May.*
to dance: dance (P) *I'd like to ~.*
Sports and games: see 5.5.

4.6 Examinations, diplomas

diploma: diploma (P); certificate (R).
examination (=testing of knowledge or ability): examination (P) *I passed my ~ last year.*
to pass (=to be successful in examination): pass (P) *I ~ed my examination last year.*
to fail (=to be unsuccessful in examination): fail (P) *I ~ed my driving-test twice.*
test: test (P) *I failed my driving-~ twice.*
final examination: final examination (R).
entrance examination: entrance examination (R).

4.7 *Future career*
(Professions, occupations: see 1.11)

to earn: earn (P) *He ~s £75 a week now.*

income: income (R); salary (R); wages (R).

tax(es): tax(es) (P).

per (week): a (week) (P) *He earns £75 a week now*; per (*week*) (R).

training: training (R).

course (instruction): course (P) *I am going to follow a ~ in book-keeping.*

to become: become (P) *I may ~ a doctor.*

unemployment (P): unemployment (O, R) *There is much ~ in our country.*

old-age pension (O): old-age pension (O, R).

5 *Free time, entertainment*

5.1 *Hobbies*
(See also 4.2–4.8)

hobby: hobby (P).

to walk: walk (P) *I like to ~ on the beach*; go for a walk (P).

to collect: collect (P) *I ~ stamps.*

to fish: fish (R) *I like to go ~ing.*

5.2 *Interests*
(See also 4.1 and 4.3–4.8)

interests: interests (R).

to be interested (in s.t.): like (P); be interested (in s.t.) (O, P).

5.3 *Radio, TV, etc.*

television: television (P); TV (R).

to watch television: watch television (P).

radio: radio (P).

programme (= list of items for broadcast): programme, (P).

news-programme: news (P); news-bulletin (R).

music: music (P).

light (music): light (P) *We listened to ~ music the whole evening.*

classical (music): classical (P) *~ music is more popular now than 10 years ago.*

popular: popular (R).

interview (n.): interview (R).

gramophone: record-player (P).

(gramophone-)record: record (P) *We listened to a ~ of Lionel Hampton.*

tape-recorder: tape-recorder (P).

tape (n.): tape (P).

to play (music): play (P) *The orchestra ~ed Beethoven.*

loud: loud (P) *The music is too ~.*

soft (opp. loud): soft (P) *I like ~ music early in the morning.*

colour: colour (P) *I'd like to see the programme in ~.*

sound: sound (P) *I don't like the ~ of this music.*

5.4 *Cinema, theatre, opera, concert, etc.*

to go out: go out (P) *When we were in Paris we went out every evening.*

afternoon: afternoon (P) *We went to the ~ performance*; matinee (O, R).

evening: evening (P).

night: night (P).

performance (O): performance (O, R).

cinema: cinema (P); movies (R).

film: film (P).

(film-)star: star (R) *Greta Garbo was a great ~.*

actor: actor (P).

actress: actress (P).

singer: singer (P).

to sing: sing (P).

song: song (P).

musician: musician (P).
music: music (P).
theatre: theatre (P).
(theatre-)play: play (P) *We saw a ~ by Noël Coward.*
stage (theatre): stage (R) *There were only two people on the ~.*
entrance (=way in): entrance (R) *There were hundreds of people before the ~ of the theatre.*
exit (=way out): exit (R) *The ~ is next to the stage.*
emergency: emergency (R) *There are five ~ exits in the theatre.*
row (=seats in a line): row (R) *Our seats are in ~ 5.*
seat: seat (P) *I want five ~s for Thursday evening.*
front (= the foremost part): front (P) *Can I have two seats in the ~?/Can I have a ~ seat?*
back (=the rearmost part): back (P) *I'd like two seats at the ~/Have you any ~ seats left?*
centre: centre (P) *I'd like to sit somewhere in the ~*; middle (R).
ticket (=theatre-ticket): ticket (P).
ticket-office: ticket-office (R).
cloakroom: cloakroom (R).
lavatory: toilet (P); lavatory (R); w.c. (R).
to book (=to reserve seats): book (P) *Where can I ~ seats for tonight?*; reserve (R).
booking-office (O): booking-office (O, R).
interval (=pause between two parts of a performance): interval (R).
opera: opera (P) *I don't like ~s by Wagner/Let's go to the ~ tonight.*
opera-house: opera-house (R).
concert: concert (P).
concert-hall: concert-hall (R).
modern (music, opera, etc.): modern (P) *I like ~ music.*
ballet: ballet (R).

to dance: dance (P).
dancer: dancer (R).
dance (=social gathering for dancing): dance (R).
night-club (O): night-club (O, P).
cabaret: cabaret (P).
floor-show (O): floor-show (O, R).
musical (=musical comedy): musical (R) *There's a nice ~ the Adelphi Theatre.*
circus: circus (R).
revue (theatrical entertainment) (O): revue (O, R) *She sings in a ~.*
Programme (=what is performed): programme (P) *There is a very good ~ at the concert-hall tonight.*
programme (=descriptive leaflet): programme (P) *Let's buy a ~ and see what the play is about.*
silence: silence (R) *~, please!*

5.5 Sports

sport(s): sport(s) (P) *Horse-racing is a popular sport in England*; name(s) of one's own favourite sport(s), if any (P); names of two or three national sports: *football* (P); *rugby* (R).
team: team (P) *The English ~ have won by 5 to 3.*
to play (games): play (P) *Do you ~ any games?*
game (=form of play): game (P) *Do you play any ~s?*; name(s) of one's own favourite game(s), if any (P).
race (=contest in speed): race (P) *There will be a boat-~ tomorrow.*
match (=contest, game): match (P) *I like watching football-~es on TV.*
to swim: swim (P).
stadium: stadium (R).
field (=sports-ground): field (P); ground (R) *There's a football-~ near the village.*
ball (=spherical object used in

games): ball (P) *If we had a ~ we could play a game.*

player: player (P).

to win: win (P).

to lose: lose (P) *The English team has lost the game.*

draw (=result of a game in which neither side has won): draw (R) *The game has ended in a ~.*

to watch: watch (P); look at (P).

5.6 Intellectual pursuits

to read: read (P).

to study: study (P); learn (P).

library: library (R).

book: book (P) *I want to buy an English ~.*

bookshop: bookshop (R).

5.7 Artistic pursuits
(See also 5.4 and 5.8)

art: art (P).

to write: write (P).

to paint: paint (P).

to make (=to produce): make (P) *Van Gogh made a beautiful picture of an old chair.*

art-forms: name(s) of one's own favourite art-forms, if any (P).

5.8 Museums, galleries, exhibitions

museum: museum (P).

gallery (=display room or building) (O): gallery (O, R).

exhibition (O): exhibition (O, R).

painting (=picture): picture (P); painting (R).

sculpture: sculpture (R) *In this cathedral you can see beautiful ~s.*

old: old (P).

antique (adj.): antique (R) *This is an ~ table.*

open (adj.): open (P) *The museum is ~ now.*

closed: closed (P) *The museum is ~ on Sundays.*

opening-hours: opening-hours (R).

to close (=to stop being open): close (P) *The exhibition ~s at 6.*

to open (=to be opened for visiting): open (P) *The museum ~s at 9.*

5.9 Press

newspaper: newspaper (P); paper (R) *Have you seen today's ~?*

magazine (=periodical): magazine (P) *I'd like to buy some ~s.*

article (=piece of writing): article (P) *There's an ~ about Wales in the* Daily Telegraph.

picture (=photograph): picture (P) *I like a magazine with many ~s.*

page: page (P) *There's an article about Wales on ~ 6.*

advertisement: advertisement (P).

to read: read (P).

6 Travel

6.1 Travel to school
(See also 6.2–6.5)

to travel: travel (P) *I have to ~ one hour to my office every day.*

early: early (P) *I have to leave very ~ in the morning.*

late (opp. early): late (P) *I always come home ~ night.*

home (=place of residence): home (P) *I leave ~ at 6 in the morning/ I come ~ at 9 in the evening.*

cheap: cheap (P).

expensive: expensive (P); be (P) *How much is a ticket to London?*

to cost: cost (R).

fare (=price of journey): fare (R) *The ~ is 15p by underground.*

ticket: ticket (P) *A ~ to London costs £1.50.*

to arrive: arrive (P).

to leave (= to go away from): leave (P) *I ~ home at 6 every morning.*

6.2 Holidays
(See also 6.1, 6.3–6.6)

holidays: holidays (P); vacation (R).

holiday: holiday (R).

summer: summer (P).

winter: winter (P).

spring: spring (P) *We always take a short holiday in ~.*

autumn: autumn (P).

season (summer, etc.): season (R) *Autumn is a good ~ for a quiet holiday.*

day: day (P).

week: week (P).

month: month (P).

Christmas: Christmas (P).

Easter: Easter (P).

tour: tour (R) *We made a ~ in the Welsh mountains.*

tourist: tourist (P).

tourist-office: tourist-office (P) *We'll ask for information at the ~.*

journey: journey (P) *We made a ~ to Spain last year*; trip (R).

group: group (P) *We went to Scotland with a ~ of friends.*

together: together (P) *We all went ~.*

abroad (= in or to a foreign country): abroad (R) *Are you going ~ this year?*; in a foreign country (P); to a foreign country (P).

to enjoy: enjoy (R) *Did you ~ your vacation?*

to visit: visit (P) *We ~ed Spain last year.*

guide (person): guide (R) *The ~ spoke several languages.*

plan (= intention): plan (R) *Have you any ~s for your summer holidays?*

sights (O): sights (O, P) *Tomorrow we are going to see the ~.*

6.3 Countries and places
(See also 2.7)

country (= state): country (P) *France is a big ~.*

town: town (P); city (R) *Coventry is an industrial ~.*

town-centre: centre (P).

castle: castle (R).

village: village (P).

place (= town, village): place (P) *Cricklewood is a nice little ~.*

small: small (P).

big: big (P); large (R).

capital town: capital (R).

Europe: Europe (P).

Africa: Africa (P).

Asia: Asia (P).

America: America (P).

Australia: Australia (P).

ocean: ocean (R).

world: world (P) *I would like to see the whole ~.*

6.4 Public transport

to travel: travel (P).

traveller: traveller (R).

to travel by ...: travel by air/car/bus/train/etc. (P).

aeroplane: plane (P); aeroplane (R).

bus: bus (P); coach (R) *We'll take the ~ to the airport.*

train: train (P).

tram: tram (P).

underground (= underground railway): underground (P) *If you want to get there fast you must take the ~.*

boat: boat (P); ferry (R); ship (R).

taxi: taxi (P).

airport: airport (P).

railway-station: railway-station (P).

bus-stop: bus-stop (P).

terminal (O): terminal (R).

railways: railways (R).

airline: airline (R).

travel bureau: travel bureau (R).

information: information (P).

information office: information office (R).

information desk: information desk (R).

enquiries: enquiries (R).

lost property office: lost property office (R).

gate (access to plane at airport) (O): gate (O, R) *Flight KL 735 to Amsterdam is boarding now through ~ 23.*

connection (=train, plane, etc., to which travellers change): connection (R) *We shall miss our ~ at Liverpool.*

to buy: buy (P).

to pay: pay (P).

to pay for ... (a ticket): pay for ... (P) *Have you paid for your ticket?*

to ask: ask (P) *Why don't you ~ him?/May I ask ~ a question?/~ him if there is a plane to London*; request (O, R).

to ask for ...: ask for ... (P) *I asked for a single ticket.*

to smoke: smoke (P).

no smoking: no smoking (R).

stewardess: stewardess (R); hostess (R).

waiting-room: waiting-room (R); lounge (R) *Passengers are requested to wait in the ~.*

refreshments (O): refreshments (O, R).

restaurant: restaurant (P).

bar (=place where drinks are served) (O): bar (O, P) *Whisky is served at the ~.*

boarding-pass (O): boarding-pass (O, R).

to change (=to leave one means of transport and get into another during a journey): change (P) *For Leeds you ~ at Sheffield.*

to check in (O): check in (O, R) *All passengers must ~ at least 30 minutes before departure.*

to board (=to go on board) (O): board (O, R) *The passengers will ~ the ship between 4 and 4.30.*

delay (O): delay (O, R) *There will be a ~ of two hours.*

delayed (O): delayed (O, R) *The train is ~.*

to cancel (O): cancel (O, R) *All services to Southend have been ~led for today.*

platform: platform (R).

direction (=course): direction (P) *This train goes in the right ~.*

to arrive: arrive (P).

arrival: arrival (R).

to reach: reach (R) *We shall ~ Amsterdam at 5 p.m.*

to leave (=to depart): leave (P) *At what time does the train ~?*

departure: departure (R).

to go to (direction): go to (P) *Where does this train ~?*

to come from (origin): come from (P) *This boat comes from Ostend.*

passenger: passenger (R).

time-table: time-table (P).

carriage: carriage (R) *Where is the first-class ~?*

fast (=quick, rapid): fast (P) *This train goes very ~.*

a fast train (=express): a fast train (P).

slow (opp. fast): slow (P) *This is a very ~ journey.*

a slow train (=stopping train): a slow train (P).

flight (=airline service) (O): flight (O, R) *~ KL173 has just arrived.*

flight (=journey by air) (O): flight

(O, R) *I hope you have enjoyed your*
~.

charter-flight (O): charter-flight (O, R).

to fly: fly (P).

harbour: harbour (R) *The ship came into the ~.*

to hurry: hurry (P) *~, or you will miss your train.*

to wait: wait (P) *We had to ~ only five minutes.*

to wait for: wait for (P) *~ me on the platform.*

to take (duration): take (P) *The journey ~s two hours.*

6.5 Private transport
(See also 11.7–11.9)

motor-car: car (P) *I always travel by ~ in my holidays*; motor-car (R).

lorry: lorry (R) *This street is not for lorries.*

petrol: petrol (P).

oil: oil (P).

to drive (a car): drive (P) *I never drink beer when I have to ~ a car.*

driver: driver (R).

petrol-station: petrol-station (P).

car-park: car-park (R).

to park: park (P) *Where can I ~ my car?*

speed: speed (P).

speed-limit: speed-limit (R).

fine (=sum of money to be paid as a penalty): fine (R) *You will have to pay a ~ of £10.*

blue zone (O): blue zone (O, R) *In the ~ you can park for one hour only.*

insurance (O): insurance (O, P).

driving-licence (O): driving-licence (O, R).

traffic-lights: traffic-lights (P).

bicycle: bicycle (P); bike (R).

motor-cycle: motor-cycle (P).

motor-scooter (O): scooter (O, R).

to hire (O): hire (O, P) *We shall ~ a car when we come to Britain*; rent (O, R).

crossing (=place where roads or road and railway cross): crossing (P) *Look out for trains when you come to the ~.*

to cross: cross (P) *Look out when you ~ the street.*

pedestrian: pedestrian (R).

motorway: motorway (P).

one-way street: one-way street (P).

danger: danger (R).

dangerous: dangerous (P).

safe (=secure): safe (R) *This is a very ~ car.*

safety: (safety (R).

busy (=full of traffic): busy (R) *Drive carefully, this is a very ~ street.*

road-sign texts (O): the commonest texts on road signs, e.g. dual carriageway (ahead); keep in lane; no entry; no parking; one-way street; turn left/right; slow down; give way (all for reading only) (O, R).

6.6 Entering and leaving a country

immigration (O): immigration (O, R).

customs (where duty is paid) (O): customs (O, P) *We had to pay duty at the ~.*

to import (O): import (O, R).

to declare (goods to be imported) (O): declare (O, R) *Have you anything to ~?*

duty (sum of money to be paid when importing goods) (O): duty (O, R) *You'll have to pay ~ on your new watch.*

frontier: frontier (P).

foreign: foreign (P).

to change (money from one country for that of another): change (P) *I want to ~ 500 French francs.*

currency (O): currency (O, R).
money: money (P).
to visit (a country): visit (P).
passport: passport (P).
to stay (in a country): stay (P) *I want to ~ in England for three weeks.*
visa (O): visa (O, R).
form (to be filled in): form (R) *All foreign visitors must fill in this ~.*
to open: open (P) *Will you ~ your bag, please?*

6.7 *Nationalities*
(See 1.8)

6.8 *Languages*
(See also 13)

language (=form of language used by a nation or race): language (P) *English is a very useful ~.*
native language: native language (R).
languages: names of one's native language, of the language of the foreign country (English), names of languages of countries neighbouring one's own country (P); names of languages of countries neighbouring the foreign language country (R).

6.9 *Hotel, camping-site, etc.*
hotel: hotel (P).
reception (=counter where guests are received) (O): reception (O, R) *Leave your key at the ~, please.*
reservation (=booking for accommodation) (O): reservation (O, R) *Have you a ~, sir?*
to book (sc. accommodation) (O): book (O, P) *I have ~ed two rooms for tonight.*
lift: lift (P) *Take the ~ to the third floor.*
to press (a button): press (R) *~ the button for the third floor.*
button (=push-button): button (R) *Press the ~ for the third floor.*

porter (=door-keeper) (O): porter (O, R) *The ~ will call a taxi for you.*
porter (=person who carries luggage) (O): porter (O, R) *The ~ will take your luggage to your room.*
hall (=space into which the main entrance opens) (O): hall (O, R) *We shall wait for the coach in the ~.*
lounge (=sitting-room for guests) (O): lounge (O, R) *The guests can watch television in the ~.*
balcony: balcony (P) *I want a room with a ~.*
view (Ger. *Aussicht*): view (R) *You have a nice ~ from this room.*
quiet (opp. noisy): quiet (P) *Can you give me a very ~ room?*
to disturb (O): disturb (O, R) *Please, do not ~.*
noise: noise (P) *Give me another room, please, there is too much ~ from the street here.*
stairs: stairs (P) *You'll have to use the ~, there is no lift here.*
inn: inn (R).
camping-site: camping-site (P).
tent: tent (P).
caravan (mobile home pulled behind a motor-car): caravan (P) *Is your car strong enough to pull this ~ in the mountains?*
youth-hostel: youth-hostel (P).
regulations (=rules to be observed): regulations (R) *It is against the ~ to walk on the grass.*
charge (=price) (O): charge (O, R) *The ~ for caravans is £1 per 24 hours;* price (P).
included: included (R) *Breakfast is ~.*
bill (=note stating amount of money due): bill (P) *Can you give me my ~, please?*
receipt (O): receipt (O, P) *May I have a ~, please?*

account (=statement of money (to be) paid or received) (O): account (O, P) *The price of the meal will be put on your* ~.

cheque (O): cheque (O, P) *I'll give you a* ~ *for £25.*

boarding-house: boarding-house (R).

guest: guest (P).

to call (=to wake) (O): call (O, P) *Please,* ~ *me at 6 tomorrow morning.*

key: key (P).

desk (=counter) (O): desk (O, R) *Please leave your key at the* ~.

message (O): message (O, R) *There is a* ~ *for you at the reception.*

to register (in a hotel, at a camping-site, etc.) (O): register (O, R) *Please* ~ *before going up to your room.*

single room: room for one person (P); single room (R).

double room: room for two persons (P); double room (R).

dormitory: dormitory (R).

to push: push (R) ~ *to open the door.*

to pull: pull (R) ~ *to open the door.*

6.10 Travel documents

passport: passport (P).

document (O): document (O, R) *Where are your insurance* ~*s?*

insurance (O): insurance (O, P).

driving-licence (O): driving-licence (O, R).

visa (O): visa (O, R).

6.11 Fares
(See also 6.4 and 6.12)

fare (price of transport): price (P); fare (R) *The* ~ *to Ostend is £15.*

6.12 Tickets

ticket (for journey): ticket (P) *Have you got the bus* ~*s?*

single (journey): single (P) *Two* ~*s to Brighton, please.*

return (journey): return (P) *A* ~ *ticket is cheaper than two singles.*

cheap: cheap (P).

adult (grown-up person): adult (P) *We are two* ~*s and three children.*

child: child (P).

group: group (P).

class (railway carriages, airline cabins): class (P) *Travelling first* ~ *is very expensive in our country.*

6.13 Luggage

luggage: luggage (P); baggage (R).

bag (=travelling-bag, handbag): bag (P) *I have two* ~*s and one suitcase.*

suitcase: suitcase (P).

box: box (P) *Can you give me a* ~ *for these glasses?*

to carry (=to take from one place to another): carry (P) *Can you* ~ *this heavy suitcase for me?*

camera: camera (P).

porter (=person who carries luggage) (O): porter (O, R) *Do you want a* ~ *for your luggage?*

weight (O): weight (O, R).

heavy: heavy (P).

light (opp. heavy): light (P) *I don't need a porter, these bags are very* ~.

6.14 Traffic
(See 6.5)

7 Relations with other people

7.1 Friendship/Aversion

friend: friend (P).

to like (a person): like (P) *I* ~ *your brother very much.*

to dislike (a person): like+negation (P) *I don't* ~ *your brother.*

7.2 Invitations (O)[1]

to invite (=to ask a person to come somewhere) (O): invite (R) *They have ~ed us for dinner tonight.*

invitation (O): invitation (O, R).

to make an appointment (=to arrange to meet a person) (O): make an appointment (O, R) *Can we ~ for next week?*

to join (=to come into the company of ...) (O): join (O, P) *May I ~ you for dinner?/Will you ~ us on our trip tomorrow?*

to expect (=to be ready to receive a person) (O): expect (O, R) *We shall ~ you at 5.*

to come to (sc. a place): come to (P) *Why don't you ~ my house?*

to have dinner: have dinner (P); dine (R).

to have lunch: have lunch (P).

to have tea: have tea (P).

to have coffee: have coffee (P).

to have breakfast: have breakfast (P).

to have a drink (O): have a drink (O, P).

to visit (=to pay a visit to a person): visit (P); come and see ... (O, R) *Why don't you ~ us tomorrow?*

present (=gift): present (P) *I've brought you a ~ from my own country.*

party (=social gathering): party (P) *We are giving a ~ for our friends tonight.*

to talk: talk (P) *We ~ed for a long time.*

to promise: promise (R) *~ you will come tomorrow.*

7.3 Correspondence

to correspond (=to exchange letters): correspond with ... (R) *I have cor-*

responded with an English friend for two years now. We write to each other every month.

pen-friend: pen-friend (R).

letter: letter (P).

envelope: envelope (P).

postcard: postcard (P).

postage-stamp: stamp (P).

pen: pen (P).

pencil: pencil (P).

note-paper: note-paper (R); paper (P) *I want to write a letter, but I have no ~.*

to send (a letter): send (P) *I sent him a letter last week.*

to receive (mail): receive (P) *I ~d a letter from him last week*; get (P) *Did you ~ a letter yesterday?*

to answer (a letter): answer (R) *Has he ~ed your letter?*

answer (to a letter): answer (P) *Have you received an ~ to your letter?*

opening formula (letter): Dear (writing only) (P) *~ Mr. Jones.*

closing formula (letter): Yours sincerely (writing only) (P).

7.4 Club-membership

club (=society of persons): club (P) *We have a sports-~ in our village.*

member (of a club): member (P) *I am a ~ of a sports-club.*

meeting (=gathering): meeting (P) *We have club ~s every week.*

to meet (=to gather): meet (P) *We ~ in a pub every Friday.*

7.5 Politics (and optional: social security)

politics: politics (P).

political: political (P).

party (=political party): party (P) *Are you a ~-member?*

government: government (P).

---

[1] Items not marked as optional occur in other sections.

to govern (=to rule): govern (R) *This king ~ed for 26 years.*

conservative (=party, politics) (O): conservative (O, P) *We have a ~ government now.*

socialist (n. and adj.) (O): socialist O P) *We have a ~ government/I an not a ~.*

communist (n. and adj.) (O): communist (O, P) *I am a member of the ~ party/Are there many ~s in your country?*

king: king (P).

queen: queen (P).

president: president (P).

minister: minister (P).

prime minister: prime minister (R).

right-wing (party, politics) (O): right-wing (O, R) *We have a ~ government now.*

left-wing (party, politics) (O): left-wing (O, R) *They are ~ students.*

state (=political community): state (P) *The ~ pays for our education.*

opinion (O): opinion (O, P).

war: war (P).

peace: peace (P).

social security (O): social security (O, R).

old-age pension (O): old-age pension (O, R).

8 Health and welfare

8.1 Parts of the body

head (part of body): head (P) *My ~ hurts.*

neck: neck (P).

back (=surface of the body from neck to buttocks): back (P) *My ~ hurts.*

arm: arm (P) *I cannot move my ~.*

hand: hand (P).

leg: leg (P).

foot (part of body): foot (P) *My ~ hurts.*

heart: heart (P).

stomach: stomach (P).

tooth: tooth (P).

hair: hair (P).

8.2 Ailments, accidents

ill (in bad health): ill (P) *I have been ~ for a week now.*

pain: pain (P); -ache (R) *I have a head~.*

fever: fever (P); temperature (R) *I have a ~.*

health: health (R).

wound: wound (P); injury (O, R).

operation (medical treatment by surgeon): operation (P) *I have had two stomach-~s.*

bandage: bandage (P) *I need a ~ for this wound.*

to be operated upon: be operated upon (R); have an operation (P).

accident (e.g. in traffic): accident (P) *I had a bad ~ yesterday.*

disease: disease (R); illness (R).

to fall ill: fall ill (R).

dead: dead (P); killed (R).

alive: alive (P).

to live (= to be alive): be alive (P) *The patient is still alive*; live (R).

cold (illness of nose or throat): cold (P) *I am afraid I have a ~.*

to hurt (tr. and intr.): hurt (P) *My leg ~s/This will ~ a little.*

to fall: fall (P) *Be careful or you will ~ on the ice.*

to break (fracture): break (P) *He has broken his leg.*

to feel (Fr. *se sentir*): feel (P) *I don't ~ quite well.*

to burn (tr.): burn (P) *I have ~t my hand.*

to cut: cut (P) *I have ~ my finger.*

to happen: happen (P) *What ~ed?*

8.3 Personal comfort

comfortable (O): comfortable (O, P)

I am quite ~ now/The chair is not very ~.

thirst: thirst (R).

thirsty: thirsty (P).

hunger: hunger (R).

hungry: hungry (P).

tired: tired (P).

well (=in good health): well (P) *I feel very ~.*

to look (=have a certain appearance): look (P) *You ~ very well.*

to rest (=to repose): rest (P) *I would like to ~ a little.*

rest (=repose): rest (P) *I will have to take a ~.*

to sleep: sleep (P).

sleepy: sleepy (P).

to wake up: wake up (P) *I woke up at 6 o'clock.*

8.4 Hygiene

to wash (tr. and intr.): wash (P) *I would like to ~ before dinner/Can you ~ these clothes for me?*

soap: soap (P).

towel: towel (P).

clean (opp. dirty): clean (P) *This shirt is not ~.*

dirty: dirty (P).

toothbrush: toothbrush (P).

toothpaste: toothpaste (P).

scissors: scissors (P).

comb: comb (P).

brush: brush (P).

to cut (hair): cut (P) *Will you ~ my hair, please?*

to shave (intr.): shave (P) *I want to ~ before dinner.*

razor: razor (P).

laundry (=laundering business) (O): laundry (O, R) *Is there a ~ in the neighbourhood?*

laundry (=clothes (to be) laundered) (O): laundry (O, R) *Has the ~ come back yet?*

8.5 Insurance (O)

to insure (O): insure (O, P).

insurance (O): insurance (O, P).

third-party (=insurance) (O): third-party (O, P) *Do you have ~ insurance?*

8.6 Medical services

doctor (=physician): doctor (P) *If you don't feel well you should go to the ~*; physician (R); surgeon (R).

ambulance: ambulance (R).

surgery-hours (O): surgery-hours (O, R) *~ 8 a.m. to 10 a.m.*

health: health (R).

patient (=person undergoing medical treatment): patient (R) *The ~ must not be moved.*

chemist: chemist (P).

medicine (=remedy): medicine (P) *Take this ~ three times a day.*

tablet (medical): tablet (P) *I must take one ~ after every meal*; pill (R).

ward (=division or room in a hospital) (O): ward (O, R) *Your daughter is in the children's ~.*

specialist (=specialized physician) (O): specialist (O, P) *I think you should go to a ~.*

dentist: dentist (P).

to fill (sc. a tooth): fill (P) *This tooth was ~ed six months ago.*

appointment (=arrangement to meet doctor or dentist) (O): appointment (O, R) *What time is your ~?*

prescription (O): prescription (O, R) *Do you want a ~ for new tablets?*

glasses (=spectacles): glasses (P).

8.7 Emergency services

fire: fire (P).

fire-service: fire-service (R).

ambulance: ambulance (R).
police: police (P).
policeman: policeman (P).
police-station: police-station (P).
consul (O): consul (O, P).
consulate (O): consulate (O, R).
embassy (O): embassy (O, R).

9 Shopping

9.1 Shopping facilities

shop: shop (P).
supermarket: supermarket (P).
department store: department store (R).
market (=public place for buying and selling goods): market (P) *We buy our vegetables at the ~.*
opening-hours: opening-hours (R).
grocer: grocer (P).
butcher: butcher (P).
baker: baker (P).
greengrocer: greengrocer (P).
tobacconist (O): tobacconist (O, P).
to buy: buy (P).
to sell: sell (P).
to change (something one has bought): change (P) *I want to ~ this shirt; it is not the right colour.*
sale (=offering of goods at low prices for a period): sale (R) *You can buy things very cheaply at the ~s.*
souvenirs: souvenirs (P).
(to pay) **cash** (O): cash (O, R).
new: new (P) *I want to buy a ~ book about England.*
to find: find (P) *Where can I ~ a tobacconist?*
it is my (etc.) **turn:** it is my (etc.) turn (R).
self-service: self-service (R).
to wrap up (O): wrap up (O, R) *Shall I wrap it up for you?*
to show: show (P) *Please ~ me another one.*

9.2 Foodstuffs

(See 10.1)

9.3 Clothes, fashion

clothes: clothes (P).
dress: dress (P).
suit: suit (P).
underwear: underwear (P).
trousers: trousers (P).
jacket: jacket (P).
shirt: shirt (P).
blouse: blouse (P).
shoe: shoe (P).
socks: socks (P).
stockings: stockings (P).
coat: coat (P).
raincoat: raincoat (P).
hat: hat (P).
skirt: skirt (P).
wool: wool (P); woollen (R).
nylon: nylon (P).
cotton: cotton (R).
leather: leather (P).
plastic: plastic (P).
real: real (P) *Is this ~ leather?*
purse: purse (P).
wallet (O): wallet (O, P).
size (=standard measurement): size (P) *What ~ shoes do you take?*
blue: blue (P).
black: black (P).
brown: brown (P).
green: green (P).
grey: grey (P).
orange: orange (P).
red: red (P).
white: white (P).
yellow: yellow (P).
light (colour): light (P) *I want a ~ colour.*
dark (colour): dark (P) *I want a ~ blue shirt.*
pair: pair (P) *I want to buy a ~ of shoes.*
pocket: pocket (P) *I want a coat with big ~s.*

watch (=timepiece): watch (P) *I want to buy a new* ∼.

to wear (clothes): wear (P) *I am not going to* ∼ *this.*

(dressed) **in:** in (R) *Did you see the girl* ∼ *the white dress?*

to try on (clothes): try on (P).

to put on (clothes): put on (P).

to take off (clothes): take off (P).

9.4 Smoking (O)

tobacco (O): tobacco (O, P).

pipe (O): pipe (O, P).

cigar (O): cigar (O, P).

cigarette (O): cigarette (O, P).

ashtray (O): ashtray (O, P).

9.5 Household-articles

pan: pan (P).

spoon: spoon (P).

fork: fork (P).

knife: knife (P).

dish: dish (R).

plate (from which food is eaten): plate (P) *I want a* ∼ *of bacon and sausage.*

cup: cup (P).

saucer: saucer (P).

bottle: bottle (P).

pot: pot (P) *Bring us a* ∼ *of tea, please.*

glass (=drinking vessel): glass (P) *I want to buy wine-*∼*es.*

glass (material): glass (P) *Is this made of* ∼ *or of plastic?*

matches (Fr. *allumettes*): matches (P) *I'd like a box of* ∼.

string (=cord): string (P) *I need a piece of* ∼.

9.6 Medicine
(See 8.6)

9.7 Prices

price: price (P).

expensive: expensive (P).

cheap: cheap (P).

high (price): high (P) *Prices are very* ∼ *in this country.*

low (price): low (P) *Prices are rather* ∼ *in this shop.*

free (=gratis): free (P) *You don't have to pay for it, it is* ∼.

how much?: how much? ∼ *are these shoes?*

to cost: be (P) *These shoes are £23;* cost (R) *These shoes* ∼ *£23.*

too (degree): too (P) *£23 is* ∼ *much for these shoes.*

discount (O): discount (O, R).

to spend (money): spend (P) *I cannot* ∼ *so much money.*

money: money (P).

bank-notes: bank-notes (R).

coins: coins (P).

monetary-system: £ (P): penny-pence (P).

to pay: pay (P) *How much did you* ∼ *for that?*

9.8 Weights and measurements

weight (=heaviness) (O): weight (O, P) *This is not the right* ∼.

to weigh: weigh (R) *This will* ∼ *5 lbs.*

heavy: heavy (P).

light (opp. heavy): light (P) *This coat is not* ∼ *enough.*

enough (=sufficiently): enough (P) *This coat is not light* ∼.

weights: kilo (P); lb. (P); oz. (P).

measures: mile (P); yard (P); foot (P) *The road is 20 ft. wide*; inch (P); kilometre (P); metre (P); centimetre (P); gallon (O, P); pint (O, P).

10 Food and drink

10.1 Types of food and drink

meal: meal (P).

food: food (P).
to eat: eat (P).
to drink: drink (P).
soup: soup (P).
meat: meat (P).
bacon: bacon (R).
sausage: sausage (R).
steak: steak (R).
beef: beef (R).
lamb: lamb (R).
pork: pork (R).
veal: veal (R).
to fry (O): fry (O, R).
to grill (O): grill (O, R).
to roast (O): roast (O, R).
to boil (O): boil (O, R).
fish: fish (P).
chicken: chicken (P).
omelette: omelette (P).
ham: ham (R).
vegetables: vegetables (P); some common national vegetables: cabbage, peas, beans (R).
potatoes: potatoes (P).
pommes frites (O): chips (O, R); pommes frites (O, R).
salad: salad (P).
tomato: tomato (R).
mushrooms (O): mushrooms (O, R).
egg: egg (P).
rice: rice (P).
spaghetti, macaroni: spaghetti (P).
salt: salt (P).
pepper: pepper (P).
mustard: mustard (P).
bread: bread (P).
(bread-)roll: roll (P) *Would you like some ~s?*
butter: butter (P).
slice: slice (P) *A ~ of bread, please.*
cheese: cheese (P).
dessert: dessert (P); sweet (R) *Have you ordered a ~?*
fruit: fruit (P).
apple: apple (P).
pear: pear (P).

banana: banana (P).
strawberry: strawberry (R).
nut: nut (R).
orange (fruit): orange (P) *I'll have an ~, please.*
ice-cream: ice-cream (P).
vanilla: vanilla (R).
chocolate: chocolate (P) *I'll have ~ ice-cream/Can I have a piece of ~?*
cake: cake (P).
pastry: pastry (R).
to bake: bake (R).
jam: jam (P).
coffee: coffee (P).
tea: tea (P).
cream: cream (R).
milk: milk (P).
sugar: sugar (P).
beer: beer (P).
wine: wine (P).
mineral water (O): mineral water (O, P).
fruit-juice: fruit-juice (P).
water: water (P).
sandwich: sandwich (P).
hot: hot (P).
cold: cold (P).
nice (= of pleasant taste): nice (P).
sweet: sweet (P) *The coffee is not ~ enough.*
bitter: bitter (P).
warm: warm (P).
thick: thick (P).
thin: thin (P).
drink (= alcoholic liquor): drink (P) *What about a ~?*
piece: piece (P) *I would like a ~ of chocolate.*

10.2 Eating and drinking out

restaurant: restaurant (P).
snackbar: snackbar (P).
café (O): café (O, R).
pub: pub (P).
bar (= counter for drinking) (O): bar (O, P) *Let's go to the ~ for a drink.*

canteen (O): canteen (O, R).

self-service: self-service (R).

help-yourself (O): help-yourself (O, R).

service (=serving of food and drink) (O): service (O, R) *No ∼ in the garden/∼ is included in the bill.*

table: table (P) *A ∼ for two, please.*

waiter: waiter (P) *The ∼ will give us the menu.*

waitress: waitress (P) *Let's ask the ∼ for the menu.*

to serve (=to provide guests with food and drink): serve (R) *We don't ∼ dinner after 10 p.m.*

to order (=to give an order to be served) (O): order (O, P) *I have ∼ed a bottle of red wine.*

menu: menu (P) *Give me the ∼, please.*

to have breakfast: have breakfast (P).

to have coffee: have coffee (P).

to have lunch: have lunch (P).

to have tea: have tea (P).

to have dinner: have dinner (P); dine (R).

to choose (=select): choose (P) *Have you chosen something from the menu?*

to decide: decide (R) *Have you ∼d yet?*

bill (=statement of money (to be) paid): bill (P) *Can I have my ∼, please.*

tip (Fr. *pourboire*) (O): tip (O, R) *The waiter will expect a ∼.*

service-charge (O): service-charge (O, R) *There is no ∼ in the canteen.*

to take away (=to remove) (O): take away (O, R) *Can I take this away?*

11 Services

11.1 Post

post-office: post-office (P).

to post (letter): post (P) *∼ this letter before 7 p.m.*

collection (=emptying of letter-boxes by postman) (O): collection (O, R) *The next ∼ is at 5 o'clock.*

letter-box: letter-box (P) *Where is the nearest ∼?*

letter (=written communication): letter (P) *I have received a ∼ from my brother.*

parcel: parcel (P).

postage stamp: stamp (P) *Do they sell ∼s at the hotel?*

postage (=payment for the carrying of letters): postage (R) *The ∼ for this parcel will be 50p.*

mail (=letters, parcels, etc., sent or delivered by post): mail (R) *The ∼ has not arrived yet.*

poste restante (O): poste restante (O, R).

postman: postman (R).

11.2 Telephone

telephone: telephone (P) *Have you got a ∼?*; phone (R).

to telephone: telephone (P); call (R) *I'll ∼ you at 5 o'clock*; ring up (R); make a (phone-)call (R).

telephone number: telephone number (P).

telephone booth: telephone booth (R); phone booth (R); call-box (R).

operator (O): operator (O, R).

to dial (O): dial (O, R).

coin: coin (P) *I have no ∼s for the telephone.*

out of order: out of order (R) *The telephone is ∼.*

11.3 Telegraph

telegraph: telegraph (R).

telegram: telegram (P).

to send: send (P).

to arrive: arrive (P).
word: word (P).
sender: sender (R) *What is the name of the ~?*

11.4 Bank

bank (=establishment for the keeping and transfer of money): bank (P) *You can cash your traveller's cheques at any ~.*
to change (money from one country for that of another): change (P) *I want to ~ 500 French francs.*
currency (O): currency (O, R).
money: money (P).
cheque (O): cheque (O, P).
traveller's cheque (O): cheque (O, P); traveller's cheque (O, R).
to cash (a cheque) (O): cash (O, P) *I want to ~ this cheque.*
bank account (O): account (O, P) *I have an ~ with the Midland Bank.*
to borrow: borrow (P).
to lend: lend (P).

11.5 Police

police: police (P).
policeman: policeman (P).
police-station: police-station (P).
thief: thief (P).
to steal: steal (P).
to lose: lose (P) *I have lost my passport.*
fine (=sum of money to be paid as a penalty): fine (R) *You will have to pay a ~ of £10.*
law: law (R).

11.6 Hospital, surgery, etc.
(See 8.6)

11.7 Repairs

to repair: repair (P); mend (R).
to fasten: fasten (P).

button (for fastening clothes): button (P) *I've lost a ~.*

11.8 Garage

garage: garage (P).
breakdown (=mechanical failure): trouble (P) *I have ~ with my car*; engine-trouble O, R).
to help: help (P).
to work (=to function): work (P) *My brakes don't ~.*
brake (O): brake (O, P) *My ~s don't work.*
engine: (engine (P).

11.9 Petrol station

petrol: petrol (P).
petrol station: petrol station (P).
oil (O): oil (O, P).
tyres (O): tyres (O, P).
to check (=to examine) (O): check (O, P) *Will you ~ the tyres, please?*
standard quantity of petrol (O): gallon (O, P).
full: full (P).
empty: empty (P).

12 Places

map: map (P).
to lose one's way: lose one's way (P).
north (=region): north (P) *He lives in the ~.*
north (=direction): north (P) *From this point you go ~.*
south (=region): south (P) *Bournemouth is in the ~.*
south (=direction): south (P) *Turn ~ when you come to the river.*
east (=region): east (P) *The snow came from the ~.*
east (=direction): east (P) *We are going to travel ~.*
west (=region): west (P) *There are beautiful beaches in the ~.*

west (=direction): west (P) *If you drive ~ you cannot miss it.*

point (=indication of place): point (P) *Turn left at this ~ on the map.*

straight on: straight on (P).

to turn (=change direction): turn (P) *~ left at the river.*

left (=position): left (P) *The town is on your ~.*

left (=direction): left (P) *Turn ~ at the crossing.*

right (position): right (P) *The town is on your ~.*

right (=direction): right (P) *Turn ~ for Liverpool.*

to cross: cross (P) *~ the river at this point.*

opposite (=facing): opposite (P) *There is a pub ~ the town hall.*

next to: next to (P) *There is a pub ~ the town hall.*

to pass (=to go past): pass (P) *You ~ a big building on your right.*

crossing (=place where roads or road and railway cross): crossing (P) *Drive 5 miles till you come to a railway ~*; crossroads (P) *Turn left at the ~.*

roundabout (=circular road at road junction): roundabout (R) *Drive on till you come to a ~.*

bridge: bridge (P).

corner: corner (P).

end: end (P) *Turn left at the ~ of the street.*

side: side (P) *Put your car at the ~ of the road.*

road: road (P).

street: street (P).

square: square (P) *I live in Portman Square.*

path: path (P).

direction (=course (to be) taken): direction (P) *In which ~ is Slough?*; way (P) *Is this the ~ to the opera?*

far: far (P).

near (opp. far): near (P) *The village is quite ~.*

distance: distance (P).

to follow: follow (P) *Just ~ me till we get to the station.*

town-hall: town-hall (R) *The post-office is opposite the ~.*

13 Foreign language

13.1 Ability

to speak: speak (P).

to understand: understand (P).

to read: read (P).

to write: write (P).

well (adv.): well (P) *I cannot write English very ~.*

a little: a little (P).

not at all: not at all (P).

easy: easy (P).

simple: simple (P).

difficult: difficult (P).

hard: hard (R) *His English is ~ to understand.*

difficulty: difficulty (R).

to say: say (P).

to know: know (P) *I don't ~ that word.*

word: word (P) *I don't know that ~.*

13.2 Understanding

to call (=to use as a name): call (P) *What do you ~ this in English?*

to be called: be called (R) *What is this called in English?*

to repeat: say again (P); repeat (R).

slowly: slowly (P) *Will you speak ~, please?*

clear (=understood): clear (P) *That's not ~ to me.*

to understand: understand (P) *I don't ~ this word*; see (R) *I ~ what you mean.*

I beg your pardon (=Will you say

that again): I beg your pardon?
(P).

to explain: explain (P).

to mean (Fr. *signifier*): mean (P)
What does this word ∼?

to mean (=to have in mind): mean
(P) *What do you ∼?*

meaning (Fr. *signification*): meaning
(R) *What's the ∼ of this word?*

to translate: translate (P).

translation: translation (P).

dictionary: dictionary (P).

13.3 Correctness

correct: right (P); correct (R).

to correct: correct (P) *Will you ∼ me
if I make mistakes?*

mistake: mistake (P).

incorrect: wrong (P).

to pronounce: pronounce (P).

pronunciation: pronunciation (R).

to spell: spell (P) *Will you ∼ that
word, please?*

spelling: spelling (R) *That's not the
correct ∼.*

question: question (P) *May I ask a
∼?*

14 Weather

14.1 Climate

cold: cold (P).
hot: hot (P).
pleasant: pleasant (P).
dry: dry (P).
rainy: rainy (P).
climate: climate (P).

14.2 Weather conditions

weather: weather (P).

fine (=sunny): fine (P) *The weather
will be ∼ tomorrow.*

bad: bad (P) *We have had three weeks
of ∼ weather.*

mild: mild (R) *We usually have ∼
weather in April.*

hot: hot (P).

warm: warm (P).

cool: cool (P).

cold (opp. hot): cold (P) *It's very ∼
today.*

sun: sun (P).

moon: moon (P).

star: star (P).

sunshine: sunshine (R).

rain: rain (P).

snow: snow (P).

ice: ice (P).

wind: wind (P).

storm: storm (R); gale (P).

thunderstorm: thunderstorm (P).

lightning: lightning (R).

heat: heat (R).

frost: frost (P).

fog: fog (P); mist (R).

shade (area without direct sunlight):
shade (P) *Shall we sit in the ∼?*

to rain: rain (P).

to snow: snow (P).

to freeze: freeze (P).

to shine: shine (P).

dark: dark (P).

light (opp. dark): light (P) *It will be
∼ soon.*

degree (temperature): degree (P) *It is
10 ∼s below zero.*

zero (zero point on thermometer):
zero (R) *It is 10 degrees below ∼.*

temperature (degree of heat and
cold): temperature (P) *The ∼ is
too high for me.*

4   Inventories

4.1   Lexical inventory

The items are arranged alphabetically. For several items, especially those which may belong to more than one grammatical category or which may have more than one meaning, a context is provided in order to indicate the category or the meaning which falls within the objective. See 4.2 for a more detailed account of the range of structurally complex items.

Each item is marked P (productive and receptive) or R (receptive) and provided with a code referring to the content-specification of chapter 3. Roman numerals refer to the divisions, Arabic numerals to the sections within each division.

Certain items are marked O as optional items.

A

a(n) P, II.8 *I'd like to buy ~ new suit. I'll give you ~ pound.*

a(n) P, II.3.15, III.4.7 *He earns £75 ~ week now.*

able P, I.2.14 *I won't be ~ to come.*

about P, II.4.1 *I have ~ £10.*

about P, I.5.1, I.5.3, II.7.6.9 *I don't want to talk ~ the war. What ~ (having) a drink? How ~ (having) a drink?* (R). *What ~ me?* (R).

above R, II.2.2 *We were flying ~ the clouds. He's in the room ~.*

abroad R, III.6.2 *Are you going ~ this year?*

accept P, II.5.2.4 *I cannot ~ (this).*

accident P, III.8.2 *I had a bad ~ yesterday.*

account O P, III.6.9, III.11.4 *The price of the meal will be put on your ~. I have an ~ with the Midland Bank.*

-ache R, III.8.2 *I have a head~.*

across R, II.2.5 *We walked ~ the street.*

active O R, III.1.15 *He is a very ~ person.*

actor P, III.5.4

actress P, III.5.4

address P, III.1.2 *What's your ~? My ~ is 15 Church Road, Cricklewood.*

adult P, II.5.1.11, III.6.12 *We are two ~s and three children. I am learning English at an institute for ~ education.*

advertisement P, III.5.9

aeroplane R, III.6.4

afraid P, I.2.5, I.3.12 *I'm ~ I cannot help you. Are you ~?*

Africa P, III.6.3

after P, II.2.7, II.3.3 *John came ~ Peter. John came ~ 6 o'clock.*

after P, II.3.3 *John came ~ I had left.*

afternoon P, I.6.1, II.3.1, III.5.4 *Good*

~! This ~ ... We went to the ~ performance.

afterwards R, II.3.3, II.3.4 *I'll do it ~.*

again P, II.3.20, III.13.2 *Will you say that ~?*

again and again R, II.3.20

against P, II.2.2, II.5.2.4 *He stood ~ the wall. I am ~ war* (R).

age R, II.5.1.11, III.1.5 *What's her ~?*

ago P, II.3.1 *Four days ~.*

agree P, I.2.1 *I ~.*

air P, III.6.4 *We'll travel by ~.*

airline R, III.6.4

airport P, III.6.4

alive P, II.5.1.12, III.8.2 *The patient is still ~.*

all P, II.8 *They ~ went home. I want ~ of it.*

all P, II.4.2 *I've lost ~ my money. ~ the shops are closed.*

all right P, I.2.1, I.2.4, I.2.24, I.4.2, II.5.1.12, II.5.2.5 *That's ~. It's ~ now. Your car is ~ now.*

allow P, I.2.25 *Are you ~ed to stay here?*

almost P, II.4.3

along R, II.2.4 *Why don't you come ~?*

along R, II.2.5 *Walk ~ this street, then turn left.*

already P, II.3.2 *I have ~ done it.*

also P, II.7.6.1, II.7.6.3 *John will ~ come.*

always P, II.3.15, II.3.18, II.8

a.m. R, II.3.1 *The train leaves at 3 ~.*

ambulance R, III.8.6, III.8.7

America P, III.6.3

among R, II.2.2 *We found a ring ~ the flowers.*

and P, II.7.6.1

animal P, III.2.8

another P, II.4.1, II.7.4.1 *Give me ~ cup of tea; I always have two. Give me ~ book; I don't like this one.*

answer P, II.6.2, III.7.3 *Have you received an ~ to your letter?*

answer R, II.6.2, III.7.3 *Has he ~ed your letter?*

antique R, III.5.8 *This is an ~ table.*

any P, II.4.2 *Have you ~ sugar? I haven't ~ money.*

anybody P, II.8 *Can ~ help us?*

anyone P, II.8 *I have not seen ~.*

anything P, II.8 *~ else, sir?*

anywhere P, II.2.1, II.8 *I have not seen it ~.*

apartment R, III.2.1

apologize O R, I.4.1 *I do ~.*

apple P, III.10.1

appointment O R, III.7.2, III.8.6 *Can we make an ~ for next week? What time is your ~?*

April P, II.3.1, III.1.4

aquarium R, III.3.5

arithmetic R, III.4.4

arm P, III.8.1 *I cannot move my ~.*

army P, III.1.11 *I am in the ~.*

arrival R, III.6.4

arrive P, II.2.4, III.6.1, III.6.4, III.11.3 *The train ~d at 11.*

art P, III.5.7

article P, III.5.9 *There's an ~ about Wales in the* Daily Telegraph.

as R, II.7.6.4 *~ you cannot come, we'll have to go without you.*

as R, II.7.3.9 *He works ~ a driver.*

as ... as R, II.7.5.2 *He is as big as his brother.*

as well as ... R, II.7.6.1 *I have bought a new car ~ a motorcycle.*

ashtray O P, III.9.4

Asia P, III.6.3

ask P, II.6.2, III.6.4 *Why don't you ~ him? May I ~ a question? ~ him if there is a plane to London. I ~ed for a single ticket.*

at P, II.2.2 *We'll wait ~ the station. I bought this book ~ Colchester.*

at P, II.3.1 *~ 4 o'clock.*

at least P, II.4.2 *I need ~ £5.*

at present P, II.3.7

August P, II.3.1, III.1.4

Australia P, III.6.3

autumn P, II.3.1, III.6.2

away P, II.1.2, II.2.5 *He walked ~. Go ~ from that car!*

B

baby P, III.1.12

back P, II.2.5 *Finally we went ~.*

back P, III.5.4 *I'd like two seats at the ~. Have you any ~ seats left?*

back P, III.8.1 *My ~ hurts.*

bacon R, III.10.1

bad P, II.5.1.7, II.5.1.8, II.5.2.2, III.1.15, III.14.2 *This soup has a very ~ taste. This meat has a ~ smell. The weather is very ~.*

bag P, III.6.13 *I have two ~s and one suitcase.*

baggage R, III.6.13

bake R, III.10.1

baker P, III.1.11, III.9.1

balcony P, III.6.9 *I want a room with a ~.*

ball P, III.5.5 *If we had a ~ we could play a game.*

ballet R, III.5.4

banana P, III.10.1

bandage P, III.8.2 *I need a ~ for this wound.*

bank P, III.11.4 *You can cash your traveller's cheques at any ~.*

bank-notes R, III.9.7

bar O P, III.6.4, III.10.2 *Whisky is served at the ~. Let's go to the ~ for a drink.*

basement R, III.2.2

bath P, III.2.6 *The ~ is upstairs.*

bathroom P, III.2.2

be P, I.1.1, I.6.2 III.1.1 *He is a nice boy. How are you? I'm fine, thank you, and how are you? I am Pete Robinson.*

be P, II.5.2.1, III.6.1, III.9.7 *How*

much is a ticket to London? The room is £10 a week.

be P, II.1.1, II.1.3 *There is no word for it. There is no water in this room.*

be P, II.3.16 *John was reading when I saw him.*

be P, III.1.9 *I am from Holland. Where are you from?*

be P, III.1.11 *I'm going to ~ a teacher.*

be R, II.7.3.1, II.7.3.2, II.7.3.3 *This castle was built in the thirteenth century. John was given a book for his birthday.*

be born P, III.1.4 *I was born in 1925.*

be called R, III.1.1 *He is called Pete.*

be going to (future intention) P, I.3.18, II.3.6 *It's going to rain. I'm going to help you.*

beach P, III.2.7 *We walked on the ~.*

beans R, III.10.1

beautiful P, III.2.7 *The mountains are very ~.*

because P, II.7.6.4, II.7.6.6 *I need a pen ~ I want to write a letter.*

become P, II.3.25, III.4.7 *Sugar has ~ very expensive. I may ~ a doctor.*

bed P, III.2.3

bedroom P, III.2.2

beef R, III.10.1

beer P, III.10.1

before R, II.2.2 *There was a tree ~ the house.*

before P, II.2.7, II.3.2 *John came ~ Peter. John came ~ 6 o'clock.*

before P, II.3.1 *John came ~ I had left.*

before P, II.3.2 *I have never done it ~.*

being R, II.3.22, III.4.2 *He began to speak. It began in 1940. We ~ the day at 8 a.m.*

behind P, II.2.2 *There's a tree ~ the house.*

believe R, I.2.18, II.6.1 *I (don't) ~ you. I (don't) ~ that this is true.*

believe in O P, III.1.13 *Do you ~ God?*

belong R, II.7.5.1 *This book ~s to me.*

below R, II.2.2 *We were flying ~ the clouds.*

beside R, II.2.2 *Come and sit ~ me.*

best P, II.5.2.2 *This is the ~ book I have ever read.*

better P, II.5.2.2, II.5.2.7 *This book is much ~ than that. Your English is much ~ now.*

between P, II.2.2 *He walked ~ two policemen. We have a holiday ~ Christmas and Easter.*

bicycle P, III.6.5

big P, II.2.8.1, II.2.8.6, III.6.3

bike R, III.6.5

bill P, III.6.9, III.10.2 *Can you give me my ~, please?*

bird P, III.2.8, III.3.5

birdcage R, III.3.5

birth R, III.1.4

birthday R, III.1.4 *When is your ~?*

a bit R, II.4.3 *He's ~ tired.*

bitter P, II.5.1.7, III.10.1 *This has a ~ taste.*

black P, II.5.1.10, III.9.3 *This is a ~ box.*

blanket P, III.2.3

blouse P, III.9.3

blue P, II.5.1.10, III.9.3 *I want a ~ dress.*

blue zone O R, III.6.5 *In the ~ you can park for one hour only.*

board O R, III.6.4 *The passengers will ~ the ship between 4 and 4.30.*

boarding-house R, III.6.9

boarding-pass O R, III.6.4

boat P, III.6.4

boil O R, III.10.1 *I want ~ed potatoes.*

book P, III.3.3, III.5.6 *I want to buy an English ~.*

book O P, III.5.4, III.6.9 *Where can I ~ seats for tonight? I have ~ed two rooms for tonight.*
bookcase P, III.2.4
booking-office O R, III.5.4
bookshop R, III.5.6
borrow P, III.11.4
both P, II.8 *They ~ went home. I want ~ of them.*
both P, II.4.2 *~ the shops are closed.*
bottle P, III.9.5 *I'd like a ~ of beer.*
bottom P, III.2.7 *We could see the ~ of the lake.*
box P, III.6.13 *Can you give me a ~ for these glasses?*
boy P, III.1.6
brake O P, III.11.8 *My ~s don't work.*
bread P, III.10.1
break P, III.4.2 *We have a ~ at 10.30.*
break P, II.5.1.12, III.8.2 *He has broken his leg.*
breakfast P, III.3.3, III.10.2 *We have ~ at 8.*
bridge P, III.12 *There's no ~ across the river.*
bring P, II.2.5 *~ me some water.*
brother P, III.1.12
brown P, II.5.1.10, III.9.3
brush P, III.8.4 *Give me a ~ for my clothes, please.*
building P, III.2.1 *I have an apartment in a big ~.*
burn P, III.8.2 *I have ~t my hand.*
bus P, III.6.4
business P, III.1.11 *I am in ~.*
business-man/woman R, III.1.11
bus-stop P, III.6.4
busy P, III.3.3 *We are very ~ in the morning.*
busy R, III.6.5 *Drive carefully, this is a very ~ street.*
but P, II.7.6.1 *I want a new car, ~ I have no money.*
butcher P, III.1.11, III.9.1

butter P, III.10.1 *I would like some bread and ~.*
button P, III.11.7 *I've lost a ~.*
button R, III.6.9 *Press the ~ for the third floor.*
buy P, III.1.11, III.2.1, III.3.4, III.6.4, III.9.1
by R, II.3.1 *He'll be here ~ 6 o'clock.*
by R, II.7.3 *This letter was written ~ Churchill.*
by P, III.6.4 *We'll travel ~ air/car/ bus/train.*
bye-bye R, I.6.4

C

cabaret P, III.5.4
cabbage R, III.10.1
café O R, III.10.2
cake P, III.10.1
call P, III.1.1, III.13.2 *We ~ him Pete. He is ~ed Pete (R). What do you ~ this in English? What is this ~ed in English? (R).*
call (=to wake) O P, III.6.9 *Please ~ me at 6 tomorrow morning.*
call (=to telephone) R, III.1.3, III.11.2 *I'll ~ you at 5 o'clock.*
call R, III.1.3, III.11.2 *I want to make a (phone-)~.*
call-box R, III.11.2
camera P, III.6.13
camping-site P, III.6.9
can (ability, capability, capacity, offering help) P, I.2.5, I.2.7, I.2.14, I,2,15, I.5.7, I.5.8, II.5.2.10
can (permission) R, I.2.24
can (possibility) P, I.2.12, I.2.13, II.1.4
canal R, III.2.7
cancel O R, III.6.4 *All services to Southend have been ~led for today.*
canteen O R, III.10.2
capital R, III.6.3 *London is the ~ of England.*
car P, III.6.5 *I always travel by ~ in my holidays.*

caravan P, III.6.9 *Is your car strong enough to pull this ～ in the mountains?*
care R, I.4.8 *I don't ～.*
careful P, I.5.5 *Be ～!*
car-park R, III.6.5
carriage R, III.6.4 *Where is the first-class ～?*
carry P, II.2.5, III.6.13 *Can you ～ this heavy suitcase for me?*
cash O R, III.9.1 *Can you pay ～?*
cash O P, III.11.4 *I want to ～ this cheque.*
castle R, III.6.3
cat P, III.2.8, III.3.5
cathedral R, III.1.13
cattle P, III.2.8
cellar P, III.2.2
centimetre P, II.2.8.2, III.9.8
central heating P, III.2.5
centre P, II.2.2, III.5.4, III.6.3 *I'd like to sit somewhere in the ～. The best shops are in the ～ of the town.*
century R, II.3.1
certain R, I.2.18, II.6.1 *I am not ～. I am ～ that this is wrong.*
certainly R, I.2.1, I.2.18 *Will you help me? ～. I ～ think that you are right.*
certificate R, III.4.6
chair P, III.2.3
change P, II.3.25 *The country has ～d since the war.*
change P, III.6.4 *For Leeds you ～ at Sheffield.*
change P, III.6.6, III.11.4 *I want to ～ 500 French francs.*
change P, III.9.1 *I want to ～ this shirt; it is not the right colour.*
charge O R, III.6.9 *The ～ for caravans is £1 per 24 hours.*
charter-flight O R, III.6.4
cheap P, III.5.2.1, III.6.1, III.6.12, III.9.7
check O P, III.11.9 *Will you ～ the tyres, please?*
check in O R, III.6.4 *All passengers*

must ～ at least 30 minutes before departure.
cheerio R, I.6.4
cheers O P, I.6.6
cheese P, III.10.1
chemist P, III.8.6
cheque O P, III.6.9, III.11.4 *I'll give you a ～ for £25.*
chicken P, III.10.1
child P, II.5.1.11, III.1.7, III.1.12, II.6.12 *We are two adults and three ～ren.*
chips O R, III.10.1 *Would you like fish and ～?*
chocolate P, III.10.1 *I'll have ～ ice-cream. Can I have a piece of ～?*
choose P, III.4.4, III.10.2 *We have to ～ one foreign language. Have you chosen something from the menu?*
Christian name R, III.1.1
Christmas: P, II.3.1, III.4.3, III.6.2
church P, III.1.13
cigar O P, III.9.4
cigarette O P, III.9.4
cinema P, III.5.4
circus R, III.5.4
city R, III.6.3 *Coventry is an industrial ～.*
class P, III.6.12 *Travelling first ～ is very expensive in our country.*
classical P, III.5.3 *～ music is more popular now than 10 years ago.*
clean P, II.5.1.14, III.8.4 *This shirt is not ～.*
clean P, II.5.1.14, III.2.5, III.2.6 *My rooms are ～ed twice a week.*
clear P, III.13.2 *That's not ～ to me.*
clerk R, III.1.11
climate P, III.14.1
cloakroom R, III.5.4
close P, II.5.1.13, III.5.8 *The exhibition ～s at 6.*
closed P, II.5.1.13, III.5.8 *The museum is ～ on Sundays.*
clothes P, III.9.3
club P, III.4.5, III.7.4 *We have several*

school-~s. *We have a sports-~ in our village.*

coach R, III.6.4 *We'll take the ~ to the airport.*

coast R, III.2.7

coat P, III.9.3 *I want to buy a new ~.*

coffee P, III.10.1, III.10.2 *Let's have some ~.*

coin P, III.9.7, III.11.2 *I have no ~s for the telephone.*

cold P, II.2.8.7, III.10.1, III.14.1, III.14.2 *It's very ~ today.*

cold P, III.8.2 *I am afraid I have a ~.*

collect P, III.5.1 *I ~ stamps.*

collection O R, III.11.1 *The next ~ is at 5 o'clock.*

college R, III.1.10 *I'll go to a ~ for business studies.*

colour P, II.5.1.10, III.5.3 *I'd like to see the programme in ~.*

comb P, III.8.4 *I want to buy a new ~.*

come P, II.2.4, III.6.4, III.7.2 *He came very late. He came to our house. This boat ~s from Ostend.*

come and see ... O R, III.7.2 *Why dont you ~ us tomorrow?*

comfortable O P, III.8.3 *I am quite ~ now. The chair is not very ~.*

communist O P, III.7.5 *I am a member of the ~ party. Are there many ~s in your country?*

concert P, III.5.4 *Let's go to a ~ tonight.*

concert-hall R, III.5.4

congratulations! P, I.6.7

connection R, III.6.4 *We shall miss our ~ at Liverpool.*

conservative O P, III.7.5 *We have a ~ government now.*

consul O P, III.8.7

consulate O R, III.8.7

cool P, II.2.8, III.14.2 *The weather is rather ~ here.*

corner P, III.12 *There is a bus-stop near the ~.*

correct R, II.5.2.7, III.13.3 *Is this word ~?*

correct P, III.13.3 *Will you ~ me if I make mistakes?*

correspond R, III.7.3 *I have ~ed with an English friend for two years now.*

cost R, II.5.2.1, III.6.1, III.9.7 *These shoes ~ £23. A ticket to London ~s £1.50.*

cotton R, II.5.1.15, III.9.3 *I want a ~ dress. This dress is made of ~.*

could (suggestion, see also: can) P, I.5.1 *We ~ go to the seaside tomorrow.*

could (in requests) P, I.5.2

country P, III.1.2, III.6.3 *France is a big ~.*

country P, III.2.7 *I'd like to live in the ~, but I have not got the money for a second house.*

course P, III.1.10, III.4.7 *I am going to follow a ~ in book-keeping.*

cow P, III.2.8

cream R, III.10.1

cross P, III.6.5, III.12 *Look out when you ~ the street. ~ the river at this point.*

crossing P, III.6.5, III.12 *Look out for the trains when you come to the ~.*

crossroads P, III.12 *Turn left at the ~.*

cup P, III.9.5

cupboard R, III.2.2

currency O R, III.6.6, III.11.4

customs O P, III.6.6 *We had to pay duty at the ~.*

cut P, II.5.1.12, III.8.2, III.8.4 *I've ~ my finger. Will you ~ my hair, please?*

D

daily R, II.3.15 *There is a ~ flight to Montreal.*

dance R, III.4.5, III.5.4 *We have a ~*

in May. Our friends give a ~
tonight.
dance P, III.4.5, III.5.4 *I'd like to* ~.
dancer R, III.5.4
danger R, III.6.5
dangerous P, III.6.5
dark P, II.5.1.4, III.14.2 *It is too* ~
to work in the garden.
dark P, II.5.1.10, III.9.3 *I want a* ~
blue skirt.
date P, III.1.4 *What's the* ~ *today?*
daughter P, III.1.12
day P, II.3.13, III.6.2
dead P, II.5.1.12, III.8.2
dear P, III.7.3 ~ *Mr. Jones.*
December P, II.3.1, III.1.4
decide R, III.10.2 *Have you* ~*d yet?*
declare O R, III.6.6 *Have you any-*
thing to ~*?*
deep P, II.2.8.1, III.2.7 *This is a very*
~ *river.*
degree P, II.2.8.7, III.14.2 *It is 10* ~*s*
below zero.
delay O R, II.3.10, III.6.4 *There will*
be a ~ *of two hours.*
delayed O R, II.3.10, III.6.4 *The train*
is ~.
delighted R, I.3.17 *I am* ~ *to hear*
this.
dentist P, III.8.6
department store R, III.9.1
departure R, III.6.4
desk P, III.2.4 *I have a big* ~ *in my*
room.
desk O R, III.6.9 *Please, leave your*
key on the ~.
dessert P, III.10.1
dial O R, III.11.2 ~ *100 for the*
operator.
dictionary P, III.13.2
differ R, II.7.4.1, II.7.4.2
difference R, II.7.4.1, II.7.4.2
different P, II.7.4.1, II.7.4.2 *England*
is quite ~ *from Holland.*
difficult P, II.5.2.13, III.13.1
difficulty R, II.5.2.13, III.13.1

dine R, III.7.2, III.10.2 *We* ~ *at 6.*
dinner P, III.3.3, III.7.2, III.10.2 *We*
have ~ *at 6.*
diploma P, III.4.6
direction P, II.2.5, III.6.4, III.12 *In*
which ~ *is Slough?*
dirty P, II.5.1.14, III.8.4
discount O R, III.9.7
disease R, III.8.2
dish R, III.9.5
distance P, II.2.2, III.12 *The* ~ *from*
A to B is 5 miles.
disturb O R, III.6.9 *Please, do not* ~.
do P, II.8, III.1.11 *What are you going*
to ~ *tonight? What do you* ~ *(for*
a living)? (R).
do P, III.4.4 *I* ~ *French at school.*
do R, II.5.2.5 *That will* ~.
do P, I.1.3, I.1.4 ~ *You know him?*
I ~*n't know him.*
do P, I.3.7 *I* ~ *hope you are right.*
do P, II.8 *He asked me to help him and*
I did.
doctor P, III.1.11, III.8.5 *If you don't*
feel well you should go to the ~.
document O R, III.6.10 *Where are*
your insurance ~*s?*
dog P, III.2.8, III.3.5
door P, III.2.2
dormitory R, III.6.9
down R, II.2.5 *We walked* ~ *the hill.*
down R, II.2.5 *Shall we walk* ~*?*
downstairs R, III.2.2 *The kitchen is*
~. *Let's go* ~ *and watch television.*
draw R, III.5.5 *The game has ended*
in a ~.
dress P, III.9.3 *I want to buy a new*
~.
drink P, III.10.1 *You cannot* ~ *this*
water.
drink O P, III.7.2, III.10.1 *Let's have*
a ~.
drive P, III.6.5 *I never drink beer when*
I have to ~ *a car.*
driver R, III.6.5
driving-licence O R, III.6.5, III.6.10

dry P, II.5.1.3, III.14.1 *My shirt is not quite ~. This is a very ~ country.*

dry P, II.5.1.3 *Where can I ~ my clothes?*

during R, II.3.1 *We met him ~ the holidays.*

duty O R, III.6.6 *You'll have to pay ~ on your new watch.*

E

each P, II.8 *Tenpence ~. ~ of us got one.*

each P, II.4.2 *~ room is the same.*

early P, II.3.11, III.6.1 *You are ~. There is an ~ flight on Sundays. You came too ~. I have to leave very ~ in the morning.*

earn P, III.3.4, III.4.7 *He ~s £75 a week now.*

east P, II.2.1, II.2.5, III.12 *The snow came from the ~. We are going to travel ~.*

Easter P, II.3.1, III.4.3, III.6.2

easy P, II.5.2.13, III.13.1

eat P, III.10.1

education P, III.1.10

egg P, III.10.1

electricity P, III.2.5

else P, II.7.4.1 *Anything ~?*

embassy O R, III.8.7

emergency R, III.5.4 *There are five ~ exits in the theatre.*

empty P, II.5.1.17, III.11.9 *The bus was ~.*

end P, II.2.2, III.12 *Turn left at the ~ of the street.*

end R, II.3.4 *In the ~ we shall win.*

end R, II.3.23, III.4.2 *The game will ~ at 4. School ~s at 4.*

engine P, III.11.8

engine-trouble O R, III.11.8

enjoy R, I.3.1, I.3.2, I.3.3, III.6.2 *Did you ~ your vacation? Did you ~ yourself? Do you ~ travelling?*

enough P, II.4.2, II.4.3, II.5.2.5,

III.9.8 *It's ~. I haven't got ~ money. This is good ~.*

enquiries R, III.6.4

entrance R, III.5.4 *There were hundreds of people before the ~ of the theatre.*

entrance examination R, III.4.6

envelope P, III.7.3

Europe P, III.6.3

even P, II.4.3 *I've ~ paid £5.*

evening P, I.6.1, II.3.1, III.5.4 *Good ~! We'll do it this ~.*

ever P, II.3.15 *Have you ~ been in Rome?*

every P, II.3.15 *We see him ~ week.*

everybody P, II.8

everyone P, II.8 *~ believes that.*

everything P, II.8

everywhere P, II.2.1, II.8

examination P, III.4.6 *I passed my ~ last year.*

excellent! R, I.4.3

except R, II.7.6.3 *We all went, ~ John.*

excursion P, III.4.5 *We made an ~ to the mountains last year.*

excuse P, I.4.1, I.6.5 *~ me, please.*

exhibition O R, III.5.8

exist P, II.1.1

exit R, III.5.4 *The ~ is next to the stage.*

expect O R, III.7.2 *We shall ~ you at 5.*

expensive P, II.5.2.1, III.6.1, III.9.7

explain P, III.13.2

F

f. (=female: writing only) P, III.1.6

factory P, III.1.11: III.2.7 *I'm going to work in a ~.*

fail P, II.5.2.8, III.4.6 *I ~ed my driving-test twice. I tried to do it, but I ~ed.*

fall P, II.2.4, III.8.2 *Be careful or you will ~ on the ice.*

fall R, III.8.2 *He fell ill three days ago.*

false R, II.5.2.7

family (=children; parents and children) R, III.1.7, III.1.12

family name R, III.1.1

fancy R, I.3.6 *~ seeing you there!*

far P, II.2.3, III.12 *We live ~ from the town. The museum is not ~.*

fare O R, III.6.1, III.6.11 *The ~ is 15p by underground. The ~ to Ostend is £15.*

farm P, III.1.11, III.2.7 *I am going to work on a ~.*

farmer R, III.1.11

farmland R, III.2.7

fast P, II.3.14, II.7.3.9, III.6.4 *We went very ~. This is a very ~ car. There is a ~ train to Edinburgh.*

fasten P, II.5.1.12, III.11.7

father P, III.1.12

february P, II.3.1, III.1.4

feel P, III.8.2 *I don't ~ quite well.*

female R, III.1.6 *A daughter is a ~ child.*

ferry R, III.6.4 *We take the ~ to Dover.*

fever P, III.8.2

few P, II.4.2 *There are only ~ people here.*

a few P, II.4.2 *I know ~ good restaurants here.*

field P, III.2.7, III.5.5 *He is working in the ~s. There were 22 players on the ~.*

fill P, II.5.1.17, III.8.6 *Please ~ this bottle with water. This tooth was ~ed six months ago.*

film P, III.5.4 *I'd like to see a ~.*

final examination R, III.4.6

finally P, II.3.4 *~ we went back.*

find P, III.9.1 *Where can I ~ a tobacconist? I cannot ~ my purse.*

fine P, I.4.3, II.5.2.4 *That's ~!*

fine P, II.5.2.2, III.14.2 *The weather will be ~ tomorrow.*

fine R, III.6.5, III.11.5 *You will have to pay a ~ of £10.*

finish R, II.3.23 *When will he ~?*

fire P, III.8.7 *My sister died in a ~.*

fire-service R, III.8.7

first P, II.2.7, III.3.4 *John came ~. ~ we went to Madrid.*

first name P, III.1.1 *His ~ is Charles.*

fish P, III.3.5, III.10.1 *We had ~ for dinner.*

fish R, III.5.1 *I like to go ~ing.*

flat P, III.2.1 *We own a ~ in London.*

flat P, III.2.7 *Our part of the country is quite ~.*

flight O R, III.6.4 *~ KL 173 has just arrived. I hope you have enjoyed your ~.*

floor P, III.2.2 *The bedrooms are on the first ~.*

floor-show O R, III.5.4

flower P, III.2.8 *I've brought you some ~s.*

fly P, III.6.4 *We'll ~ from London to Paris.*

fly P, III.2.8 *There's a ~ in your soup.*

fog P, III.14.2

follow P, II.2.5, III.12 *Just ~ me till we get to the station.*

fond R, III.1.14 *My sister is ~ of sweets.*

food P, III.10.1

foot P, III.8.1 *My ~ hurts.*

foot P, II.2.8.2, III.9.8 *The road is 20 ft. wide.*

football P, III.5.5

for R, II.2.5 *He's leaving ~ Rome.*

for P, II.3.13, II.3.19 *I've waited here ~ two hours.*

for P, II.7.3.5 *I want to buy a present ~ my wife.*

forbid R, I.2.26, II.6.2

foreign P, III.1.8, III.6.2, III.6.6 *We have a ~ guest. We often go to ~ countries.*

foreigner P, III.1.8

forename R, III.1.1

forest P, III.2.7

forget P, I.2.10, I.2.11 *I have for-gotten to bring my glasses. I have forgotten my passport.*

forgive R, I.4.1 *Please ~ me.*

fork P, III.9.5

form P, III.1.10 *I'm in the fifth ~.*

form R, III.6.6 *All foreign visitors must fill in this ~.*

formerly P, II.3.8

free P, III.9.7 *You don't have to pay for it, it is ~.*

free P, III.3.3 *We are ~ on Satur-days.*

freeze P, III.14.2 *It was freezing last week.*

Friday P, II.3.1

fridge P, III.2.6

friend P, III.3.3, III.7.1

from P, II.3.22 *I lived here ~ 1940 till 1945.*

from P, II.2.5, II.2.6 *The wind is ~ the east. We came ~ London.*

front P, III.5.4 *Can I have two seats in the ~? Can I have a ~ seat?*

in front of P, II.2.2 *There's a tree ~ the house.*

frontier P, III.6.6

frost P, III.14.2

fruit P, III.10.1

fruit-juice P, III.10.1

fry O R, III.10.1 *Would you like fried potatoes?*

full P, II.5.1.17, III.11.9 *The bus is ~ of children. The train is quite ~.*

furnished O R, III.2.1 *We have rented a ~ apartment.*

furniture R, III.2.3

G

gale P, III.14.2

gallery O R, III.5.8 *We went to a picture ~ yesterday.*

gallon O P, II.2.8.5, III.9.8, III.11.9

game P, III.5.5 *Do you play any ~s?*

garage P, III.2.6, III.11.8 *There's a ~ behind the house. Where is the nearest ~?*

garden P, III.2.2, III.2.6 *There's a ~ behind our house.*

gas P, III.2.5 *We have ~ heating. I can smell ~.*

gate O R, III.6.4 *Flight KL 735 to Amsterdam is boarding now through ~ 23.*

gentlemen (as on lavatory doors) R, III.1.6

geography P, III.4.4

get R, II.3.25 *He's ~ting old.*

get (see also: have got) P, II.7.5.1, III.7.3 *I got a nice present from him. Did you ~ a letter yesterday?*

get up P, II.2.4, III.3.3 *I got up at six.*

girl P, III.1.6

give P, II.7.5.1 *I gave him a nice present.*

glad P, I.2.4, I.3.17 *I shall be very ~ to help you. I am very ~ to see you.*

glass P, III.9.5 *Is this made of ~ or of plastic?*

glass P, III.9.5 *I want to buy wine-~es.*

glasses P, III.8.6 *I cannot read; I've lost my ~.*

go P, II.2.4 *The car would not ~.*

go P, II.2.4, III.1.10, III.3.3, III.6.4 *Why did you ~? He went to Lon-don. Where does this train ~ (to)?*

go P, II.3.22 *Let's ~ sailing.*

go away P, II.2.4 *Why did you ~?*

go for a walk P, III.3.3, III.5.1

go on P, II.3.16 *It will ~ for five years.*

go out P, II.2.4, III.3.3, III.5.4 *I often ~ in the evenings. When we were in Paris we went out every evening.*

God P, III.1.3

gold P, II.5.1.15 *I have bought a ~ watch. This watch is made of ~.*

good P, I.3.1, I.4.3, II.5.2.2 *This is a very ~ book. ~!*

good-bye P, I.6.4
govern R, III.7.5 *This king ~ed for 26 years.*
government P, III.7.5
grandchild R, III.1.12
grandfather R, III.1.12
grandmother R, III.1.12
grass P, III.2.8
grateful R, I.3.16 *I am very ~ to you.*
green P, II.5.1.10, III.9.3 *I've bought a ~ suit.*
greengrocer P, III.1.11, III.9.1
grey P, II.5.1.10, III.9.3
grill O R, III.10.1 *We'll have ~ed sausages.*
grocer P, III.1.11, III.9.1
ground R, III.5.5 *There's a football ~ near the village.*
ground-floor P, III.2.2
group P, II.7.6.1, III.6.2, III.6.12 *We went to Scotland with a ~ of friends.*
guest P, III.6.9
guide R, III.6.2 *The ~ spoke several languages.*

H

hair P, III.8.1
half P, II.3.1 *It's ~ past three.*
half P, II.4.2 *Give me ~ of it. Give me the other ~.*
hall O R, III.6.9 *We shall wait for the coach in the ~.*
hallo P, I.6.1
ham R, III.10.1 *Would you like ~ and eggs?*
hand P, III.8.1 *I've hurt my ~.*
happen P, II.1.5, III.8.2 *What ~ed?*
harbour R, III.6.4 *The ship came into the ~.*
hard P, II.7.3.9, III.3.3 *We have to work very ~ at school.*
hard R, II.5.2.13, III.13.1 *His English is ~ to understand.*

hard P, II.5.1.9 *This leather has become very ~.*
hardly R, II.4.3 *This is ~ correct.*
hardly any P, II.4.2 *I have ~ money.*
hardly ever P, II.3.15 *I ~ see him.*
hat P, III.9.3
hate R, I.3.2, III.1.14 *I ~ porridge. I ~ watching television. I would ~ to go there.*
have P, II.1.3 *I ~ a nice house in the country. I ~ plenty of time.*
have P, II.3.16 *I ~n't seen you for a long time.*
have (causative) P, I.5.2, II.7.3.6 *Can I ~ my skirt washed, please?*
have P, III.7.2, III.10.2 *We ~ breakfast at 8. Let's ~ coffee now.*
have got P, II.1.3, II.7.5.1 *I ~ a small caravan.*
have to P, I.2.20 *I ~ finish this first.*
he P, I.1.1, II.8
head P, III.8.1 *My ~ hurts.*
health R, III.8.2, III.8.6
hear P, II.5.1.6 *I cannot ~ it. I am afraid I cannot ~ very well. Can you ~ me now?*
heart P, III.8.1
heat R, III.14.2
heating P, III.2.5 *We have no ~ in this room.*
heavy P, II.2.8.2, III.6.13, III.9.8 *This blanket is too ~.*
help P, I.5.7, I.5.8, III.11.8 *Can you ~ me, please? Can I ~ you?*
help yourself O R, III.10.2
her P, II.8 *I've seen ~.*
her P, II.7.5.1, II.8 *Give me ~ book.*
here P, II.1.2, II.2.1, II.8
here's to ... O P, I.6.6 *~ your vacation!*
hers P, II.7.5.1, II.8 *This is ~. ~ is better* (R).
herself R, II.8 *She's done it ~.*
high P, II.2.8.1, II.5.2.1, III.2.7, III.9.7 *This mountain is very ~. Prices are very ~ in this country.*

hill P, III.2.7

him P, II.8

himself R, II.8 *He's done it* ∼.

hire O P, III.6.5 *We shall* ∼ *a car when we come to Britain.*

his P, II.7.5.1, II.8 *It's* ∼. ∼ *is better* (R).

his P, II.7.5.1, II.8 *Give me* ∼ *book.*

history P, III.4.4 *I like* ∼ *lessons very much.*

hobby P, III.5.1

holiday R, III.6.2

holidays P, III.4.3, III.6.2

home P, II.2.4, III.3.3, III.6.1 *I go* ∼ *at 6. I leave* ∼ *at 6 in the morning. I come* ∼ *at 9 in the evening.*

homework P, III.3.3

hope P, I.3.7, II.6.1 *I* ∼ *so. I* ∼ *that you'll win.*

horse P, III.2.8

hospital P, III.1.11, III.8.6 *I want to work in a* ∼.

hostess R, III.6.4 *There are* ∼*es at the airport who will give you further information.*

hot P, II.2.8.7, III.10.1, III.14.1, III.14.2

hotel P, III.6.9

hour P, II.3.13

house P, III.2.1 *We've bought a new* ∼.

how P, I.1.4, II.7.3.9 ∼ *far is it?* ∼ *can I do it?* ∼ *nice!*

how do you do? P, I.6.3

hunger R, III.8.3

hungry P, III.8.3

hurry P, II.2.4, III.6.4 ∼, *or you will miss your train.*

hurt P, III.8.2 *My leg* ∼*s. This will* ∼ *a little.*

husband P, III.1.7, III.1.12

I

I P, I.1.1, II.8

ice P, III.14.2 *There is* ∼ *on the lake.*

ice-cream P, III.10.1

if P, II.7.6.8 *I'll help you* ∼ *I can.*

if P, I.2.16, II.6.2 *Ask him* ∼ *there is a plane to London. I wonder* ∼ *you could help me.*

ill P, II.5.1.12, III.8.2 *I have been* ∼ *for a week now.*

illness R, III.8.2

immigration O R, III.6.6

import O R, III.6.6 *If you want to* ∼ *wine you must pay duty.*

important P, II.5.2.11

impossible P, I.2.12, II.1.4 *It is* ∼.

in P, II.3.1, II.3.6 *I'm leaving* ∼ *four days.*

in P, II.2.2 *I live* ∼ *London. The letter was* ∼ *the envelope.*

in P, II.2.5 *Shall we go* ∼?

in R, III.9.3 *Did you see the girl* ∼ *the white dress?*

inch P, II.2.8.2, III.9.8

included R, III.6.9 *Breakfast is* ∼.

income R, III.4.7

incorrect R, I.2.1, II.5.2.7 *That's* ∼.

indeed P, I.3.16 *Thank you very much* ∼.

industry R, III.2.7 *There's too much* ∼ *near this lake.*

information P, III.6.4

information desk R, III.6.4

information office R, III.6.4

initials R, III.1.1 *Are your* ∼ *G.B.S.?*

injury O R, III.8.2

inn R, III.6.9

insect P, III.2.8

inside P, II.2.1 *Put the car* ∼.

inside R, II.2.2 *I have never been* ∼ *this museum.*

institute R, III.1.10

insurance O P, III.6.5, III.6.10, III.8.5

insure O P, III.8.5

intend P, I.3.18 *I* ∼ *to study English.*

interested P, I.3.4, I.3.5, III.5.2 *I am* ∼ *in foreign countries.*

interesting P, I.3.4, I.3.5 *That's (very)* ∼.
interests R, III.5.2 *What are your* ∼?
interval R, III.5.4 *We'll have a cup of coffee during the* ∼.
interview R, III.5.3 *There is an* ∼ *with the Prime Minister on the radio.*
into P, II.2.5 *Let's go* ∼ *the museum.*
introduce O R, I.6.3 *May I* ∼ *you to ...*
invitation O R, III.7.2
invite O R, II.6.2, III.7.2 *They have* ∼*d us for dinner tonight.*
island P, III.2.7
it P, I.1.1, II.8 ∼ *is a very nice picture. I have never seen* ∼ *before.*
it P, II.8 ∼*'s raining.*

J

jacket P, III.9.3
jam P, III.10.1 *I like* ∼ *for breakfast.*
January P, II.3.1, III.1.4
job P, III.1.11, III.3.4
join O P, III.7.2 *May I* ∼ *you for dinner? Will you* ∼ *us on our trip tomorrow?*
journey P, III.6.2 *We made a* ∼ *to Spain last year.*
July P, II.3.1, III.1.4
June P, II.3.1, III.1.4
just P, II.3.8 *I've* ∼ *seen him.*

K

keep P, II.7.5.1 *May I* ∼ *this?*
key P, III.6.9
kill R, III.8.2 *Three people were* ∼*ed in the accident.*
kilo P, II.2.8.4, III.9.8
kilometre P, II.2.8.2, III.9.8
kind P, I.3.16, III.1.15 *It's very* ∼ *of you to help me. He is a very* ∼ *man. Would you be so* ∼ *as to ...* (R). *Would you be* ∼ *enough to ...* (R).

king P, III.7.5
kitchen P, III.2.2
knife P, III.9.5
know P, I.2.8, I.2.9, I.2.19, II.6.1, III.13.1 *I don't* ∼ *that word. I don't* ∼ *him. I* ∼ *that it's true.*

L

labourer O R, III.1.11
ladies (as on lavatory doors) R, III.1.6
lake P, III.2.7
lamb R, III.10.1 *We'll have* ∼ *for dinner.*
lamp P, III.2.3
land P, III.2.7 *When the plane flew very high we could not see the* ∼.
language P, III.6.8 *English is a very useful* ∼.
large R, II.2.8.1, III.6.3
last P, II.3 *I saw him* ∼ *week/month/year/etc.*
last P, II.2.7 *Peter came* ∼. *The* ∼ *guest arrived at 10.*
late P, II.3.12, III.6.1 *We'll have to hurry, we are* ∼. *We came* ∼ *for the show. We were too* ∼, *the train had left. I always come home* ∼ *at night.*
lately R, II.3.8
later P, II.3.3, II.3.10 *The train will come* ∼.
later on P, II.3.3, II.3.4 *I'll do it* ∼.
laugh P, II.6.2 *I had to* ∼.
laundry O R, III.8.4 *Has the* ∼ *come back yet?*
laundry O R, III.8.4 *Is there a* ∼ *in the neighbourhood?*
lavatory R, III.2.2, III.5.4
law R, III.11.5 *It is against the* ∼ *to do this.*
lazy R, III.1.15
lb. P, II.2.8.4, III.9.8
learn P, III.1.10, III.5.6
leather P, II.5.1.15, III.9.3 *I've*

bought a ~ jacket. These gloves are made of ~.

leave P, II.2.4, III.1.10, III.6.1, III.6.4 *We left the station at 10. I shall ~ school in two years. I ~ home at 6 every morning. At what time does the train ~?*

left P, II.2.5, III.12 *Turn ~ at the crossing. The town is on your ~.*

left-wing O R, III.7.5 *They are ~ students.*

leg P, III.8.1

lend P, III.11.4

lesson P, III.1.10, III.4.2

let R, I.2.24 *Please, ~ me help you.*

let's ... P, I.5.1 *~ go to a show tonight.*

letter P, III.7.3, III.11.1 *I have received a ~ from my brother.*

letter P, III.1.1 *What is the last ~ of your name?*

letter-box P, III.11.1 *Where is the nearest ~?*

library R, III.5.6

lie P, II.3.24 *He has been lying here for half an hour now.*

lie down P, II.2.4 *I would like to ~ for an hour.*

lift P, III.2.2, III.6.9 *Take the ~ to the third floor.*

light P, II.5.1.4, III.14.2 *We'll go for a walk as soon as it gets ~.*

light P, II.5.1.10, III.9.3 *I want a ~ colour.*

light P, II.2.8.3, III.5.3, III.6.13, III.9.8 *I want a very ~ blanket. We listened to ~ music the whole evening. I don't need a porter, these bags are very ~.*

lightning R, III.14.2

like P, I.3.1, I.3.3, I.3.9, I.3.20, I.3.21, II.5.2.6, III.1.14, III.5.2, III.7.1 *I ~ your brother very much. I don't ~ swimming. I'd ~ to buy that. Would you ~ to swim?*

like R, II.7.3.9 *You do it ~ this.*

like P, II.7.4.2 *It's ~ an orange.*

listen P, II.5.1.6, III.3.3 *~ to me, please. ~, the train is coming.*

little P, II.4.2 *I have ~ money.*

a little P, II.4.2, II.4.3, III.13.1 *I'd like ~ sugar in my tea. He's ~ worried.*

live P, III.1.2, III.2.1 *Where do you ~? I ~ in France.*

live R, III.8.2 *He will not ~ much longer.*

living R, III.1.11 *What do you do for a ~?*

living-room P, III.2.2

long P, II.2.8.2 *This road is very ~.*

long P, II.3.13 *We had to wait (a) ~ (time).*

look P, II.5.1.4, III.5.5 *Don't ~ now, this is not very nice. ~ at his new car!*

look P, II.5.1.12, III.8.3 *You ~ very well.*

look out! P, I.5.5

lorry R, III.6.5 *This street is not for lorries.*

lose P, III.5.5 *The English team has lost the game.*

lose P, III.11.5, III.12 *I've lost my passport. I have lost my way.*

lost property office R, III.6.4

a lot R, II.4.3 *He's ~ better now.*

a lot of P, II.4.2 *He earns ~ money.*

loud P, II.5.1.6, III.5.3 *The music is too ~.*

lounge O R, III.6.4, III.6.9 *Passengers are requested to wait in the ~. The guests can watch television in the ~.*

love P, I.3.1 *I ~ you. I ~ baseball.*

low P, II.2.8.1, II.5.2.1, III.9.7 *There is a ~ hill near our town. Prices are rather ~ in this shop.*

luggage P, III.6.13

lunch P, III.3.3, III.7.2, III.10.2 *We have ~ at 1 p.m.*

M

m. (=male: writing only) P, III.1.6

magazine P, III.5.9 *I'd like to buy some ~s.*

mail R, III.11.1 *The ~ has not arrived yet.*

make P, II.1.1, II.5.1.3, III.5.7, III.11.2 *Van Gogh made a beautiful picture of an old chair. We ~ bicycles here. You've made my floor wet! Can we ~ an appointment for next week?* (R). *I'd like to ~ a (phone-)call* (R).

male R, III.1.6 *A son is a ~ child.*

man P, III.1.6 *There were five men and seven women in the bus.*

man R, II.8 *There were animals here before ~ came.*

many P, II.3.20, II.4.2 *How ~ times have you been to Paris?*

map P, III.12

March P, II.3.1

market P, III.9.1 *We buy our vegetables at the ~.*

married P, III.1.7 *Are you ~?*

master R, III.1.10 *Mr. Jones is our English ~.*

match P, III.5.5 *I like watching football-~es on TV.*

matches P, III.9.5 *I'd like a box of ~.*

mathematics P, III.4.4

matinée O R, III.5.4

matter P, II.5.2.3 *What's the ~?*

matter P, I.4.2 *It doesn't ~ (at all).*

may (uncertainty) P, I.2.18

may (permission) P, I.2.24

may (request) P, I.3.20

May P, II.3.1, III.1.4

me P, II.8

meal P, III.3.3, III.10.1 *Let's have a ~ in a restaurant.*

mean P, III.13.2 *What does this word ~?*

mean P, I.3.8, III.13.2 *This is just what I ~t. What do you ~?*

by means of R, II.7.3.9

meaning R, III.13.2 *What's the ~ of this word?*

meat P, III.10.1

medicine P, III.8.6 *Take this ~ three times a day.*

meet R, I.6.3 *I'd like you to ~ ...*

meet P, III.7.4 *We ~ in a pub every Friday.*

meeting P, III.7.4 *We have club ~s every week.*

member P, III.7.4 *I am a ~ of a sports-club.*

mend O R, III.11.7 *Can you ~ these shoes for me?*

menu P, III.10.2 *Give me the ~, please.*

message O R, III.6.9 *There is a ~ for you at the reception.*

metal P, II.5.1.15 *I use a ~ box for these papers. Is this box made of ~?*

metre P, II.2.8.2, III.9.8

middle R, III.5.4 *The table was in the ~ of the room.*

might (suggesting a course of action) R, I.5.1

mild R, III.14.2 *We usually have ~ weather in April.*

mile P, II.2.8.2, II.3.14, III.9.8

milk P, III.10.1 *A glass of ~, please.*

mind R, I.3.8 *This is just what I had in ~.*

mind R, I.2.24, I.4.8, I.5.2 *Do you ~ if I smoke? I don't ~. I don't ~ if he joins us. Would you ~ opening the window?*

mind R, I.5.5 *~ your head!*

mine P, II.7.5.1, II.8 *This is ~. ~ is better* (R).

mineral water O P, III.10.1

minister P, III.7.5 *There is a new ~ in our government.*

minute P, II.3.1, II.3.13 *It's 23 ~s past 3. Can you wait a few ~s?*

Miss P, III.1.1 *This is ~ Jones.*

mist R, III.14.2

mistake P, III.13.3 *You don't make many* ~s.

modern P, III.5.4 *I like* ~ *music.*

moment P, II.3.13

Monday P, II.3.1

money P, III.3.4, III.6.6, III.9.7, III.11.4

month P, II.3.1, II.3.13, II.5.1.11, III.1.5, III.1.10, III.6.2 *Our baby is six* ~*s old.*

monthly R, II.3.15 *We have* ~ *meetings.*

moon P, III.14.2

more P, II.4.2 *I want* ~ *money.*

more P, II.4.3, II.7.4.2 *London is* ~ *interesting than Birmingham.*

morning P, I.6.1, II.3.1 *Good* ~*! I saw him this* ~.

most P, II.4.2 ~ *people don't know this.*

most P, II.4.3 *London is the* ~ *interesting place I know.*

mother P, III.1.12

motor-car R, III.6.5

motor-cycle P, III.6.5

motorway P, III.6.5

mountain P, III.2.7

mountains P, III.2.7 *I like to spend my holidays in the* ~.

move P, II.2.4 *The car did not* ~.

movies R, III.5.4

Mr. P, III.1.1 *This is* ~ *Jones.*

Mrs. P, III.1.1 *This is* ~ *Jones.*

much P, II.4.2, II.4.3, II.5.2.1, III.9.7 *There isn't* ~ *food in the fridge. This is* ~ *better. How* ~ *are these shoes?*

museum P, III.5.8

mushrooms O R, III.10.1

music P, III.5.3, III.5.4

musical R, III.5.4 *There's a nice* ~ *at the Adelphi Theatre.*

musician P, III.5.4

must (logical conclusion) P, I.2.16 *This* ~ *be true.*

must (obligation) R, I.2.20 *I* ~ *go home now.*

must not (prohibition) R, I.2.26

mustard P, III.10.1

my P, II.7.5.1, II.8

myself R, II.8 *I've done it* ~.

N

name P, III.1.1 *What's your* ~*?*

narrow R, II.2.8.1

nationality R, III.1.8

native language R, III.6.8

near P, II.2.3, III.12 *The village is quite* ~.

near P, II.2.3 *We live* ~ *the cathedral.*

necessarily R, I.2.16

necessary P, I.2.22

neck P, III.8.1 *He has broken his* ~.

need R, I.2.22 *You* ~ *not do it.*

need P, I.3.8 *This is just what I* ~.

neighbourhood R, II.2.3 *We live in the* ~ *of a big town.*

never P, I.1.3, II.3.15, II.8

New P, II.5.1.11, III.9.1 *I want to buy a* ~ *book about England.*

news P, III.5.3

news-bulletin R, III.5.3

newspaper P, III.5.9

next P, II.3.6 *I'll do it* ~ *week.*

next R, II.3.4 *What did you do* ~*?*

next to P, II.2.2, III.12 *Please, sit* ~ *me at dinner. There is a pub* ~ *the town-hall.*

nice P, I.2.4, I.3.1, I.3.6, I.3.16, II.5.1.7, II.5.1.8, II.5.2.4, III.1.15, III.10.1 *That will be very* ~. *How* ~ *to see you! It was very* ~ *of you to come. It's a very* ~ *taste. The flower has a* ~ *smell. He's a very* ~ *man.*

night P, I.6.4, II.3.1, III.5.4 *Good* ~*! I saw him last* ~.

night-club O P, III.5.4

no P, I.1.3, I.2.5 ~, *thank you.*

no P, I.1.3, II.4.2 *I have* ~ *time.*

no doubt R, I.2.18, II.6.1 ~ *this is right.*

no-one P, II.8

nobody P, I.1.3, II.8

noise P, II.5.1.6, III.6.9 *Give me another room, please, there is too much ~ from the street here.*

normal P, II.5.2.12

north P, II.2.5, II.2.1, III.12 *From this point you go ~. He lives in the ~.*

not P, I.1.3 *I have ~ seen him.*

not always P, II.3.17, II.3.19

not ... at all P, III.13.1 *I cannot understand her at all.*

not...either P, II.7.6.1 *I cannot swim either.*

not so ... as R, II.7.4.2 *He is not so big as his brother.*

not...till/until R, II.3.1 *He won't be here till/until 6 o'clock.*

note-paper R, III.7.3

nothing P, I.1.3, II.8

November P, II.3.1, III.1.4

now P, II.3.1, II.3.7, II.8

nowhere P, II.2.1, II.8

number P, III.1.2 *I live at ~ 15.*

nurse R, III.1.11 *She is a ~ in a hospital.*

nut R, III.10.1 *These ~s are too hard to eat.*

nylon P, II.5.1.15, III.9.3 *I don't want ~ sheets. This shirt is made of ~.*

O

occupation O R, III.1.11 *What's your ~?*

ocean R, III.6.3

o'clock P, II.3.1 *It's 4 ~.*

October P, II.3.1, III.1.4

of P, II.7.5.1 *I want some seats in the front ~ the room.*

of course P, I.2.1, I.2.24

off P, III.9.3 *Can I take my jacket ~?*

off P, III.2.5 *The heating is ~.*

office P, III.1.11 *I want to work in an ~.*

office worker R, III.1.11

often P, II.3.15

oil O P, III.2.5, III.6.5, III.11.9 *Will you check the ~, please?*

old P, II.5.1.11, III.1.5, III.5.8 *I am too ~ for this. How ~ are you? I am 18 years ~. This is an ~ chair.*

old-age pension O R, III.4.7, III.7.5

omelette P, III.10.1

on P, II.2.2 *The meat was ~ the table.*

on P, II.3.1, II.3.15 *I'll do it ~ Monday. We never go there ~ Sundays.*

on R, II.7.6.9 *I cannot give you any information ~ train-services.*

on P, III.2.5 *The heating is ~.*

once P, II.3.15, II.3.21 *I go there ~ every day. He came (only) ~.*

one P, II.8 *I like the red ~ better.*

one-way street P, III.6.5

only P, II.7.6.9 *I ~ wanted to help you. He came ~ once.*

open P, III.6.6 *Will you ~ your bag, please?*

open P, II.5.1.13, III.5.8 *The museum is ~ now.*

open P, II.5.1.13, III.5.8 *The museum ~s at 9.*

opening-hours R, III.5.8, III.9.1

opera P, III.5.4 *I don't like ~s by Wagner. Let's go to the ~ tonight.*

opera-house R, III.5.4

operate R, III.8.2 *Have you ever been ~d upon?*

operation P, III.8.2 *I have had two stomach-~s.*

operator O R, III.11.2 *Dial 100 for the ~.*

opinion O P, III.7.5

opposite P, II.2.2, III.12 *There is a pub ~ the town-hall.*

or P, II.7.6.2 *I'll go to London ~ to Rome.*

orange P, II.5.1.10, III.9.3 *I don't want an ~ dress.*

orange P, III.10.1 *I'll have an* ~, *please.*

order O P, III.10.2 *I have* ~*ed a bottle of red wine.*

in order to R, II.7.6.7 *He came* ~ *help me.*

ordinary R, II.5.2.12

origin O R, III.1.9 *What's your country of* ~?

other P, II.7.4.1 *Give me the* ~ *book.*

ought R, I.5.4, II.5.2.3 *You* ~ *to help your friend.* •

our P, II.7.5.1, II.8 *We'll have to send postcards to* ~ *friends.*

ours P, II.7.5.1, II.8 *This is* ~. ~ *is better* (R).

ourselves R, II.8 *We've done it* ~.

out P, II.2.5 *We walked* ~.

out of P, II.2.6 *He came* ~ *the house.*

out of order R, II.5.1.12, III.11.2 *The telephone is* ~.

outside P, II.2.1 *The children are playing* ~.

outside P, II.2.2 *He spends most of his time* ~ *the house.*

over P, II.2.2 *We flew* ~ *the city.*

own R, II.7.5.1 *We* ~ *a house in the country.*

own P, II.7.5.1 *This is my* ~ *book.*

oz. P, II.2.8.4, III.9.8

P

page P, III.5.9 *There's an article about Wales on* ~ *6.*

pain P, III.8.2 *I feel* ~ *in my leg.*

paint P, III.5.7 *Van Gogh* ~*ed a chair.*

painting R, III.5.8 *They have beautiful* ~*s in this gallery.*

pair P, II.7.6.1, III.9.3 *I want to buy a* ~ *of shoes.*

pan P, III.9.5

paper R, III.5.9 *Have you seen today's* ~?

paper P, III.7.3 *I want to write a letter, but I have no* ~.

parcel P, III.11.1

pardon P, III.13.2 *I beg your* ~?

parents R, III.1.12

park P, III.1.2 *My house is near Hyde* ~.

park P, III.6.5 *Where can I* ~ *my car?*

part P, III.2.7 *In our* ~ *of the country there are many farms.*

party P, III.7.5 *Are you a* ~-*member?*

party P, III.4.5, III.7.2 *We have a nice Christmas-* ~. *We are giving a* ~ *for our friends tonight.*

pass P, II.2.4, III.12 *You* ~ *a big building on your right.*

pass P, III.4.6 *I* ~*ed my examination last year.*

passenger R, III.6.4

passport P, III.6.6, III.6.10

past P, II.2.5 *We drove* ~ *the castle.*

past P, II.3.1 *It's half* ~ *three.*

pastry R, III.10.1

path P, III.12

patient R, III.8.6 *The* ~ *must not be moved.*

pay P, III.6.4, III.9.7 *How much did you* ~ *for that?*

peace P, III.7.5

pear P, III.10.1

peas R, III.10.1

pedestrian R, III.6.5 *This is a crossing for* ~*s.*

pen P, III.7.3

pencil P, III.7.3

pen-friend R, III.7.3

penny P, III.3.4, III.9.7

people P, II.8 *What do* ~ *think about the government? There are five* ~ *present.*

pepper P, III.10.1

per R, II.3.14, II.3.15, III.4.7 *I earn £75* ~ *week now.*

performance O R, III.5.4

perhaps P, I.2.18

person R, II.8 *There are five ~s present.*

pet R, III.3.5 *Have you any ~s?*

petrol P, III.6.5, III.11.9

petrol-station P, III.6.5, III.11.9

phone R, III.1.3, III.11.2

phone-booth R, III.11.2

physician R, III.1.11, III.8.6

picture P, III.2.4, III.5.8, III.5.9 *I have a nice ~ on the wall. I like a magazine with many ~s. They have several ~s by Rembrandt here.*

piece P, III.10.1 *I would like a ~ of chocolate.*

pig P, III.2.8

pill R, III.8.6

pillow P, III.2.3

pint O P, II.2.8.5, III.9.8 *Let's have a ~ of beer.*

pipe O P, III.9.4 *I like to smoke a ~ after dinner.*

pity P, I.3.11, I.4.7 *That's a (great) ~.*

place P, III.1.4, III.6.3 *Cricklewood is a nice little ~.*

plan R, III.6.2 *Have you any ~s for your summer holidays?*

plane P, III.6.4 *We are going to take a ~ to London.*

plant P, III.2.4, III.2.8 *There are many beautiful ~s in the wood.*

plastic P, II.5.1.15, III.9.3 *I don't like ~ plates. This plate is made of ~.*

plate P, III.9.5 *I want a ~ of bacon and sausage.*

platform R, III.6.4 *We'll wait for you on the ~.*

play P, III.3.3, III.5.5 *Do you ~ any games?*

play P, III.5.3 *The orchestra ~ed Beethoven.*

play P, III.5.4 *We saw a ~ by Noël Coward.*

player P, III.5.5

pleasant P, I.3.1, II.5.1.8, III.14.1 *This is very ~. The flower has a*

very ~ smell. We had ~ weather in June.

please P, I.5.2 *~, help me!*

pleasure R, I.2.4 *With ~.*

p.m. R, II.3.1 *The train leaves at 3 ~.*

pocket P, III.9.3 *I want a coat with big ~s.*

pocket-money P, III.3.4

point P, III.12 *Turn left at this ~ on the map.*

police P, III.8.7, III.11.5

policeman P, III.8.7, III.11.5

police-station P, III.8.7, III.11.5

political P, III.7.5

politics P, III.7.5

pommes frites O R, III.10.1

popular R, III.5.3

pork R, III.10.1

port of embarkation O R, III.1.9

porter O R, III.6.9 *The ~ will call a taxi for you.*

porter O R, III.6.9, III.6.13 *The ~ will take your luggage to your room.*

possible P, I.2.12, I.2.13, II.1.4 *It is ~.*

post P, III.11.1 *~ this letter before 7 p.m.*

postage R, III.11.1 *The ~ for this parcel will be 50p.*

postcard P, III.7.3

poste restante O R, III.11.1

poster P, III.2.4 *I have a ~ on the wall.*

postman R, III.11.1

post-office P, III.11.1

pot P, III.9.5 *Bring us a ~ of tea, please.*

potato P, III.10.1

£ (=pound) P, III.3.4, III.9.7

prefer P, I.3.14 *I ~ steak. I ~ swimming in the lake* (R).

prescription O R, III.8.6 *Do you want a ~ for new tablets?*

present P, III.3.3, III.7.2 *I've brought you a ~ from my own country.*

president P, III.7.5

press R, III.6.9 ∼ *the button for the third floor.*

price P, II.5.2.1, III.6.9, III.6.11, III.9.7 *The* ∼ *is £10.*

prime minister R, III.7.5

profession O R, III.1.11 *What's your* ∼?

programme P, III.5.3, III.5.4 *There is a very good* ∼ *at the concert-hall tonight.*

programme P, III.5.4 *Let's buy a* ∼ *and see what the play is about.*

promise R, III.7.2 ∼ *you will come tomorrow.*

pronounce P, III.13.3 *How do you* ∼ *this word?*

pronunciation R, III.13.3

pub P, III.10.2

pull R, II.2.5, III.6.9 ∼ *to open the door.*

pupil P, III.1.10

purpose R, II.7.6.7 *This car is used for many* ∼*s.*

purse P, III.9.3 *I've lost my* ∼.

push R, II.2.5, III.6.9 ∼ *to open the door.*

put P, II.2.5, III.3.4 *Where shall I* ∼ *your coat? I* ∼ *some money in the bank.*

put on P, III.9.3 ∼ *your hat.*

Q

quality P, II.5.2.2 *I don't like the* ∼ *of this material.*

quarter P, II.3.1 *It's a* ∼ *to 3.*

queen P, III.7.5

question P, II.6.2, III.13.3 *May I ask a* ∼?

quick P, II.3.13 *We'll have a* ∼ *meal.*

quiet O R, III.1.15 *He is a very* ∼ *boy.*

quiet P, III.6.9 *Can you give me a very* ∼ *room?*

quite P, II.4.3 *He is* ∼ *old.*

R

race P, III.5.5 *There will be a boat-* ∼ *tomorrow.*

radio P, III.2.6, III.5.3 *I like to listen to the* ∼.

railways R, III.6.4

railway-station P, III.6.4

rain P, III.14.2 *We had too much* ∼ *last week.*

rain P, III.14.2 *It is* ∼*ing again.*

raincoat P, III.9.3

rainy P, III.14.1

rarely P, II.3.15

rather P, I.3.14 *I'd* ∼ *go for a walk than stay at home. I'd* ∼ *not.*

rather P, II.4.3 *He is* ∼ *old.*

razor P, III.8.4

reach R, II.2.4, III.6.4 *We shall* ∼ *Amsterdam at 5 p.m.*

read P, III.3.3, III.5.6, III.5.9, III.13.1 *I like* ∼*ing books about England. I cannot* ∼ *this letter.*

reading P, III.4.4 ∼ *is taught in primary schools.*

ready P, II.3.23 *When will you be* ∼?

real P, II.5.1.16, III.9.3 *Is this* ∼ *leather?*

reason R, II.7.6.6 *The* ∼ *is that he is afraid.*

receipt O P, III.6.9 *May I have a* ∼, *please?*

receive P, III.7.3 *I* ∼*d a letter from him last week.*

recently R, II.3.8

reception O R, III.6.9 *Leave your key at the* ∼, *please.*

recommend O R, I.5.4, II.6.2 *I can* ∼ *a trip to Rome.*

record P, III.3.3, III.5.3 *We listened to a* ∼ *of Lionel Hampton.*

record-player P, III.3.3, III.5.3

red P, II.5.1.10, III.9.3 *I bought a* ∼ *dress.*

refreshments O R, III.6.4

register O R, III.6.9 *Please ~ before going up to your room.*

regulations O R, III.6.9 *It's against the ~ to walk on the grass.*

religion R, III.1.13

remain R, II.3.24 *How long will you ~ here? Will it ~ dry today?*

remember P, I.2.10, II.6.1 *I ~ my first visit to your country. I ~ seeing him last year. I ~ that he went there last year.*

rent O P, III.2.1, III.6.5 *We shall ~ an apartment. Here we can ~ a car* (R).

repair P, II.5.1.12, III.11.7 *Can you ~ this for me?*

repeat R, III.13.2 *Will you ~ this, please?*

request O R, II.6.2, III.6.4 *Guests are ~ed to leave their keys at the desk.*

reservation O R, III.6.9 *Have you a ~, sir?*

reserve R, III.5.4 *Have you ~d a room?*

rest P, III.8.3 *I will have to take a ~.*

rest P, III.8.3 *I would like to ~ a little.*

restaurant P, III.6.4, III.10.2

result R, II.7.6.5 *The ~ is that I cannot go to Spain.*

return P, III.6.12 *A ~ ticket is cheaper than two singles.*

revue O R, III.5.4 *She sings in a ~.*

rice P, III.10.1

right P, I.2.1, I.3.8, II.5.2.3, II.5.2.7, III.13.3 *That's ~. This is the ~ thing to do. The answer is ~. You are ~.*

right P, II.2.5, III.12 *Turn ~ for Liverpool. The town is on your ~.*

right-wing O R, III.7.5 *We have a ~ government now.*

ring up R, III.1.3, III.11.2 *I'll ring you up from Amsterdam.*

river P, III.2.7

road P, III.1.2. III.12

roast O R, III.10.1 *We'll have ~ beef.*

roll P, III.10.1 *Would you like some ~s?*

room P, II.2.8.6, III.2.2 *You have plenty of ~ here.*

room P, III.2.2 *We have two ~s on the ground-floor.*

single room R, III.6.9

double room R, III.6.9

rough P, II.5.1.9 *I want a coat of ~ wool.*

round P, II.2.2 *There's a wall ~ our garden.*

round P, II.5.1.1 *I saw a ~ thing on the road.*

roundabout R, III.12 *Drive on till you come to a ~.*

row R, III.5.4 *Our seats are in ~ 5.*

rugby R, III.5.5

S

safe R, III.6.5 *This is a very ~ car.*

safety R, III.6.5

salad P, III.10.1

salary R, III.4.7

sale R, III.9.1 *You can buy things very cheaply at the ~s.*

salt P, III.10.1 *Give me some ~, please.*

same P, II.3.5, II.7.4.1, II.7.4.2 *They came at the ~ time. They are not the ~. This book is the ~ as that.*

sandwich P, III.10.1

Saturday P, II.3.1

saucer P, III.9.5

sausage R, III.10.1

save P, III.3.4 *I ~ money for the holidays.*

say P, I.1.2, I.6.5, II.6.2, III.13.1 *He said that he was ill. I ~ ... (R). How do you ~ that in English?*

school P, III.1.10, III.1.11, III.3.3, III.4.2 *I am going to work in a ~. ~ begins at 8.30. After ~ I first do my homework.*

primary school P, III.1.10

secondary school P, III.1.10

scissors P, III.8.4

scooter O R, III.6.5

sculpture R, III.5.8 *In this cathedral you can see beautiful ~s.*

sea P, III.2.7 *We live near the ~.*

seaside R, III.2.7

season R, III.6.2 *Autumn is a good ~ for a quiet holiday.*

seat P, III.5.4 *I want five ~s for Thursday evening.*

see P, II.5.1.4, II.5.1.5 *I cannot ~ very well, it's too dark. Can you ~ something?*

see P, I.6.4 *I'll ~ you tomorrow.*

see R, III.13.2 *I ~ what you mean.*

seldom R, II.3.15

self-service R, III.9.1, III.10.2

sell P, III.1.11, III.9.1 *Do you ~ matches?*

send P, II.2.5, III.7.3, III.11.3 *I sent him a letter last week.*

sender R, III.11.3 *What is the name of the ~?*

September P, II.3.1, III.1.4

serve R, III.10.2 *We don't ~ dinner after 10 p.m.*

service O R, III.10.2 *No ~ in the garden. ~ is included in the bill.*

service O R, III.1.13 *There are three ~s in this church on Sundays.*

service-charge O R, III.10.2 *There is no ~ in the canteen.*

several R, II.3.20 *I've been there ~ times.*

sex R, III.1.6

shade P, III.14.2 *Shall we sit in the ~?*

shall P, I.2.7, I.5.1 *~ I help you? ~ we go home now?*

shave P, III.8.4 *I want to ~ before dinner.*

she P, I.1.1, II.8

sheep P, III.2.8

sheet P, III.2.3 *I don't like nylon ~s on my bed.*

shelf P, III.2.4 *I have a ~ for my books.*

shine P, III.14.2 *The sun is shining again.*

ship R, III.6.4 *A big ~ came into the harbour.*

shirt P, III.9.3

shoe P, III.9.3

shop P, III.1.11, III.9.1 *I work in a ~.*

shop-assistant R, III.1.11

short P, II.2.8.1, II.2.8.2, II.3.13 *It is only a ~ distance. We waited only a ~ time.*

should (advice) P, I.5.4 *You ~ visit the castle.*

should(n't) (right, wrong, disapproval) P, I.4.4. II.5.2.3 *You shouldn't say that. We shouldn't have left you. This should be the right answer.*

show P, II.1.6, III.9.1 *Please, ~ me another one.*

shower P, III.2.6 *I prefer a ~ to a bath.*

side P, II.2.2, III.12 *Put your car at the ~ of the road.*

sights O P, III.6.2 *Tomorrow we are going to see the ~.*

sign R, III.1.1 *Have you ~ed your cheque?*

signature R, III.1.1 *Before we can pay this cheque we must have your ~.*

silence R, III.5.4 *~, please!*

silver P, II.5.1.15 *I'd like to buy some ~ spoons. These spoons are made of ~.*

simple P, III.13.1 *Isn't there a ~ word for it?*

since P, II.3.13, II.3.22 *I've lived here ~ 1960.*

sing P, III.5.4

singer P, III.5.4

single R, III.1.7 *Are you married or ~?*

single P, III.6.12 *Two ~s to Brighton, please.*

sister P, III.1.12

sit P, II.3.24 *Don't ~ on that table!*

sit down P, II.2.4 *Would you like to ~?*

size P, II.2.8.1, III.9.3 *What ~ shoes do you take?*

skirt P, III.9.3 *I want to buy a ~.*

sleep P, III.8.3 *You've slept long enough now.*

sleepy P, III.8.3

slice P, III.10.1 *A ~ of bread, please.*

slow P, II.3.14, III.6.4, III.13.2 *We went very ~ly. We have a ~ car. There was only a ~ train to Brighton. This is a very ~ journey. Will you speak ~ly, please?*

slow down (reading only) O R, III.6.5

small P, II.2.8.1, II.2.8.6, III.6.3

smell P, II.5.1.8 *This flower has a very pleasant ~.*

smell P, II.5.1.8 *The food ~s good. Can you ~ gas?*

smoke P, III.6.4 *Would you like to ~? No smoking* (R).

smooth R, II.5.1.9 *This material is very ~.*

snackbar P, III.10.2

snow P, III.14.2 *There is ~ on the mountains.*

snow P, III.14.2 *It will ~ tomorrow.*

so P, I.2.16, II.7.6.5 *~ I was right. He ate too much ~ he didn't feel well.*

so P, II.8 *He wanted to leave, but he didn't say ~.*

so P, II.4.3, II.7.4.2 *I'm ~ sorry. He is not ~ big as his brother* (R).

soap P, III.8.4

socialist security O R, III.7.5

socialist O P, III.7.5 *We have a ~ government. I am not a ~.*

socks P, III.9.3

soft P, II.5.1.6, III.5.3 *I like ~ music when I wake up.*

soft P, II.5.1.9 *I want a ~ pillow.*

soldier P, III.1.11

some P, II.8 *~ of them went home.*

some P, II.4.2 *I'd like ~ bread. I'd like ~ chips.*

somebody P, II.8

someone P, II.8

something P, II.8

sometimes P, II.3.15, II.8

somewhere P, II.2.1, II.8

son P, III.1.12

song P, III.5.4 *This is an old English ~.*

soon P, II.3.6

as soon as R, II.3.5 *I'll help you ~ I can.*

sorry P, I.3.11, I.4.1, I.4.7 *I'm very ~ to hear that you have to go. I'm very ~ that this has happened. I'm ~ if I have hurt you. ~!*

sort P, III.1.15 *What ~ of man is he?*

sound P, II.5.1.6, III.5.3 *We could not hear a ~. I don't like the ~ of this music.*

soup P, III.10.1

south P, II.2.1, II.2.5, III.12 *Bournemouth is in the ~. Turn ~ when you come to the river.*

souvenirs P, III.9.1

spaghetti P, III.10.1

spare R, III.3.3 *What do you do in your ~ time?*

speak P, II.6.2, III.13.1 *Can you ~ French?*

specialist P, III.8.6 *I think you should go to a ~.*

speed P, III.6.5

speed-limit R, III.6.5

spell P, III.1.1, III.13.3 *Can you ~ your name, please? Will you ~ that word, please?*

spelling R, III.13.3 *That's not the correct ~.*

spend P, III.3.4, III.9.7 *I cannot ~ so much money. I ~ my money on clothes.*

spoon P, III.9.5

sport(s) P, III.5.5 *Horse-racing is a popular ~ in England.*

spring P, II.3.1, III.6.2 *We always take a short holiday in* ~.

square P, III.1.2, III.12 *I live in Port-man* ~.

square P, II.5.1.1 *I received a* ~ *box.*

stadium R, III.5.5

stage R, III.5.4 *There were only two people on the* ~.

stairs P, III.2.2, III.6.9 *You'll have to use the* ~ *there is no lift here.*

stamp P, III.7.3, III.11.1 *Do they sell* ~*s at the hotel?*

stand P, II.3.24 *I cannot* ~ *any longer, I am too tired.*

stand still R, II.2.4 *Try to* ~, *please.*

star P, III.14.2 *I cannot see any* ~*s tonight.*

star R, III.5.4 *Greta Garbo was a great* ~.

start P, II.3.22 *The game* ~*ed at 7. He* ~*ed to speak. We* ~ *at 6 o'clock.*

state P, III.7.5 *The* ~ *pays for our education.*

stay P, II.3.24, III.6.6 *I will* ~ *here for a week. It won't* ~ *dry for long.*

steak R, III.10.1

steal P, III.11.5

stewardess R, III.6.4

still P, II.3.7 *Are you* ~ *here?*

stockings P, III.9.3

stomach P, III.8.1 *I had a* ~ *operation last year.*

stop P, II.3.23 *The game will* ~ *at 9. He* ~*ped talking. We* ~ *at 5 p.m.*

stop P, II.2.4 *The car* ~*ped suddenly.*

storm R, III.14.2 *Don't go sailing in such a* ~.

straight on P, II.2.5, III.12

strange P, II.5.2.12

strawberry R, III.10.1

street P, III.1.2, III.12

string P, III.9.5 *I need a piece of* ~.

strong P, II.5.1.9 *This is a very* ~ *material.*

student P, III.1.10

study P, III.4.4, III.5.6 *I've studied English for two years.*

subject P, III.4.4 *What* ~*s do you take at school?*

succeed P, II.5.2.8 *He tried but did not* ~.

success P, II.5.2.8

successful R, II.5.2.8

such P, II.4.3, II.8 *I don't like* ~ *people. He's* ~ *a nice boy!* (R). *It was* ~ *fun!* (R).

suddenly P, II.3.25

sugar P, III.10.1

suit P, III.9.3 *I've bought a new* ~.

suitcase P, III.6.13

summer P, II.3.1, III.6.2

summer-holidays P, III.4.3

sun P, III.14.2 *The* ~ *is shining again.*

Sunday P, II.3.1

sunshine R, III.14.2

supermarket P, III.9.1

suppose R, I.2.18, II.6.1 *I* ~ *that you are right. I* ~ *so.*

suppose R, I.2.25 *Are you* ~*d to walk on the grass?*

sure P, I.2.18, II.6.1 *Are you* ~? *I'm* ~ *that he will come.*

surgeon R, III.8.6

surgery-hours O R, III.8.6 ~ *8 a.m. to 10 a.m.*

surname P, III.1.1 *His* ~ *is Robinson.*

surprise P, I.3.6 *This is a* ~!

surprising R, I.3.6

surprised R, I.3.6

sweet P, II.5.1.7, III.10.1 *The coffee is not* ~ *enough.*

sweet R, III.10.1 *Have you ordered a* ~?

swim P, III.5.5 *Do you like* ~*ming?*

T

table P, III.2.3, III.10.2 *A* ~ *for two, please.*

tablet P, III.8.6 *I must take one* ~ *after every meal.*

take P, II.2.5 *I'll* ~ *you to your room.*

take P, III.1.10 *We are going to* ~ *lessons in English.*

take P, II.3.13, III.6.4 *The journey* ~*s two hours.*

take away R, II.2.5, III.10.2 *Can I take this away?*

take off P, III.9.3 *Can I* ~ *my jacket?*

talk P, II.6.2, III.7.2 *We* ~*ed for a long time.*

tall P, II.2.8.1

tape P, III.5.3 *There are twelve English songs on this* ~.

tape-recorder P, III.5.3

taste P, II.5.1.7 *I don't like this* ~.

taste P, II.5.1.7 *How does your soup* ~? *Would you like to* ~ *this cheese?*

tax(es) P, III.4.7

taxi P, III.6.4

tea P, III.10.1, III.10.2 *I'd like a cup of* ~. *We have* ~ *at 5.*

teach P, P, III.1.10

teacher P, III.1.10, III.1.11

team P, III.5.5 *The English* ~ *have won by 5 to 3.*

telegram P, III.11.3

telegraph R, III.11.3

telephone P, III.1.3, III.2.5, III.11.2 *Have you got a* ~?

telephone P, III.1.3, III.11.2 *I'd like to* ~ *to Holland.*

telephone-booth R, III.11.2

telephone number P, III.1.3, III.11.2

television P, III.2.6, III.5.3

tell P, II.6.2 ~ *me what you've done.* ~ *me about your work.*

temperature P, II.2.8.7, III.14.2 *The* ~ *is too high for me.*

temperature R, III.8.2 *I have a* ~.

tent P, III.6.9

term P, III.4.3 *During the first* ~ *we often play football.*

terminal O R, III.6.4 *The train arrived at the* ~ *at 2 p.m.*

test P, III.4.6 *I failed my driving-*~ *twice.*

than P, II.7.4.2 *John is bigger* ~ *his brother.*

thank P, I.2.4, I.3.16, II.6.2 ~ *you (very much (indeed)).*

that P, I.1.1, II.2.1, II.8 *I want* ~ *book. Will you take* ~?

that R, II.8 *This is food* ~ *I like.*

that P, I.2.10 *He thought* ~ *I was ill.*

the P, II.4.3, II.8 *That's* ~ *best coffee I know. Can you give me* ~ *teapot, please?* ~ *Italians don't like this opera.*

theatre P, III.5.4

their P, II.7.5.1, II.8

theirs P, II.7.5.1, II.8 *It's* ~. ~ *is better* (R).

them P, II.8

themselves R, II.8 *They've done it* ~.

then P, II.3.1, II.7.6.5, II.8 ~ *he saw me. First we went to Madrid,* ~ *we travelled to Gibraltar. He ate very much and* ~ *he didn't feel well.*

there P, II.1.1, II.1.3, II.8 ~ *is no word for it.* ~ *is no water in this room.*

there P, I.2.1 ~ *he is.*

therefore R, I.2.16 ~ *I cannot help you.*

these P, I.1.1, II.2.1, II.8 ~ *houses are nice.* ~ *are nice.*

they P, I.1.1, II.8

thick P, II.2.8.1, III.10.1 *I don't want a* ~ *slice of cake.*

thief P, III.11.5

thin P, II.2.8.1, III.10.1 *I want a* ~ *slice of cake.*

thing P, II.8 *What do you call that* ~?

think P, I.2.1, I.2.18, I.3.18, II.6.1 *I don't* ~ *so. I* ~ *that you are right. I'm* ~*ing of going home tomorrow* (R). *I'll have to* ~ *about that.*

third-party O P, III.8.5 *Do you have a* ~ *insurance?*

thirst R, III.8.3

thirsty P, III.8.3

this P, I.1.1, II.2.1, II.8 ~ book is nice. ~ is nice.

those P, I.1.1, II.2.1, II.8 ~ books are nice. ~ are nice.

through P, II.2.5 We drove ~ the centre of the town.

thunderstorm P, III.14.2

Thursday P, II.3.1

ticket P, III.5.4, III.6.1, III.6.12 A ~ to London costs £1.50. Have you got ~s for the cinema?

ticket-office R, III.5.4

till P, II.3.13, II.3.23 I'll be here ~ 5 o'clock. Drive on ~ you come to a church.

time P, II.3.1 What ~ is it?

time P, II.3.15 I go to London four ~s a/per week.

time-table P, III.6.4

tip O R, III.10.2 The waiter will expect a ~.

tired P, III.8.3

to P, II.2.5 Let's go ~ London.

to P, II.3.23 I work from 9 ~ 12 every morning.

to P, II.7.3.3 I'll give the ticket ~ your brother.

to P, II.7.6.7 He came ~ help me.

to P, I.3.20 I want ~ go home.

tobacco O P, III.9.4

tobacconist O P, III.9.1

today P, II.3.1, II.3.7

together P, II.7.6.1, III.6.2 We all went ~.

toilet P, III.2.2, III.5.4

tomato R, III.10.1

tomorrow P, II.3.1, II.3.6

the day after tomorrow P, II.3.1, II.3.6

tonight P, II.3.1, II.3.6

too P, II.4.3, III.9.7 £23 is ~ much for these shoes.

too P, II.7.6.1, II.7.6.3 Do you think so, ~? John is coming ~.

tooth P, III.8.1

toothbrush P, III.8.4

toothpaste P, III.8.4

top P, III.2.7 We could see the ~s of the mountains.

tour R, III.6.2 We made a ~ in the Welsh mountains.

Tourist P, III.6.2

tourist P, III.6.2

tourist-office P, III.6.2 We'll ask for information at the ~.

towards R, II.2.5

towel P, III.8.4 I need a clean ~.

town P, III.6.3

town-hall R, III.12 The post-office is opposite the ~.

traffic-lights P, III.6.5

train P, III.6.4 We'll take a ~ to London.

train P, III.1.10 She was ~ed to be a nurse.

training R, III.4.7

tram P, III.6.4

translate P, III.13.2

translation P, III.13.2

travel P, III.6.1, III.6.4 I have to ~ one hour to my office every day.

travel bureau R, III.6.4

traveller R, III.6.4

traveller's cheque O R, III.11.4

tree P, III.2.8 There's a beautiful ~ in our garden.

trip R, III.6.2

trouble P, III.11.8 I have ~ with my car.

trousers P, III.9.3

true P, II.5.2.7

try P, II.5.2.8 Let me ~.

try on P, III.9.3 Can I try this on?

Tuesday P, II.3.1

turn R, III.9.1 It's my ~ now.

turn P, II.2.5, III.12 ~ left at the river.

turn off P, III.2.5 How do you ~ the gas?

turn on P, III.2.5 How do you ~ the gas?

TV R, III.2.6, III.5.3
twice P, II.3.20
typist R, III.1.11
tyres O P, III.11.9

U

unable R, I.2.14 *I am ~ to help you.*
under P, II.2.2 *The dog slept ~ the table.*
underground P, III.6.4 *If you want to get there fast you must take the ~.*
understand P, III.13.1, III.13.2 *I don't ~ this word.*
underwear P, III.9.3
unemployment O R, III.4.7 *There is much ~ in our country.*
unfortunately R, I.2.5 *~ I cannot help you.*
unimportant R, II.5.2.11
university P, III.1.10
unpleasant O P, II.5.1.8, III.1.15 *These flowers have an ~ smell. He is an ~ person.*
until R, II.3.23 *We'll wait ~ you are ready.*
up R, II.2.5 *We walked ~ the hill.*
up R, II.3.5 *We looked ~.*
upstairs R, III.2.2 *The bathroom is ~. Let's go ~ and go to bed.*
us P, II.8
use P, II.5.2.9 *We cannot ~ this.*
useful P, II.5.2.9
usually P, II.3.15

V

vacation R, III.6.2
valley P, III.2.7
vanilla R, III.10.1
veal R, III.10.1
vegetables P, III.10.1
very P, II.4.3 *He is ~ old.*
view R, III.6.9 *You have a nice ~ from this room.*
village P, II.6.3

visa O R, III.6.6, III.6.10
visit P, III.3.3, III.6.2, III.6.6, III.7.2 *We ~ed Spain last year. I hope you'll ~ us when you are in Holland.*

W

wages R, III.4.7
wait P, III.3.24, III.6.4 *We had to ~ only five minutes. ~ for me on the platform.*
waiter P, III.10.2 *The ~ will give us the menu.*
waiting-room R, III.6.4
waitress P, III.10.2 *Let's ask the ~ for the menu.*
wake up P, III.3.3, III.8.3 *I woke up at 6 o'clock.*
walk P, II.2.4, III.5.1 *Try to ~ to the car. I like to ~ on the beach.*
wall R, III.2.2
wallet O P, III.9.3
want P, I.3.8, I.3.20 *This is just what I ~ed. I ~ a new suit. I ~ to go home.*
war P, III.7.5
ward O R, III.8.6 *Your daughter is in the children's ~.*
warm P, II.2.8.7, III.10.1, III.14.2 *The soup is ~. It's rather ~ today.*
wash P, II.5.1.14, III.2.6, III.8.3 *Can you ~ these clothes for me? I would like to ~ before dinner.*
washing-machine R, III.2.6
watch P, III.9.3 *I want to buy a new ~.*
watch P, II.5.1.4, III.3.3, III.5.3, III.5.5 *I like ~ing a game of cricket. I like ~ing TV.*
water P, III.2.5, III.2.7, III.10.1 *There is a lot of ~ in Holland. Can I have a glass of ~?*
way P, III.12 *Is this the ~ to the opera?*
way P, II.7.3.9 *You do it in this ~.*
w.c. R, III.2.2, III.5.4

we P, I.1.1, II.8

weak R, II.5.1.9 *This material looks rather ∼.*

wear P, III.9.3 *I'm not going to ∼ this.*

weather P, III.14.2

Wednesday P, II.3.1

week P, II.3.1, II.3.13, III.6.2

weekdays R, II.3.1

weekend R, II.3.1

weekly R, II.3.15 *There is a ∼ flight to Kuala Lumpur.*

weigh R, II.2.8.4, III.9.8 *This will ∼ 5 lb.*

weight O P, II.2.8.4, III.6.13, III.9.8 *This is not the right ∼.*

well P, I.6.2, II.5.1.12, III.8.3 *I feel very ∼. I'm very, thank you, and how are you?* (R).

well P, II.5.2.2, III.13.1 *I cannot write English very ∼.*

west P, II.2.1, II.2.5, III.12 *There are beautiful beaches in the ∼. If you drive ∼ you cannot miss it.*

wet P, II.5.1.3

what P, I.1.4, I.3.6, II.8 *∼ do you want? ∼ drinks do you like? ∼ a surprise!* (R).

what P, II.8 *∼ you say is wrong.*

when P, I.1.4, II.3.1 *∼ can you come?*

when P, II.3.5 *I'll go out ∼ it is dark.*

where P, I.1.4, II.2.1 *∼ are you?*

where R, II.2.2 *Put it back ∼ it came from.*

which P, II.8 *France is a country ∼ I like very much.*

which P, I.1.4, I.3.15, II.8 *∼ do you prefer? ∼ flowers do you like best?*

while R, II.3.5 *I'll write a letter ∼ you go to the dentist.*

white P, II.5.1.10, III.9.3 *She bought a ∼ dress.*

who P, I.1.4, II.8 *∼ is going with us?*

who P, II.8 *Guests ∼ want to visit the town can take a bus.*

who(m) R, II.8 *∼ did you give it to? He is a man ∼ I have never seen.*

whose R, II.8 *He is the man ∼ car was stolen last night.*

whose R, II.8 *∼ suitcase is this? ∼ is this?*

why P, I.1.4, II.7.6.4, II.7.6.6 *∼ did you go there? ∼ don't you go home?*

wide R, II.2.8.1

wife P, III.1.7, III.1.12

will P, I.2.6 *∼ you come?*

will P, I.3.18, I.3.19 *I'll help you as soon as I can.*

will P, II.5.2.10 *This medicine ∼/ won't help you.*

will P, II.3.6 *I won't be able to help you.*

win P, III.5.5 *Which team has won?*

wind P, III.14.2 *There is a strong ∼ from the east today.*

window P, III.2.2

wine P, III.10.1

winter P, II.3.1, III.6.2 *We are going to the mountains this ∼.*

with P, II.7.3.4 *You can open the door ∼ this key.*

with P, II.2.2 *I shall be ∼ you in five minutes.*

with P, II.7.6.3 *We'll take John ∼ us.*

with P, II.7.5.1 *Did you see a man ∼ a big suitcase?*

without P, II.7.5.1 *You cannot travel here ∼ a passport.*

without P, II.7.6.3 *We'll go ∼ John.*

woman P, III.1.6

wonder R, I.2.18, II.6.1 *I ∼. I ∼ if you could help me.*

wood R, III.2.7 *We'll go for a walk in the ∼.*

wood P, II.5.1.15 *This box is made of ∼.*

wooden R, II.5.1.15

wool P, II.5.1.15, III.9.3 *This is made of ∼.*

woollen R, II.5.1.15, III.9.3

word P, III.11.3, III.13.1 *I don't know that* ∼.

work P, III.1.11 *Where do you* ∼. *How long do you* ∼ *every day?*

work O P, III.11.8 *My brakes don't* ∼.

working hours R, III.3.4

world P, III.6.3 *I would like to see the whole* ∼.

worried P, I.3.12, I.3.13 *I'm* ∼ *about your health.*

worse P, II.5.2.2, II.5.2.7 *The weather is much* ∼ *now.*

worst P, II.5.2.2 *This is the* ∼ *weather I've ever seen.*

would P, I.3.3, I.5.2, II.5.2.6 ∼ *you like ice-cream?* ∼ *you like to go out tonight?* ∼ *you be so kind as to help me?* (R).

wound P, III.8.2 *I have a* ∼ *in my leg.*

wrap up O R, III.9.1 *Shall I wrap it up for you?*

write P, II.6.2, III.5.7, III.7.3, III.13.1 *We* ∼ *to each other every month. We have not learned to* ∼ *English.*

writing P, III.4.4 ∼ *is taught in primary schools.*

wrong P, II.5.2.3 *What's* ∼*? It is* ∼ *to be lazy.*

wrong P, II.5.2.7, III.13.3 *The answer is* ∼.

wrong P, II.5.2.7 *I'm afraid you are* ∼.

Y

yard P, II.2.8.2, III.9.8 *I need 3* ∼*s of this material.*

year P, II.3.1, II.3.13, II.5.1.11, III.1.5, III.1.10 *I'm 18* ∼*s old.*

yellow P, II.5.1.10, III.9.3

yes P, I.2.1, I.2.4 ∼, *please.*

yesterday P, II.3.1, II.3.8

the day before yesterday P, II.3.1, II.3.8

yet P, II.3.2 *Has he come* ∼*? I have not* ∼ *seen John.*

you P, I.1.1, II.8 *Are* ∼ *coming, John? It is a nice record if* ∼ *like modern music.*

young P, II.5.1.11, III.1.5 *This is a party for* ∼ *people.*

yours P, II.7.5.1, II.8, III.7.3 *That's* ∼. ∼ *is better* (R). ∼ *sincerely.*

your P, II.7.5.1, II.8

yourself/-ves R, II.8 *You've done it* ∼.

youth-hostel P, III.6.9

Z

zero R, III.14.2 *It is 10 degrees below* ∼.

Items not included in the lexicon:

Cardinal numerals up to 4 digits P, II.4.1, III.1.2

Other cardinal numerals up to 9 digits R, II.4.1

Ordinal numerals up to 2 digits P, II.4.1, III.1.4

Names of letters of the alphabet P, III.1.1

Names of one's own country, country (major countries) of foreign language, neighbouring countries of one's own country P, III.1.2

Names of neighbouring countries of foreign language country (countries) R, III.1.2

Names of one's own nationality, of nationality of native speakers of the foreign language, of inhabitants of countries neighbouring one's own country. P, III.1.8

Names of nationality of inhabitants of countries neighbouring the foreign language country (countries) R, III.1.8

Name of learner's vocational school, if any P, III.1.10

Name of one's own intended occupation P, III.1.11

Name of one's own religion, if any P, III.1.13

Any foreign language equivalents of the names of the principal units of the learner's own monetary system P, III.3.4

The foreign language words for the learner's own pets, if any P, III.3.5

Names of the learner's own school-subjects P, III.4.4

Names of one's own favourite sports, if any P, III.5.5

Names of two or three national sports P, III.5.5

Names of one's own favourite games, if any P, III.5.5

Names of one's own favourite art-forms, if any P, III.5.7

Names of one's own native language, of the language of the foreign country, names of languages of countries neighbouring one's own country P, III.6.8

Names of languages of countries neighbouring the foreign language country R, III.6.8

4.2   Structural inventory

by L. G. Alexander

This is an inventory and not a reference grammar: that is, it does not set out to provide information about the use of English. It is assumed that the potential user is reasonably conversant with English grammatical structure. The listed items and their exponents are not meant to be in any way exhaustive or prescriptive. They merely demonstrate the range of structures and possible utterances that would have to be taught if threshold-level specifications were assumed.

An alphabetical ordering has been preferred to any other form of presentation since it is the least prescriptive model. It can be manipulated creatively by the user, who is free to decide on his own sequence for teaching purposes.

The entries are in **bold type**: all structural words and problematical lexical items **unspaced**, all grammatical categories **s p a c e d**. Exponents are in *italics*. s. means: see under.

When using this inventory, the following should be noted:

1. A great many (though by no means all) of the structural words and problematical lexical items which appear in the lexicon are listed in this inventory. Occasionally, single items (e.g. "give", "explain", etc.) are included to represent a particular grammatical category and the user is referred to the relevant entries.
2. Compounds and derivatives are possible providing that their meaning is fully predictable from the content-specification. For instance, "put up (your hand)" would fall within threshold-level specifications even though it is not listed in the lexicon or this inventory, but "put up with" (=*tolerate*) would not.
3. Students would be expected to acquire a productive command of all the entries except those marked "R" which are for receptive recognition only.

Every effort has been made to ensure a close correlation between the T-level specifications and this inventory. Other works which were extensively consulted during the preparation of this list:

A Grammar of Contemporary English, R. Quirk, S. Greenbaum, G. Leech and J. Svartvik, Longman, 1972.

Advanced Learner's Dictionary of Current English, A. S. Hornby, Oxford University Press, 1974 edition.

English Grammatical Structure, R. A. Close, L. G. Alexander, W. S. Allen and R. O'Neill, Longman, 1975.

Modern English, W. R. Rutherford, Harcourt Brace, 1968.

Volkshochschul Zertifikat Englisch: Strukturenliste, edited and revised by W. S. Allen, D.V.V., 1974.

A

a(n)
- indefinite article: *She's ∼ nurse*; *He's ∼ office worker.*
- distributive: *I see him once ∼ week*; *I earn £75 ∼ week now.*
- after half/such/what: *Half ∼ slice please*; *He's such ∼ nice boy* (R); *What ∼ surprise* (R); s. such; what.

ability s. able to; can; could; unable to.

able to
- interchangeable with can: *He's ∼ speak English* (R); s. adjective + to.
- future: *I'll be ∼ see you tomorrow.*
- past (=managed to): *I was ∼ get some tickets* (R).

about
- (=approximately): *It costs ∼ £2.*
- (=concerning): *I don't want to think ∼ the war.*
- after what: *What ∼ (having) a drink?*; focussing: *What ∼ me?* (R).
- after how: *How ∼ (having) a drink?* (R).

above
- as adverb: *He's in the room ∼* (R).
- as preposition: *We were flying ∼ the clouds* (R).

across
- indicating motion: *We walked ∼ the street* (R).

addresses *15 Church Road (Street, Avenue), etc.*; s. at.

adjectives
- after get/become: *He's getting old* (R); *Oil has become very expensive*; s. inchoative verbs.
- attributive/predicative: *It's a nice book*; *It's nice.*
- comparison: s. comparative forms; comparison.
- +to-infinitive: *I'm (glad) to (see you)*; also: able (R), afraid, allowed, delighted (R), sorry, supposed (R); *It's (nice) of you to (help me)*; also: good, kind.
- order: *It's a big black car*; *It's a big American car.*
- possessive: s. pronouns.
- +that-clause: *I'm sorry (that) this has happened*; also: afraid, certain (R), delighted (R), glad, sure; *It's possible (that) he is here*; also: bad, certain (R), good, interesting.
- with too/enough + to-infinitive: *I'm too tired to go out*; *I'm old enough to see that film*; also: lazy, short, tall, strong, weak, young, etc.; *It's too cold to go out*; *It's not cheap enough to buy*; also: dangerous, difficult, easy, expensive, hard, hot, near, etc.

adverbial
- clause: s. clauses.
- comparison: s. comparative forms.
- form +-ly: *He drives badly*; +-y/ -ily: *It rained heavily.*
- particle: *Come in*; *Sit down*; *Stand up.*
- same form as adj.: *He drove fast*; *It rained hard.*
- of degree: *It's very/quite hot.*
- of manner: *He drove carefully/fast*; *He travelled by air.*
- of place: *It's here/there/in the garden.*
- of time: *He arrived today/yesterday/on Sunday/at four o'clock/in winter/two hours ago*; *He will arrive tomorrow, etc.*
- too and also: *I went to Paris, too*; *I also went to Paris.*
- of frequency: *He's always late.*
- transposable particle: *Put on your coat*; *Put your coat on*; *Put it on.*

afraid
- to express fear: *I'm ~.*
- +of: *I'm ~ of trouble.*
- +to-infinitive: *I'm ~ to go there;* s. adjective+to-infinitive.
- +that (introductory polite formula): *I'm ~ (that) I can't help you;* s. adjective+that-clause.

after
- as preposition: *John came ~ 6 o'clock.*
- as subordinating conj.: *He came ~ I had left; I'll speak to him ~ he arrives.*

afterwards *I'll do it ~.*

against
- as preposition (place): *We stood ~ the wall.*
- (opposition): *He's ~ me* (R).

age *How old (What age) is she? She's three (years old);* s. how.

ago
- exact time reference with past tense: *How long ~ were you in Paris? I was in Paris three days;* s. for; since; past tense.

all *They ~ went home; I want ~ of it; ~ the shops are closed; I've lost ~ my money;* s. both.

allowed to
- permission: *Are we ~ go inside?;* s. adjective+to.
- prohibition: *You're not ~ smoke in the theatre.*

almost *It's ~ full; I'm ~ ready;* s. quite.

along
- as adv. particle: *Why don't you come ~?* (R).
- as preposition: *Walk ~ this street, then turn left* (R).

already *I've ~ done it;* s. still; yet; present perfect tense.

also s. adverbial, too and also.

always *He's ~ late;* s. adverbial, of frequency.

among *He's ~ those people* (i.e. among several; s. between).

and
- in double imperatives: *Come/go/try ~ see.*
- joining words and phrases: *It's black ~ white.*
- joining clauses: *He speaks ~ writes English; I'm staying here ~ John is too.*

another
- (=one more): *Give me ~ cup of tea.*
- (=a different): *I don't like this book; I'd like ~ (one).*

any s. some; hardly.

anybody, anyone s. some-compounds.

anything s. some-compounds.

anywhere s. some-compounds.

apostrophe 's' s. contractions; genitive.

articles s. a; the; zero.

as
- manner: *He works ~ a driver.*
- as conj.: *~ you can't come, we'll have to go without you;* s. comparison.

as soon as
- as subordinating conj.: *We had dinner ~ he had left; I'll ring you ~ he arrives.*

as well as *I've bought a new car ~ a motor cycle.*

ask *Why don't you ~ him?; I ~ed for a single ticket;* s. indirect speech; verb+object+to; verb+if.

aspect s. present progressive tense; past progressive tense; past perfect tense.

at
- referring to place: *Somebody's ~ the door; She stayed ~ home; We stayed ~ the Metropole.*
- referring to time: *I'll see you ~ 4 o'clock.*

at all *I haven't got any* ∼.
– polite formula: *Not* ∼*!*
at least *I need* ∼ *£6.*
attributive s. adjectives.
auxiliaries s. be; do; have.
away
– as particle: *He walked* ∼*; Put it*
∼*; It's far* ∼.
– +from: *Go* ∼ *from that car!*

B

back
– as particle: *We went* ∼ *(home)*;
Put/give it ∼*; It is a long way*
∼.
bad irregular comparison; s. comparative forms.
be
– as a full verb: *He's a nice boy*; *He was ill.*
– auxiliary: s. passive; past progressive; present perfect; present progressive.
– contrasted with go: *I was at the station*; *I went to the station.*
– +going to: s. future.
– imperative: ∼ *careful!* ∼ *quiet!*
because
– as subordinating conj.: *He didn't come* ∼ *he was ill.*
– why? because: *Why did you leave?*
∼ *I was late*; s. clauses, cause.
become s. inchoative verbs.
been s. present perfect tense.
before
– as adverb: *I've never done it* ∼.
– as preposition: *John came* ∼ *6 o'clock.*
– as subordinating conj.: *John came*
∼ *I had left*; *I'll speak to him* ∼
he leaves.
behind
– as adv. particle: *He's far* ∼.
– as preposition: *There's a tree* ∼
the house.

believe
– +so: *I* ∼ *so.*
– +(that): *I* ∼ *(that) you're right*;
s. verb+that.
belong to *Who(m) does this book* ∼
to?; *It* ∼*s to me.*
below
– as adverb: *He's in the room* ∼.
– as preposition: *We were flying* ∼
the clouds.
between *I was standing* ∼ *two trees*
(i.e. between two; s. among).
a bit
– as intensifier: *He's* ∼ *tired.*
both *They* ∼ *went home*; *They're* ∼
ready; *I want* ∼ *of them*; ∼ *the shops are closed*; s. all.
bring ∼ *me it*; ∼ *it to me*; s. direct object; indirect object.
but *He's not very tall,* ∼ *he's very strong*; *I'm tired* ∼ *John isn't*; *He reads English* ∼ *doesn't speak it.*
by
– an author: *It's* ∼ *Shakespeare*
(R).
– as agent in passive: *This letter was written* ∼ *Churchill* (R).
– in adv. phrases of manner: *We'll travel* ∼ *air.*
– +time reference: *He'll be here* ∼
6 o'clock (R) (i.e. at some time before); s. till/until.

C

can
– ability: *I* ∼ *drive a car.*
– in offers of help: ∼ *I open the door for you?*
– giving and seeking permission: ∼
I smoke please? (R); *You* ∼ *smoke if you like* (R).
– referring to possibility/impossibility/deduction: *She* ∼*'t be Danish*; *she must be Swedish.*
– with future time reference: *I* ∼ *see*

you tomorrow; s. *could*; *may*; *might*; *able to*; *unable to*.

cardinal numbers up to four digits; over four digits and up to nine (R); O pronounced /ou/ when making telephone calls; the use of "zero" to refer to degrees.

causative form in requests: *Can I have my shirt washed, please?*

certain

- to express certainty/uncertainty: *I'm (not) ~ (R)*.
- +of: *I'm ~ of that* (R).
- +that: *I'm ~ (that) he'll come* (R); s. adjective+that-clause.

clauses

- cause/reason: because: *He hasn't come because he's ill*; *Why isn't he here? Because he's ill*; As: *As you can't come, we'll have to go without you*.
- condition: *I'll help you if I can*; *If he's here, I'll see him*; *If he comes tomorrow, I'll speak to him*; s. verb+if.
- place: *Put it back where it came from* (R).
- purpose: to/in order to: *He came to help me*; *He came here in order to help me* (R); s. verb+to.
- relative: s. relative clauses.
- result: so: *He ate too much so he didn't feel well*.
- that: *He thought (that) I was ill*; *I'm certain (that) he's ill*; *It's a pity (that) you can't come*; s. adjectives; verb.
- time: *I'll go out when it's dark*; *I'll write a letter while you go to the dentist*; other temporal conjunctions: after, as soon as, before, till, until (R).

come

- from a source/origin: *These tomatoes came from Holland*; *Where do you ~ from?*; *I ~ from England*.

- +for a walk/drive: *~ for a walk*.
- +home: *I'll ~ home late*.
- +to+NP: *He came to the cinema with me*.
- +-ing form: *~ swimming with us* (R).
- +particle: *~ on! ~ in! ~ out!*

comparative forms

- adj. with -er (than): *He's taller than John*.
- adj. with -y/-ier (than): *He arrived earlier than John*.
- adj. with -est: *He's the tallest in the class*.
- adj. with -y/-iest: *It's the heaviest in the (world)*.
- adj. with more/most: *It's more expensive than mine*; *It's the most expensive in the (shop)*.
- irregular forms: better/best; worse/worst; less/least; more/most; farther/further/farthest/furthest.
- adverb with more/most: *He drove more carefully than I did*.
- adverb with -er/-est: *He drove faster than I did*.

comparison

- as+adj.+as: *He's as tall as I am* (R).
- not so/as+adj.+as: *He's not so/as tall as I am* (R).
- as+adv.+as: *He drove as carefully as I did* (R).
- not so/as+adv.+as: *He didn't drive so/as carefully as I did* (R); s. different; like; same.

complex sentences s. clauses.

compounds of some, any, no, every s. some-compounds.

compound nouns e.g. post-office; bus-stop; letter-box; police-station. Compare: teapot/pot of tea; s. nouns, partitive.

compound sentences s. and; but; or.

Concord e.g. *Jane is a nurse. Mary is a nurse. Jane and Mary are nurses*; *I want a cup of coffee. He wants a cup of coffee*; *I don't smoke. He doesn't smoke.*

conditionals s. clauses, condition.

conjunctions s. and; as well as; but; or; so.

continuous tenses s. present progressive; past progressive.

contractions e.g. *I'm late*; *You're early*; *He can't come*; *He doesn't like it*; *He's ill*; *He went to the party after he'd finished work*; *I'd like some.*

copula s. be; inchoative verbs; semi-copula.

cost/price *How much is it? It's £2.00/$4.00*; *It costs £2.00/$4.00*; *It's 10p/10 cents.*

could

– past ability: *I* ∼ *swim very well when I was a boy.*

– in offers of help: ∼ *I open the door for you.*

– in requests for help: ∼ *you open the door (for me), please?*

– in requests for permission: ∼ *I smoke, please?*

– in suggestions: *We* ∼ *go to the seaside tomorrow.*

– referring to possibility/impossibility/deduction: *She* ∼*n't be Danish; she must be Swedish.*

– with future time reference: *I* ∼ *see you tomorrow*; s. can; may; might; able to; unable to.

countable nouns s. nouns, unit.

countries e.g. *He comes from France*; *France is a big country*; s. zero article.

D

dates

– spoken convention: e.g. *January the first*; *The first of January.*

– written convention: e.g. *January 1st*; *January 1*; *1st January*; *1 January.*

– abbreviations: *Jan., Feb., Aug., Sept., Oct., Nov., Dec.* (R).

days of the week

– including abbreviations: *Mon., Tue., Wed., Thurs., Fri., Sat., Sun.* (R).

deduction s. can; could; must.

definite article s. the; zero article.

demonstratives

– adjectives: *This/that car is new*; *This/that one is new*; *These/those cars are new*; *These/those are new.*

– pronouns: *Give me this/that one*; *What are these/those?*; s. pronouns.

determiners s. a; demonstratives; possessives; some; the; zero article; s. quantifiers.

did/didn't s. do.

different *This one is* ∼; *It's* ∼ *from that*; s. same; *I want a* ∼ *one.*

direct object *She gave the money to me*; other verbs from Lexicon: bring, lend, read, send, show, write; *She bought a present for me*; other verbs from Lexicon: answer, correct, fill, keep, sign, translate.

– +object+to: *He explained it to me*; s. verb+object+to for list.

distance *How far is it? It's 2 miles/ 2 kilometres away*; s. how.

do/did

– as auxiliary: interrogative present and past (yes/no questions): *Do you like ice-cream?*; *Does he like ice-cream?*; *Did you write a letter?*; *Did he write a letter?*

– as auxiliary: negative present and

past: *I don't like ice-cream*; *He doesn't like ice-cream*; *He didn't enjoy the meal.*
- as full verb: *What are you doing?*; *What did you do?*; *That will do* (R).
- contrasted with make: *What is she doing?* (=performing); *What is she making?* (=creating).
- in imperatives (negative): *Don't smoke.*
- in place of verb: *Who does/did? I do/did*; *John doesn't like ice-cream, but I do*; *John didn't enjoy the meal but I did.*

down
- as adverb particle: *Sit ~.*
- as preposition: *We walked ~ the hill* (R).

duration s. during; for; since; while; how (long).

during
- while the event was in progress: *He brought us some wine ~ the meal* (R).
- during a period of time: *We met him ~ the holidays* (R).

E

each *Ten pence ~*; *~ room is the same*; *They gave us one ~*; *~ of us got one*; s. every.

echoed questions e.g. *I'm tired. Are you?*; *I'm not tired. Aren't you?*; *I went out last night. Did you?*; s. question tags; short answers.

either *I can't swim ~*; s. too.

else used after some, any, no, every compounds (s. some), and who, what.

enjoy
- +reflexive: *~ yourself!* (R).
- +noun: *Did you ~ your holiday?* (R).

- +gerund: *Do you ~ listening to music?* (R); s. verb+-ing.

enough
- predicatively: *That's ~, thank you.*
- after adj. or adv.: *That's not good ~*; *He doesn't swim well ~.*
- +to-infinitive: *I don't feel well ~ to go out*; select other suitable examples from the list given under adjective+to.
- as determiner/quantifier: *I haven't got ~ money.*

even
- used to invite comparisons: *I've ~ paid £5*; *I can't ~ lift it*; *I paid ~ more.*

ever
- after hardly: *I hardly ~ see him.*
- with the present: *Do you ~ play football?*
- with the past: *Did you ~ meet John?*
- with the present perfect: *Have you ~ been to Rome?*; *Have you ~ met John?*; s. adverbial of frequency; never; present perfect tense.

every *We see him ~ week*; *~ boy will get a present*; *~ house has a white door*; s. each.

everybody, everyone
- as singular subject: *~ believes that.*
- as singular object: *I can't tell ~*; s. some-compounds.

everything
- as singular subject: *~ is ready.*
- as singular object: *I've seen ~*; s. some-compounds.

everywhere *I've looked ~*; s. some-compounds.

except *Everyone came ~ John* (R).

exclamations
- after what: *What a (beautiful) day!*
- after how: *How nice!*

existence s. there.

explain *Please ～!* ; *Please ～ it to me* ;
s. direct object, and verb+
object+to for list.

F

fall s. inchoative verbs.
far
– basic use: *The museum isn't ～.*
– +away: *It's ～ away.*
– +from: *We live ～ from the town*;
compare: near.
– in comparisons: s. comparative
forms.
– +to: s. adjective+to.
fast
– as adj.: *It's a ～ train.*
– as adv.: *We went very ～.*
Feel
– as semi-copula: *He ～s ill*; s. semi-
copula.
few
– with plural unit nouns: *There are
～ good restaurants here.*
– comparisons: *I have ～er postcards
than you have*; *I have the ～est.*
a few
– (=a number of): *I know ～ good
restaurants here*; s. little; quantifiers.
first
– as adj.: *The ～ guest arrived at 10.*
– as adv.: *Peter came ～.*
– as ordinal: *I saw him on January
1st.*
fond of
– +gerund: *I'm ～ sweets*; *I'm ～
reading.*
for
– after adj.+gerund: *I'm sorry ～
troubling you.*
– destination/purpose: *He's leaving
～ Rome* (R); *This present is ～ my
wife.*
– duration: *I've waited here ～ two
hours*; s. present perfect tense.

forget
– +to-infinitive: *I've forgotten your
name*; *I forgot to send you a card*;
s. verb+to.
– +that: *I forgot that it's Tuesday.*
frequency s. adverbial.
from
– a source/origin: *I bought this ～
Selfridges*; *Where do you come
～?*
– direction (movement): *The wind is
～ the east*; *We flew ～ London.*
– duration: *We lived here ～ 1940 till
1945*; *The bank is open ～ 9.30 to
3.00.*
future, ways of expressing
– be going to: *We're going to fly to
Rome tomorrow.*
– will ('ll): *I'll see you tomorrow.*
– with present progressive: *He's
leaving tomorrow.*
– with simple present: *He leaves
tomorrow* (R).

G

genitive
– of personal pronouns: *My name's
Tom.*
– with apostrophe ('s or s'): *It's
John's book*; *It's James'(s) book*;
They're the children's books; *The
girls' clothes*; *They're my
brother's*; *I bought it at the
butcher's.*
– with of-phrase: *It's at the back of
the station.*
gerund
– as subject/object: *Reading is
taught early* (R); *I like reading.*
– after prepositions: *I'm afraid of
losing my way.*
– after certain verbs: *I don't like
swimming*; s. verb+-ing.
– after fancy, mind: *Fancy meeting
you!* (R); *I don't mind waiting* (R).

get
- referring to possession: *I've got a new car.*
- referring to physical action: *I got up at 6.*
- (=become): *He's ~ting old* (R); s. inchoative verbs.
- (=receive): *I got a letter from my brother.*
- +particle: *I got up/down/out/over, etc.*

give s. direct object; indirect object.

glad
- to express pleasure: *I'm ~.*
- +to-infinitive: *I'm ~ to see you*; s. adjective+to-infinitive.
- +that: *I'm ~ (that) you're here*; s. adjective+that-clause.

go
- (=depart): *Where did he ~ (to)?; He went to London; Why did he ~?*
- (=function): *The car would not ~.*
- +for a walk/drive: *I went for a walk* (R).
- +home: *I went home.*
- +to+NP: *I went to bed/the cinema.*
- +-ing form: *We went shopping* (R).
- +particle: *I went out; We went on; Why did you ~ away?*

going to s. future; intention.

gold *This ring is made of ~; It's a ~ ring*; compare: wood/wooden (R), wool/woollen (R); words from Lexicon which act as nouns and adjectives: glass, leather, metal, nylon, plastic.

good irregular comparison; s. comparative forms; s. adjective+to.

got s. have.

H

habit s. present tense.

half *It's ~ past three; Give me ~ of it; I want ~ a bottle.*

hard
- as adj.: *It's ~ work.*
- as adv.: *We worked ~*; s. adjective+to.

hardly *I can ~ keep awake.*

hardly any *I've got ~ money.*

hardly ever *He's ~ late*; compare: adverbial, of frequency.

hate
- expressing emotion, strong feeling, etc.: *I ~ him; I ~ ice-cream.*
- +gerund: *I ~ watching TV.*
- +to-infinitive: *I'd ~ to go there.*

have
- as full verb (=possess): *I ~ some money; ~ you any money?; Do you ~ any money?*
- (=eat, drink, etc.): *Let's ~ breakfast; ~ a drink.*
- (with ailments): *I ~ a headache; I ~ toothache.*
- as auxiliary: *I've been there; He's written to me.*
- causative: *Can I ~ this shirt washed, please?*
- +got: *I've got a small caravan.*
- +to (necessity): *Do you ~ to leave? I ~ to/don't have to see him; I had to/didn't have to see him.*
- in present perfect: *I've been to Paris; I've bought a dress.*
- in past perfect: *I saw him after I had finished work.*

hear
- after can: *I can ~ you.*
- as stative verb: *I ~ very well*; s. present simple tense, with stative verbs.

height
- with reference to people: *How tall are you? I'm 5 ft. 6/1 metre 80.*
- with reference to things: *How tall/ high is it? It's 50 ft. (tall/high); It's 20 metres (tall/high)*; s. how.

here
- adv. place (stressed): *It's* ∼; ∼ *he is.*
- to indicate: ∼ *it is*; ∼*'s the bus.*
- to wish well: ∼*'s to* ...

high
- with reference to things only: *That's a* ∼ *building/mountain*; s. low, tall.

home *I go* ∼ *at 6*; *I leave* ∼ *at 6 in the morning*; *I come* ∼ *at 6 in the evening.*

hope
- +so: *I* ∼ *so/not.*
- +(that): *I* ∼ *(that) you're right*; s. verb+that.
- +to-infinitive: *I* ∼ *to see you soon*; s. verb+to.

how
- +about: ∼ *about (having) a drink?* (R) (see entry for *about*).
- asking for adv. manner: ∼ *does he drive?*
- in exclamations: ∼ *nice!* s. what.
- +adj. with reference to
  age: ∼ *old is he?*
  cost/price: ∼ *much is it?*
  distance: ∼ *far/near is it?*
  height: ∼ *high/tall is it?*; ∼ *tall is he?*
  length: ∼ *long is it?*
  quantity: ∼ *much/many do you want?*
  size: ∼ *big/small/wide* (R) *is it?*
  temperature: ∼ *hot/cold is it?*
  weight: ∼ *heavy/light is it?*
  width: ∼ *wide* (R) *is it?*
- +adv.: ∼ *soon/often* ...? etc.
- duration/time: ∼ *long were you in Rome?*; ∼ *long ago were you in Rome?*
- repeated actions: ∼ *many times* ...?; s. many; present perfect tense.

I

if
- in indirect yes/no question: *I wonder* ∼ *you could help me*; s. indirect speech.
- in conditional clauses: s. clauses, conditional.
- verb+if: s. verb+if.

imperatives *Sit down!*; *Don't say that!*; *Be careful!*; *Have a cigarette!*; *Put your coat on!*

impersonal construction s. it.

in
- as adv. particle: *Come* ∼!
- referring to things worn: *Which boy? The one* ∼ *the white shirt* (R).
- referring to place: *He's* ∼ *bed*; *He's* ∼ *the garden*; *He's* ∼ *Sweden.*
- referring to time: *I'll see you* ∼ *July 19–*; *It often rains* ∼ *(the) winter*; *I'll see you* ∼ *two weeks (time).*

in front of *There's a tree* ∼ *the house.*

in order to *He came here* ∼ *help me* (R); s. clauses, purpose.

inchoative verbs
- become: *Oil has become very expensive.*
- get: *He's getting old* (R).
- fall: *He fell ill* (R).

indefinite article s. a(n); zero article.

indefinite pronoun s. some-compounds.

indirect object *She gave the money to me*; for other verbs: s. direct object; *She brought me a present*; for other verbs: s. direct object.

indirect speech
- statements: *He says/tells me he is ill/likes ice-cream/can/may/will come.*

- tense changes: *He said/told me he was ill/liked ice-cream/could/would come.*
- no tense change: *He asks if he can/ may go*; *He asks if you like it*; s. verb + if.
- tense changes (+question word): *He asked if he could go*; *He asked if you were enjoying it*; *He asked me when I would arrive.*
- imperatives: *He told me to go*; *I told him to go.*

infinitive
- after let: *Please let me help you.*
- as object: e.g. *I want to go*; s. verb + to.
- complementation of adj.: e.g. *I'm afraid to go*; s. adjective + to; clauses.
- expressing purpose: e.g. *I've come here to help you.*
- to: *It's hard to say.*
- or -ing: *I like to lie/lying in the sun*; s. verb + to; verb + -ing.

-ing form: s. gerund; infinitive.

inside
- as particle: *He's ∼.*
- as preposition: *He's ∼ the museum.*

instrument s. with; without.

intensifiers *It's a lot/a bit/a little/ much better*; s. quite; rather; too; very.

intention
- with going to: *I'm going to write him a letter.*
- with will: *I will write him a letter.*

interrogative form
- of auxiliaries/modals: *Is he here?*; *Has he (got) a car?*; *Can you speak English?* etc.
- negative questions: *Isn't he here?*; *Hasn't he (got) a car?*; *Can't he speak English?* etc.
- with do/does/did: *Do you like ice-cream?*; *Does he like ice-cream?*;

Did he write to you?
- negative questions: *Don't you like ice-cream?*; *Doesn't he like ice-cream?*; *Didn't he write to you?*
- with question words (who and which) as subject (no inversion): *Who told you that?*; *Which bus goes to Oxford Circus?*
- who(m)? what? which? whose? how? when? where? why? (with inversion): *Who(m) did you see?*; *What is she doing?*; *Which one have you bought?* etc.
- prepositional ending: *What are you looking at?*

into *Let's go ∼ the house.*

intonation
- especially with reference to: wh-questions and yes/no-questions; echoed questions; a question in statement form; requests and commands.

intransitive verb s. verb.

invitations s. can; could; will; would.

irregular adjectives s. comparative forms.

irregular plurals s. plural nouns.

irregular verbs The following occur in the Lexicon:

```
be – was – been
become – became – become
begin – began – begun (R)
break – broke – broken
bring – brought – brought
burn – burnt – burnt
buy – bought – bought
choose – chose – chosen
come – came – come
cost – cost – cost (R)
cut – cut – cut
do – did – done
drink – drank – drunk
drive – drove – driven
fall – fell – fallen
feel – felt – felt
find – found – found
fly – flew – flown
```

forbid – forbade – forbidden (R)
forget – forgot – forgotten
freeze – froze – frozen
get – got – got (gotten R)
give – gave – given
go – went – gone
have – had – had
hear – heard – heard
hurt – hurt – hurt
keep – kept – kept
know – knew – known
learn – learnt – learnt
leave – left – left
lend – lent – lent
let – let – let
lie – lay – lain
lose – lost – lost
make – made – made
mean – meant – meant
meet – met – met
pay – paid – paid
put – put – put
read – read – read
say – said – said
see – saw – seen
sell – sold – sold
send – sent – sent
show – showed – shown
sing – sang – sung
sit – sat – sat
smell – smelt – smelt
speak – spoke – spoken
spend – spent – spent
stand – stood – stood
swim – swam – swum
take – took – taken
teach – taught – taught
tell – told – told
think – thought – thought
understand – understood – understood
wear – wore – worn
write – wrote – written

it as subject: *~'s fine*; *~'s raining*; *~ tastes good*; *~ hurts*; *What's ~ like?*
- +adj.+to-infinitive: *~'s nice to see you*; s. adjective+to; pronouns.

J

just
- in present perfect: *I've ~ seen him*; s. adverbial, of frequency.

L

last
- as adj.: *The ~ guest arrived at 10.*
- as adv.: *Peter came ~.*
- in time references: *I saw him ~ night, etc.*; s. next.

late
- as adj.: *We are ~.*
- as adv.: *We arrived ~.*

lately *Have you seen John ~?*

least
- comparisons: *This one is the ~ expensive.*

length *How long is it? It's 2 yards/2 metres long*; s. how.

less
- with mass nouns: *I want ~ (sugar), please.*
- comparisons: *I have less time than you have*; *It's less expensive than yours.*

let
- (=allow) *~ me help you*; *Rooms to ~*; s. infinitive.

let's
- in suggestions: *~ go to a show tonight*; s. shall.

like
- after would: *Would you ~ ...?*
- as an adv.: *You do it ~ this.*
- as a verb: *I ~ your brother very much*; *I ~ ice-cream.*
- in comparisons: *What's it ~? It's ~ an orange/~ tea.*
- +to-infinitive: *I'd ~ to see a film.*

little
- with mass nouns: *There's very ~ time.*

– comparisons: *I have less money than you have.*

a little

– (=a quantity of): *May I have ~ sugar, please?*
– as intensifier: *It's ~ better.*

long

– distance: *It's a ~ way.*
– duration: *I haven't seen him for a ~ time.*

look

– as semi-copula: *You ~ ill; It ~s nice.*
– as verb: *~ at this!*
– +particle: *~ out!*

a lot

– as intensifier: *He's ~ better now.*

a lot of/lots of

– in affirmative statements with mass and unit nouns: *I've got ~ time/books.*

love

– expressing emotion/strong feeling, etc.: *I ~ you; I ~ ice-cream.*
– +gerund: *I ~ watching TV* (R).
– +to-infinitive: *I ~ to watch TV* (R).
– after would: *I'd ~ to see that film* (R).

low

– with reference to things only: *That's a ~ building/mountain;* s. high.

M

make

– basic meaning: *I made it myself; This dress is made of wool.*
– contrasted with do: *What is she making?* (=creating); *What is she doing?* (=performing).

many

– as quantifier: *I've got too ~.*
– in negative statements with unit

nouns: *There aren't ~ taxis in this town.*

– +times: *How ~ times have you been to Paris? Four times.* s. how; present perfect tense.

mass nouns s. nouns.

matter

What's the ~?; It doesn't ~.

may

– permission: *~ I leave now?*
– requests: *~ I have some please?*
– uncertainty/possibility: *Perhaps I ~ see you again.*
– with future time reference: *I ~ see you tomorrow.*

meals

– no article before meals: *I'm going to have breakfast/lunch, etc.;* s. zero article.

measures/volume: pint, gallon, as given in the Lexicon.

might

– possibility: *I ~ go there tomorrow.*
– suggestion: *We ~ go to a show tonight;* s. may.

mind

– basic meaning: *I don't ~* (R).
– +if: *I don't ~ if he joins us* (R).
– polite requests: *Would you ~ opening the window?* (R); s. gerund.
– warning: *~ the gap!* (R).

modals s. can, could, may, might, must, need, ought to, shall, should, will, would.

months of the year s. dates.

more

– with mass and unit nouns: *I need ~ stamps/time.*
– comparisons: *I have ~ than you have; It's ~ expensive than yours.*

most

– with mass/unit nouns: *~ people don't know this.*
– in comparisons: *This one is the ~ expensive.*

motion s. prepositions.
much
- as adverb: *You smoke too* ∼; *I shouldn't smoke so* ∼; *I don't like it very* ∼.
- as quantifier: *I've got too* ∼; compare: many.
- as intensifier: *This is* ∼ *better*.
- in negative statements with mass nouns: *There isn't* ∼ *sugar*; s. how.

must
- deduction: *She* ∼ *be Danish; she can't be Swedish*.
- necessity/obligation: *I* ∼ *leave immediately* (R); s. have + to.
- prohibition: *We* ∼*n't smoke in the theatre*; needn't: s. need.
- with future reference: *I* ∼ *see you tomorrow*.
- with past reference: had to: s. have + to.

N

names s. nouns; zero article.
nationalities as required.
near
- as adverb: *The village is quite* ∼.
- as preposition: *We live* ∼ *the cathedral*; compare: far from.

necessity s. have; must; need (absence of necessity).
need
- as full verb: *I* ∼ *a new coat; I don't* ∼ *a new coat; Do you* ∼ *a new coat?*
- as modal (absence of necessity): *We* ∼*n't do it* (R); mustn't: s. must.

negative form
- of be/auxiliaries/modals: *He isn't here; He hasn't got a car; He can't speak English, etc.*
- negative questions: *Isn't he here?*; *Hasn't he got a car?*; *Can't he speak English? etc.*
- with do/does/did: *I don't like ice-cream; He doesn't like ice-cream; He didn't write to me.*
- negative questions: *Don't you like ice-cream?*; *Doesn't he like ice-cream?*; *Didn't he write to you?*

negative interrogative s. interrogative forms; negative form.
never
- with the present: *I* ∼ *play football.*
- with the present perfect: *I've* ∼ *been to Rome; I've* ∼ *met John*; s. adverbial of frequency; ever; present perfect tense.

new
- with reference to things: *His car is* ∼; s. old; young.
next
- as adj.: *He's in the* ∼ *room.*
- as adv.: *What's* ∼? (R).
- in time references: *I'll see you* ∼ *week, etc.*; compare: last.
- + to (preposition): *I sat* ∼ *to John.*

no
- in negative answers: ∼, *thank you.*
- (= not any): s. some.
- no-compounds: s. some-compounds.

nobody, no one s. some-compounds.
nominalization s. it.
none s. some.
not s. interrogative form; negative form; hope; rather; suppose.
not ... any s. some.
not ... much/many s. much; many.
nothing s. some-compounds.
nouns
- common: a camera, an orange, etc.: as specified in Lexicon.
- compound: post-office, letter-box, etc.: as specified in Lexicon.
- count/countable: a camera, an orange, etc.: as specified in Lexicon.

– mass: sugar, coffee, etc.: as specified in Lexicon.
– mass or unit: beer/a beer, coffee/a coffee, etc.: as specified in Lexicon.
– partitive: a piece/slice, etc., of: as specified in Lexicon.
– plural: s. plural nouns.
– proper: names of people and places as required.
– unit: s. count/countable above; s. a(n); plural nouns; some; the; zero article.

nowhere s. some-compounds.

number s. plural nouns.

numbers cardinal and ordinal.

O

of s. genitive; prepositions; a cup of coffee: s. nouns: partitive.

off
– as particle: *Keep ~!*; *Take it ~.*

offers s. can, could, let, shall.

often *He's ~ late*; s. adverbial, of frequency.

old
– as opposite of new: *His car is ~*; and young: *He is ~.*
– comparisons: people and things: *He's ~er/the ~est*; *It's ~er/the ~est.*

on
– in adv. manner: *~ foot.*
– as adv. particle: *Come ~!*; (=forwards): *We went ~.*
– focussing: *I cannot give you any information ~ train services* (R).
– referring to place: *It's ~ the table.*
– referring to time: *I'll see you ~ Monday*; *I go there ~ Mondays*; *I went there ~ July 17th*; *I went there ~ Monday, July 17th.*

once *He came (only) ~*; *He comes here ~ a week*; s. a(n).

one
– as pronoun/propword: *Which ~?* *The red ~*; *I like the red ~ better.*
– distinguishing from a(n): *I want ~ book and not two.*
in place of a(n)+unit *I've got ~.*

ones
– as pronoun/propword: *Which ~?* *The red ~*; *I like the red ~ better.*
– in place of plural unit: *I've got some big ~.*

only
– positions: *I ~ wanted to help you*; *He came ~ once.*

or
– joining words or phrases: *It's black ~ white.*
– joining clauses: *We can go to the beach ~ stay at home.*

ordinal numbers up to two digits: e.g. 20th, 21st, 22nd, 23rd, 24th, etc.

other
– (=alternative): *Give me the ~ book*; *Give me the ~ one/ones*; s. another.

ought to
– advisability / desirability / duty: *You ~ see a doctor* (R).
– inadvisability/disapproval: *You oughtn't to do that* (R); s. should.

out as particle: *We walked ~.*

out of *He came ~ the house.*

outside
– as particle: *He's ~.*
– as preposition: *He's ~ the museum.*

over *We flew ~ the city.*

own
– (my own=mine, etc.): *This is my ~ (book).*
– as stative verb: *He ~s a house in the country.*

P

particle s. adverbial particle; adverbial, transposable particle.

participle s. past participle; present participle.

partitive s. nouns, partitive.

passive

– simple present: *The train is delayed* (R).

– simple past: *The train was delayed* (R).

– present perfect: *The train has been delayed* (R).

– future and modals: *The train will be delayed* (R).

– with by-phrase: *This book was written by Churchill* (R).

– direct/indirect: *John was killed* (R); *I was given a book* (R).

past

– as preposition: *It's half ∼ 3; He walked ∼ the house.*

past continuous tense s. past progressive tense.

past participle

– after have/had in present/past perfect: *I've broken my watch.*

– in passive construction: *He was killed in an accident* (R).

– used adjectivally: *My watch is broken; The shops are closed; I found a broken watch.*

past perfect tense

– with after: *After I had finished I left.*

– with before: *I left before I had finished.*

– with when: *When I had finished I left.*

past progressive tense

– with e.g. when (progressive and past: interrupted actions): *When I was leaving the hotel I met Harry.*

– adv. place (stressed): *It's ∼; ∼ he was working in the garden while my wife was cooking the dinner.*

past tense

– with irregular verbs: s. irregular verbs.

– with regular verbs: s. regular verbs.

– with exact time reference: *He left a week ago, etc.*

period of time s. by; during; for; since; while.

permission s. allowed to; can; could; may.

personal pronouns s. pronouns.

phrasal verbs

– intransitive: e.g. *Come in.*

– transitive: e.g. *Put on your coat; Put your coat on; Put it on.*

piece of s. nouns, partitive.

place s. adverbial; prepositions.

plural nouns

– form and spelling:

– +-s: cars, socks, cups, etc.

– +-es: potatoes, glasses, watches, brushes, boxes, etc.

– consonant -y to -ies: babies, lavatories (R), etc.

– -fe to -ves: knives, wives, thieves, lives, etc.

– irregular: children, feet, men, pence, teeth, women.

– used only as plural: glasses, people, police, scissors, trousers.

– used only as singular: hair, information, baggage (R), luggage, furniture, news, spaghetti, and mass nouns (sugar, coffee, etc.).

point

– in space: s. adverbial, place; prepositions.

– of time: s. adverbial, time; prepositions; at; by; in; on; since.

possession s. have, own.

possessive s. pronouns; genitive.

possibility s. can; may; might; could.

predicative s. adjectives.

preference s. rather.

prepositions s. about; above; across (R); against; along (R); among (R); at; behind; between; by; down; during (R); for; from; in; inside; into; next to; of; on; out of; outside; round; since; through; to; up; with.

– after adjective/verb: s. adjectives; verbs.

– at the end of a question: *What are you looking at?*

– before a gerund: s. gerund.

– of motion: to, from, etc.

– of position: in, at, etc.

– of time: in, at, etc.

present continuous tense s. present progressive tense.

present participle

– as adj.: *It's surprising.*

– in progressive aspect: *He's writing; He was writing.*

present perfect tense

– been and gone: *Have you ever been to Paris? I went there last year.*

– no time reference: *He has left.*

– repeated actions: *I've been there again and again; I've met him several times.*

– with ever, never: *Have you ever met John? No, I've never met him.*

– with (not) ... yet/already: *Has your friend come yet? No, he hasn't come yet; He's already left.*

– with since + exact time reference: *I've been here since Thursday; I haven't seen him since Monday.*

– with for + a period of time: *I've been here for a month.*

present progressive tense

– current action: *What are you doing (now)? I'm reading.*

– with future reference: *He's leaving tomorrow.*

present simple tense

– habitual: *He washes his hands before a meal; He usually arrives at 8.*

– with future reference: *The train leaves at 6.27.*

– with stative verbs: *He wants some coffee*; compare: believe, belong to (R), forget, hear, know, like, live, love, mean, need, own, remember, see, smell, understand.

progressive aspect s. present progressive tense; past progressive tense.

prohibition s. allowed to; must.

pronouns

– indefinite: s. some, some-compounds.

– personal: subject: I, we, he, she, it, they, you; object: me, us, him, her, it, them, you.

– possessive adjectives and pronouns: my, mine; our, ours; his, his; her, hers; its; your, yours; their, theirs.

– reflexive: myself, himself, herself, itself, ourselves, yourselves, themselves.

pronunciation:

– [s] after 'k', 'p', 't': socks, pots, cups, etc.

– [z]: cars, dogs, letters, etc.

– [iz]: houses, watches, etc.

proper nouns s. nouns.

purpose s. clauses, purpose.

put on ~ *your hat; Put your hat on; Put it on*; s. adverbial, transposable particle.

Q

quantifiers/determiners s. all; a lot of; some; many; much; hardly any; enough; little; few; several; half; nouns, partitive.

quantity
- of mass: *How much do you want? I want a slice/a pound (lb.)/a kilo (kg.)/a little/etc.*
- of units: *How many do you want? I want 5/2 pounds (lb.)/2 kilos (kg.)/a few/etc.*; s. how; many; much: quantifiers; some.

questions s. echoed questions; indirect speech; interrogative form; prepositions.

question tags *He's here, isn't he?*; *He isn't here, is he? etc.*

quite
- as intensifier: *He's ~ old*; s. rather; too; very.

R

rarely *He's ~ late*; s. adverbial, of frequency.

rather
- as intensifier: *He's ~ old*; s. quite; too; very.
- preference: *I'd ~ go for a walk than stay at home; I'd ~ not.*

reason s. clauses, cause/reason.

reflexive pronouns s. pronouns.

regular verbs verbs as given in Lexicon.
- +-d, +-ed [d]: e.g. served, answered, etc.
- +-ed [t]: e.g. washed, etc.
- +-ed [id] after [t], [d]: e.g. posted, etc.
- +-ied [aid] or [i:d] in place of consonant +-y: e.g. tried, carried, etc.

relative clauses
- included subject: *She's the girl who works in the office; They're the girls who work in the office; She's the girl that works in the office (R); They're the girls that work in the office (R); That's the train which/that (R) leaves at 6.*
- included or deleted object: *That's*

the girl (whom) I met yesterday; They're the girls (whom) I met yesterday; That's the book (which/ that) I bought yesterday; They're the books (which/that) I bought yesterday.
- prepositional ending: *That's the man (whom) I told you about; That's the hotel (which/that) I stayed at.*

remember
- +object: *I ~ my first visit to your country.*
- +to-purpose: *Please ~ to post my letter.*
- +-ing (recollection): *I ~ seeing him last year.*
- +that: *I ~ (that) he went there last year.*

reported speech s. indirect speech.

requests s. can, could, may, will, would, causative form in requests; suggestions.

right
- after be: *The answer is ~; You're ~.*

round
- as adj.: *It's ~.*
- as prep.: *There's a wall ~ the garden.*

S

same *This one is the ~; It's the ~ as that; They came home at the ~ time*; s. different.

say s. indirect speech; verb+obj.+ to; verb+that.

see
- after can: *I can ~ you.*
- as stative verb: *I ~ quite well*; s. present simple tense; stative verbs.
- (=understand): *Oh – I ~! (R).*
- (=meet; also progressive aspect): *I'll ~ you tomorrow; I'm ~ing him tomorrow.*

seldom *He's* ∼ *late* (R); s. adverbial,
of frequency.
semi-copula
- feel: *He feels ill.*
- look: *He looks ill*; *It looks nice.*
- smell: *It smells good* (it has a nice
smell).
- taste: *It tastes good* (it has a nice
taste).
send ∼ *me it*/∼ *it to me*; s. direct
object; indirect object.
several
- as adj.: ∼ *people were there* (R).
- repeated actions: *I've been there* ∼
times (R); s. present perfect tense.
sequence of tenses s. clauses, con-
dition/time; indirect speech; since.
shall
- in offers and suggestions: ∼ *I help
you?*; ∼ *we go home now?*; s. let;
let's.
shape *It's round/square, etc.*; s.
how; what.
short
- as adj. opposite of long and tall:
It's ∼; *He's* ∼.
- duration: *For a* ∼ *time.*
short answers e.g.
- adj. complement: *What colour is
it? Black.*
- adv. place/prep. phrase: *Where is
he? In the garden.*
- adv. time: *When will he be here? On
Monday.*
- NP object: *What's he reading? A
book.*
- NP subject/subject + be/auxiliary/
modal: *Who's waiting? Bob is.
Who likes ice-cream? I do. Who
broke the window? I did. Who can
help me? I can, etc.*
- yes/no tag answers: *Is he here?
Yes, he is/No, he isn't, etc.*
should
- advisability / desirability / duty:
You ∼ *see a doctor.*

- inadvisability/disapproval: *You*
∼*n't do that*; s. ought to.
show ∼ *me it*/∼ *it to me*; s. direct
object; indirect object.
simple past tense s. past tense.
simple present tense s. present
simple tense.
simple sentences
- not more than two complements:
I'll see you on Monday; *Let's go
into the garden now.*
since
- +exact time reference: *I've been
here* ∼ *Thursday*; *I haven't seen
him* ∼ *Monday*; s. present perfect
tense.
size *How big is it? It's very big. What
size do you want? Size 8/Size 42,
etc.* s. how; what.
smell
- as semi-copula: *It* ∼*s good.*
- as verb of perception: *I can* ∼ *gas*;
I ∼ *gas*; ∼ *it!* s. hear; see; present
simple tense; stative verbs.
so
- (=therefore): ∼ *I was right*; *He
didn't arrive* ∼ *I left.*
- +adj.: *I'm* ∼ *glad.*
- after believe, hope, suppose and
think: *I believe/hope/suppose/think*
∼.
- not so/as ... as: *He's not* ∼/*as big
as his brother.*
some, any, no+mass/plural units
- some: affirmative: *I've got* ∼
sugar/magazines; questions, ex-
pecting 'yes': *Would you like* ∼
sugar/magazines?
- any: negatives: *I haven't got any
sugar/magazines*; questions: *Have
you got any sugar/magazines?*
- no+noun (=not any): *I've got no
sugar/magazines.*
some-/any-/no-/every-compounds:
someone – anyone – no one –
                                    – everyone

somebody – anybody – nobody –
– everybody
something – anything – nothing –
– everything
somewhere – anywhere – nowhere –
– everywhere
some-/any-/no-compounds follow
basic some/any/no pattern; s.
everybody, everyone; everything;
everywhere.

sometimes ~ *he's late*; *He's* ~ *late*;
He's late ~; s. adverbial, of frequency.

soon
- (=early): *We're too* ~.
- with future reference: *I'll see you*
  ~; s. as soon as.

sorry
- to apologize: *I'm* ~.
- +to-infinitive: *I'm* ~ *to hear that.*
- +that: *I'm* ~ *(that) you can't*
  come; s. adjective + to/that.
- +if: *I'm* ~ *if I have hurt you.*

speak
- a language: *Do you* ~ *English?*;
  compare: say and tell.

spelling s. plural nouns; regular
verbs.

stative verbs s. present simple
tense; stative verbs.

still
- affirmative: *He is* ~ *here.*
- to emphasize continuity: *He's*
  been here since yesterday and he's
  ~ *here*; *He's* ~ *working on it*; *Is*
  he ~ *here?*

stop
- +gerund: *We* ~*ped at 9*; *He*
  ~*ped talking.*

subordinating conjunctions
after, because, before, if, in order
to, since, that, till, to + inf., until
(R), when, where (R), while (R),
passim; s. clauses.

such a(n)
- (+adj.)+noun: *He's* ~ *a nice*

boy! (R); *He's* ~ *an interesting*
man! (R); *It was* ~ *fun* (R).

suggestions *Why don't you* ...?
(R); *Shall we* ...?; *Let's* ...?; *Will*
you ...?; *Would you* ...?; *We*
might ... (R); *What about* ...?

suppose
- +so: *I* ~ *so/not* (R).
- +(that): *I* ~ *(that) you're right*
  (R); s. verb+that.
- obligation: *Are you* ~*d to do that?*
  (R); s. adjective + to.

T

tags s. question tags; short answers.
take *How long does it* ~? *It* ~*s two*
hours.
tall
- with reference to people and
  things: *He's* ~; *It's a* ~ *building*;
  s. high, short.

taste
- as semi-copula: *It* ~*s good* (It has
  a good taste).
- as verb: ~ *it!*

tell s. indirect speech; verb +
object + to; verb + that.
- +about: ~ *me about it.*

temperature *How hot/cold is it? It's*
70° (Fahrenheit); *It's 20° (Centi-*
grade/Celsius); s. how.

temporal clauses s. clauses, time.
temporal conjunctions s. clauses,
time.
tenses s. future; present; past.
than s. comparisons; rather.
that s. adjectives; clauses,
demonstrative; relative clauses.
the
- definite article: *Which one?* ~ *red*
  one; *Which ones?* ~ *red ones.*
- singular unit: ~ *car in* ~ *garage*
  is new.

– plural units: ~ *cars in* ~ *garage are new.*
– mass noun: ~ *tea in that pot is cold.*
– topographical: *We went down* ~ *Thames*; *We went to* ~ *Alps*; s. zero article.
– referring to one only: ~ *sun is hot*; *Close* ~ *door.*
– referring to place: *I'm going to* ~ *butcher's/* ~ *cinema/* ~ *seaside.*

then
– (=at the time): *I'll see you* ~.
– (=after that): *I was at the corner.* ~ *he saw me.*

there
– adv. place (stressed): *It's* ~; ~ *he is!*
– existential (unstressed): ~ *'s a man at the door*; ~ *was no one there*; ~ *'s been an accident.*
– (=take place): ~ *will be a concert tomorrow.*

these s. demonstratives.

think
– +so: *I (don't)* ~ *so.*
– +(that): *I* ~ *that you're right*; s. verb+that.
– +of: *I'm* ~*ing of going home tomorrow.*

this s. demonstratives.

those s. demonstratives.

through *We drove* ~ *the centre of the town.*

till/until *I'll be here* ~ (R) *6 o'clock.*

not . . . till/until *I won't be here till/until 6 o'clock* (R); compare: by.

time
– telling the time, including reference to the 24-hour clock.
– of day/greetings, etc.: *this morning, etc.*; *good morning, etc.*
– point of time: s. adverbial, of time; at; in; on.

titles
– as in: *Mr. (Tom) Jones*; *Mrs.* *(Mary) Smith*; *Miss (Jane) Brown*; *Ms. (Jane) Brown*; *Dr. (Frank) Wright.*
– when addressing a physician: e.g. *Yes, doctor.*

to
– after adjectives: *I'm sorry* ~ *hear this.*
– after too+adj.: *It's too heavy* ~ *lift.*
– after adj.+enough: *It's cheap enough* ~ *buy*; s. adjectives.
– as preposition: *He went* ~ *the cinema*; *He went* ~ *bed.*
– in infinitive constructions: *I want* ~ *see him*; s. verbs.
– purpose: *I went there* ~ *meet him*; s. clauses, purpose.

too
– (=also): *I'll come to the party,* ~; s. either.
– as intensifier (=excessively): *It's* ~ *heavy*; *It's* ~ *heavy to lift*; s. quite; rather; very; adjective with too/enough+to-infinitive.

transitive verb s. verb.

U

unable to
– interchangeable with can't: *He's* ~ *speak English* (R).
– future: *He'll be* ~ *see you tomorrow* (R).
– past (=didn't manage to): *I was* ~ *get any tickets* (R).

uncountable noun s. nouns.

until s. till.

up
– as particle: *Wake* ~!
– as preposition: *We walked* ~ *the hill.*

V

verb s. be, do, have (auxiliaries); inchoative; irregular; phrasal; regular; stative (see present simple); tense (under present; past).

- +if: some verbs from the Lexicon that will combine with if: ask, forget, know, mind (R), remember, wonder (R).
- +-ing: some verbs from the Lexicon that will combine with -ing: begin (R), enjoy (R), finish (R), hate (R), like, love, mind (R), remember (R), start, try (=experiment).
- +to: some verbs from the Lexicon that will combine with to: agree, allow, begin (R), decide, dislike (R), expect (R), fail, forget, hate (R), hope, intend, learn, like, love, need (R), promise (R), remember, say, speak, try (=attempt to).
- +object+to: some verbs from the Lexicon which will combine with object+to: ask, explain, help, introduce (R), order (R), promise (R), request (R), say, tell.
- +that: some verbs from the Lexicon that will combine with that: agree, believe (R), decide, expect (R), feel, forget, know, mean, promise (R), remember, see, suppose (R), tell someone, understand.
- +preposition: prepositions that will combine with some of the verbs in the Lexicon: apologize for (R), arrive at, ask for, borrow from, correspond with (R), differ from (R), excuse for, leave for, look at, smell of, wait for.

verb used intransitively *I'm waiting*; *I'm reading, etc.*; *Look! Listen! etc.*

verb used transitively *I'm reading a book*; *I'm putting on my coat*; *Look at this picture.*

very
- as intensifier: *He's ~ old*; s. quite; rather; too.

W

want *I ~ a new suit*; s. present simple tense; stative verbs.

want to *I ~ go home*; s. verbs: +to-infinitive.

weather *What's the ~ like (today)?*; *What's it like (today)?*

well
- as predicative adj.: *I feel ~.*
- as adverbial of manner: *I can't write English very ~.*

what
- in wh- questions: s. interrogative form.
- in exclamations: *~ a surprise!* (R); compare: how.
- (=the thing which): *~ you say is wrong.*
- with reference to size: *~ size is it?*; s. how.

when
- in wh- questions: s. interrogative form.
- as temporal conjunction (=the time when): *I'll go out ~ it is dark.*

where
- in wh- questions: s. interrogative form.
- as conjunction (=the place where): *Put it back ~ it came from* (R).

which
- in wh- questions: s. interrogative form.
- as relative: s. relative clauses.

while
- (=during the time when): *I'll write a letter ~ you go to the dentist* (R); s. clauses, of time; past progressive tense.

who
- in wh- questions: s. interrogative form.
- as relative pronoun: s. relative clauses.

who(m)
- in wh- questions: s. interrogative form.
- as relative pronoun: s. relative clauses.

whose
- in wh- questions: ~ *case is this?* (R); ~ *is this case?* (R).
- as relative: *I don't know* ~ *it is* (R).

width *How wide is it?* (R); *It's 2 yards/metres (wide)* (R); s. how.

will, 'll
- plain future: *I'~/I won't see you tomorrow.*
- promise: *I'~ help you as soon as I can.*
- in invitations, requests: ~ *you come?*
- instructions: ~ *you help me?*; ~ *you open the window?*
- in predictions: *This medicine* ~/ *won't help you.*

with
- (=accompanying; in the company of): *We'll take John* ~ *us*; *I'll be* ~ *you in five minutes.*
- instrumental: *You can open the door* ~ *this key.*
- possession, personal characteristics: *The man* ~ *the black bag*; *The girl* ~ *the blue eyes*; s. in.

without
- (=not accompanying): *We'll go* ~ *John.*
- instrumental: *You can't open the door* ~ *the key.*
- not possessing: *I've come* ~ *my bag.*
- +gerund: *We sat there* ~ *talking.*

wonder
- +if: *I* ~ (R); *I* ~ *if you could help me?* (R).

wood/wooden *This box is made of wood*; *It's a wooden box*; compare: gold; wool/woollen.

wool/woollen *This dress is made of wool*; *It's a woollen dress*; compare: gold; wood/wooden.

would
- in offers, invitations: ~ *you like some ice-cream?*; ~ *you like to go out tonight?*
- requests: ~ *you open the window, please?*; ~ *you mind opening the window?* (R).

word order
- basic statement pattern: (time)/subject/verb/object/manner/place/(Time); for changes from this pattern s. adverbial, of frequency; interrogative form.

wrong
- after be: *The answer is* ~; *You're* ~.
- +to infinitive: *It's* ~ *to ask*; s. adjective+to-infinitive for list.

Y

years
- spoken convention: e.g. *nineteen hundred, nineteen one, nineteen two, etc.*
- written convention: *1900, 1901, 1902, etc.*

yes/no
- questions: s. interrogative form.
- tags: s. short answers.

yet
- in questions: *Has he come* ~?
- in negatives: *He hasn't come* ~; s. already; still; present perfect tense.

you (=one) *It's a nice record if* ~ *like modern music.*

young
- with reference to people: *He's* ∼;
s. old.

Z

zero article
- abstract nouns: *Information/news
is hard to get.*
- a place or means of transport as
defined by its purpose: *in/to pri-
son, hospital, school, church, bed,
by train, bus, car, plane;* N.B. also:
go/come home.

- meals: *We're going to have break-
fast/lunch/tea/dinner.*
- mass nouns: *Ice-cream is nice; I
like ice-cream.*
- personal pronouns: *That's my
book; It's mine.*
- plural units: *Cars are expensive.*
- topographical names; names of
people; titles; languages; proper
nouns: *I live in Bridge Street/Lon-
don/England;* N.B. *the* U.S.A.,
U.S.S.R., etc. *John rang me yesterday; Mr. Jones has arrived; I speak
English.*

4.3   Grammatical summary

1   Sentence types

1.1   **Types**
1. Declarative sentences.
2. Interrogative sentences:
– yes/no questions;
– question-word sentences. $\left.\right\}$ Affirmative and negative (P).
3. Imperative stentences:
– commands;
– polite requests.

1.2   **"Short" sentences**
1 Short answers (type: *(Yes,) I am*; *(No,) I can't* (P).
2. Short questions (type: *Are you? Can't you?*) (P).
3. Question tags (type: *You aren't afraid, are you?*) (R).

1.3   **Complexity**
1. Simple sentences, up to those containing two complements (P).
2. Compound sentences: coordination with *and* (P), *but* (P), *or* (P); without conjunction (R).
3. Complex sentences: sentences containing object-clauses (P), subject-clauses (type: *It is a pity that you cannot come*) (P), adverbial clauses of time (P), place (R), condition (P), cause/ reason (P), relative clauses (P).

2   Verbs

2.1   **Types**
1. Main verbs (see lexicon).
2. Copula: be (P).
semi-copulas:
become (P) *I may become a doctor*;
get (P) *He's getting old*;
fall (P) *He's fallen ill*;
feel (P) *I don't feel quite well*;
look (P) *You look very well*;

remain (R) *Will it remain dry today?*;
stay (P) *It won't stay dry for long.*
3. Auxiliaries and semi-auxiliaries:
– tense/aspect:
have, perfect and pluperfect (P);
be, present continuous and past continuous (P);
be going to, future (P);
will, future (P).
– Voice: *be* (R).
– Periphrasis: *do* (P).
– Modality:
can, ability, capability, capacity (P), possibility (P), permission
(R);
could, see *can*; also: suggestion (P);
be able to, ability, capability (P);
be going to, intention (P), future (P);
may, uncertainty (P), permission (P);
might, see *may*;
be allowed to, permission (P);
be supposed to, permission (R);
must, logical conclusion (P), obligation (R);
have to, obligation (P);
need (+not), absence of obligation (R);
ought to, advisability (R), right/wrong (R);
shall (in questions), offer (P), suggestion (P);
should, right/wrong (P), disapproval (P);
will, intention (P), request (P), capacity (P), future (P);
would, see *will*; also; enquiry (P), request (P).

2.2   **Forms**
1. Finite forms (P).
2. Infinitive:
– Plain infinitive (V_{inf}) with auxiliaries (P); with *let's* (P), *let me*
(R), *I'd rather* (P).
– Infinitive with *to* (V_{to}) with semi-auxiliaries (*have to, ought to,*
be going to, etc.) (P); with main verbs (*hate, like, try, want*)
(P); with predicative adjectives (how *nice,* be *sorry,* be *glad,*
be *delighted*) (P).
3. Imperative (P).
4. Past participle (V_{ed}): in perfect and pluperfect (P); in passive
(R); after causative *have* (P).
5. Present participle/gerund (V_{ing}): in continuous tenses (P); after
come (R), *enjoy* (R), *go* (R), *hate* (R), *like* (P), *remember* (R);
after prepositions (R).

2.3   **Voice**
1. Active (P).
2. Passive (R).

2.4   **Aspect**
1. Simple (P).
2. Perfect/pluperfect (P).
3. Continuous (P).

2.5   **Tense**
1. Present (P).
2. Past (P), including "modal past" of auxiliaries: *could* (P), *might* (P), *ought to* (R), *should* (P), *would* (P).
3. Future (P), with *will*, *be going to*, and continuous tenses of verbs of motion.

3   Nouns

3.1   **Number**
1. Singular (P).
2. Plural (P).

3.2   **Case**
1. Common case (P).
2. Genitive singular (-*'s*) of personal nouns (P).
For other (functional) distinction of cases, see division II of content-specification (3.3.1–3.3.5).

3.3   **Function**
1. Nouns as head of NP (P).
2. Attributive nouns, esp. material nouns (P).

4   Adjectives

4.1   **Function**
1. Attributive (P).
2. Predicative (P).

4.2   **Form**
1. Positive degree (P).

2. Comparative degree (*-er, more*) (P); irregular forms of those "irregulars" which occur in the lexicon.
3. Superlative degree (*-est, most*) (P); irregular forms of those "irregulars" which occur in the lexicon.

4.3 **Comparison**
1. Equality: as ... as (R).
2. Inequality: not so ... as (R); comparative + *than* (P); superlative (P).

5 Adverbs

5.1 **Form**
1. Derivation with *-ly* (P).
2. Non-derived adverbs, e.g. *soon, fast* (R/P): see lexicon.

5.2 **Comparison**
See under Adjectives.

6 Articles

1. Definite article: *the* (P).
2. Indefinite article: *a(n)* (P).
3. Absence of definite article in cases such as *to go to school, in summer, to have dinner* (P).

7 Pronouns (including pronominal adjectives)

1. Personal: subject forms and object forms (P).
2. Possessive:
   – adjectives: *my, your, their, etc.* (P);
   – pronouns: *mine, yours, theirs, etc*; used as complement (P), used as subject (R).
3. Demonstrative:
   – adjectives: *this, that, these, those, such* (P);
   – pronouns: *this, that, these, those* (P).

4. Interrogative:
- adjectives: *whose* (R), *what* (P), *which* (P);
- pronouns: *who* (P), *whom* (R), *whose* (R), *what* (P), *which* (P).
5. Relative: *who* (P), *whose* (R), *whom* (R), *which* (P), *that* (R), without relative pronoun (R).
6. Indefinite: *someone* (P), *somebody* (P), *no one* (P), *not ... anyone* (P), *nobody* (P), *everybody* (P), *something* (P), *nothing* (P), *everything* (P), *all* (as in: *They all went home*, and in: *I want all of it*) (P), *some* (as in: *Some of them went home*) (P), *any* (as in: *Have you got any money? I haven't any money*) (R), *it* (as in: *It rains*) (P).
7. Emphatic: *myself, yourself, etc.* (type: *I've done it myself*) (R).
8. Propword: *one* (type: *I like the red one better*) (P).

8 Numerals

1. Cardinal: up to 4 digits (P), up to 9 digits (R).
2. Ordinal: up to 2 digits (P).
Also: *half, quarter* (P).

9 Word order

9.1 Basic pattern
Subject-predicate-complement(s) (P).

9.2 Derived patterns
1. Yes/no-question pattern (P).
2. Wh- question pattern (P).
3. Negative sentence pattern with *not* (P).
4. Passive voice pattern (P).
5. Imperative pattern (P).
6. Indirect object replacement by to-adjunct (P).

9.3 Position of adverbials
The normal positions of the adverbials listed in the content-specification, excluding M_2 (P).

10 Word formation

1. Adverb-derivation with -*ly* (P).
2. Compounds and derivatives as listed in the content-specification (R/P).
3. Compounds and derivatives not listed in the content-specification as far as their meaning is fully predictable from component parts occurring in the content-specification (R).

5 Bibliography

K. Bung – The input-output relation in language behaviour. *CCC/EES* (73), 12, Strasbourg, 1973.
- The foreign language needs of waiters and hotel staff. *CCC/EES* (73), 16 rev., Strasbourg, 1973.
- The specification of objectives in a language learning system for adults. *CCC/EES* (73), 34, Strasbourg, 1973.
J. A. van Ek – Analysis of the problems involved in defining, in operational terms, a basic competence level (or threshold-level) in foreign language learning by adults. *CCC/EES* (72), 17, Strasbourg, 1972.*
- Proposal for the definition of a threshold-level in foreign language learning by adults. *CCC/EES* (72), 72, Strasbourg, 1972.*
- *Systems Development in Adult Language Learning, the Threshold-Level*, Council for Cultural Cooperation, Council of Europe, Strasbourg, 1975.
C. M. Lindvall – *Defining Educational Objectives*, Pittsburgh, 1969.
R. F. Mager – *Preparing Instructional Objectives*, Belmont, Cal., 1962.
R. Richterich – Analytical classification of the categories of adults needing to learn foreign languages. *CCC/EES* (71), 55, Strasbourg, 1971.*
- A model for the definition of language needs of adults learning a modern language. *CCC/EES* (72), 49, Strasbourg, 1972.*
J. L. M. Trim – Modern languages in adult education, with special reference to a projected European unit/credit system: consolidated report. *EES/Symposium 57*, 3, Strasbourg, 1973.
- Draft outline of a European unit/credit system for modern language learning by adults. *CCC/EES* (73), 9, Strasbourg, 1973.*
- Research and development programme for a European unit/credit system for modern language learning by adults: progress report. *CCC/EES* (73), 26, Strasbourg, 1973.
D. A. Wilkins – An investigation into the linguistic and situational content of the common core in a unit/credit system. *CCC/EES* (72), 67, Strasbourg, 1972.*

Studies marked * have been published together in *Systems Development in Adult Language Learning* by the Council for Cultural Cooperation, Council of Europe, Strasbourg, 1973.

Modern languages in adult education. *EES/Symposium 57*, 10, Strasbourg, 1974.

Schools Council Modern Language Project at the University of York:

A Syllabus for GCE O-Level Examinations in Russian (Draft).

A Syllabus for German Audio-Visual/Lingual Courses (Draft).

A GCE O-Level Syllabus for French (Draft).

Supplement: Threshold level and methodology

by L. G. Alexander

1 Introductory remarks

Threshold Level Specifications have profound implications for language course design and, by extension, for language teaching and learning. For this reason the term 'methodology' must be taken to refer both to course design and actual teaching and learning. While we must accept without question that there is no single "best method", we must also allow that not all methods are of equal value. There are many roads to Rome, but some are more direct than others and quite a number never arrive at all. When discussing methodology, our main concern must be cost effectiveness. The difficulty of learning a language should not be under-estimated and there are no short cuts, but this realization should never inhibit us from constantly seeking more effective (and therefore less time-consuming) ways of fulfilling this formidable undertaking. It is precisely this search that has led to the formulation of Threshold Level Specifications.

It is worth beginning any discussion of methodology with a broad definition of the term "language course". It is easier to say what a course isn't than what it is: the present Specifications, for instance, are not a language course; nor is any kind of syllabus; nor is a grammar book or a dictionary. All of these present some of the raw facts of language. A course differs from specifications and inventories in that it constitutes an attempt to process the raw facts of a language into an organized system which will facilitate its acquisition. (That is why it is rarely possible to learn a language directly from a grammar book or a dictionary.) At best, a language course can only lubricate the process of acquisition so that learning is motivated, enjoyable and effective. We must assume that most general courses will set out to communicate the four skills of understanding, speaking, reading and writing, though the degree to which each of these is developed may vary enormously. The challenge to the course designer is to create an integrated and above all teachable system which will develop these skills; the challenge to the teacher is to interpret the system creatively and adapt it to suit the needs of his class in order to communicate the four skills; the challenge to the learner is to acquire these skills to the limit of his potential in the time available.

Broadly speaking, course design can be considered under three headings: Why?, What? and How?

"Why?" refers to the establishment of priorities: Why am I going to do this and not that? We can only arrive at these priorities after we have taken into account all the *constraints* which will influence our decision. "What?" refers to *overall framework*: What am I going to teach?; and "How?" refers to *method*. These three headings, *Constraints*, *Overall framework* and *Method*, can provide a useful schema for discussion of the methodological implications of Threshold Level Specifications.

2   Constraints ("Why?")

In the Threshold Level Introduction (1.1.4) the communication need of the learner is established as an important constraint. In the context of course design as a whole, this must be seen as one of a large number of possible limitations which are too numerous to list exhaustively. But here, in random order, are some of the most important ones:

Age range: How old are the learners? Are they all the same age? Are there different age-groups in the same class?

Motivation: Why are they learning the language? Is it to achieve something highly specific, like passing an examination or doing a job? Or is it for some general reason: e.g. to occupy their spare time, or because the educational system requires it? Do they want to integrate with a foreign language community or not? Are they attending classes of their own volition or are they a "captive audience"?

Washback: To what extent does an external syllabus or examination influence the teaching/learning set-up? Is this influence desirable? If it is undesirable, can it be modified or altered, or does it have to be endured?

Student background: Do the learners have roughly the same educational background or not? How do they vary in terms of individual ability? Are they streamed into ability groups? What is their past learning history: are they zero beginners or false beginners?

Teacher background: How fluent is the teacher's command of the language he is teaching? How much training has he had? How many opportunities does he have for re-training? How did the teacher acquire command of the foreign language he is teaching? How does the teacher's learning experience influence his choice of materials?

Opportunity: Will the learners put the foreign language to immediate use while they are still learning? Will they hope to put the language to use after a course of study? Are they unlikely to have any opportunity to use the foreign language in the foreseeable future?

Materials: Does the teacher have freedom of choice, or does he have to use what is available? What resources are there in terms of hardware (tape-recorders, overhead projectors, etc.) or software (tapes, slides, etc.)?

Time (duration): How much time is allocated to language study? Is it a short-term course (e.g. six weeks) or a long-term course (e.g. up to eight years)? What is the total number of teaching/learning hours available? How much extra time can be assumed for homework? How much time has to be realistically written off for holidays, etc.?

Time (frequency): How is the time distributed: e.g. how many lessons are there per week and how long is each lesson?

Physical: How many students are there in a class? What are the class conditions? Is there a lot of outside noise? Is the classroom comfortable (not too hot, cold, etc.)?

Day-to-day: At what time of the day are lessons held: e.g. early in the day or after the students have done a full day's work, etc.? How many other commitments (work, study, etc.) has the learner got? How many hours per day is the teacher expected to teach – including extra-institutional work?

Over and above these factors, there are publishing constraints to the extent that course designers have to develop materials within a limited number of pages and there are the constraints imposed by page layout and design. The likely cost of the end-product to the consumer may seriously affect methodological decisions (determining such questions as, for example, the number of tapes to be made available) and may take priority over everything else.

Threshold Level Specifications indicate for a defined public what has to be taught if effective communication is to be achieved. The problem for the course designer and the teacher is how to manipulate this information, given the constraints which must be taken into account. While it is possible to define a large target audience which shares a number of these constraints, there will always be variations and conflicts even within quite small groups of learners. Teacher and learner must resolve their conflicts together by constantly modifying materials and techniques and by constantly responding imaginatively and intelligently to an ever-changing situation.

3   Overall framework ("What?")

In Threshold Level Specifications the principle of selection has already been applied: *what* we have to teach is clearly defined, but, drawing on this definition, the individual user must decide on his own priorities and must develop his own framework for a course, while at the same time ensuring that the specifications are adequately covered. The elementary nature of the utterances we are trying to teach at zero and near-zero should not lull us into thinking that a rudimentary framework will provide an adequate vehicle: quite the contrary. The simpler the utterances to be taught, the more complex the framework that will be required to carry them.

3.1 Orthodox specifications compared with Threshold Level

Orthodox Specifications (e.g. as often defined by Ministries of Education and published as syllabuses in different parts of the world) usually consist of two inventories: one grammatical and the other lexical. The implication is that learning a language involves the mastery of a grammatical system and the concurrent acquisition of a serviceable "minimum adequate" vocabulary. Threshold Level Specifications, by comparison, bring together a number of different factors which are considered indispensable for verbal communication. As is clearly indicated (see Threshold Level Introduction, 1.1.1) the objectives are behavioural (note that this term has nothing to do with behaviouristic stimulus/response language teaching techniques). Verbal communication is seen to be highly complex (compared with the components of the Orthodox Syllabus) for it is recognized that not only are there "grammatical rules" but rules which are part of the system of social behaviour (which we may think of as "rules for use"): what we say and how we say it depends on such factors as what the speakers want to *do* through language, what their relationship is, what the setting is and so on. In Threshold Level Specifications the grammatical and lexical components remain limited, but they are seen as only a small part of the total system of language behaviour: the Specifications set out to identify and describe many of the different factors which influence verbal communication.

Of course, the very best language courses based on Orthodox Specifications set out to teach the skills of understanding, speaking, reading and writing, and to that extent they are likely to have much in common with materials based on a functional/notional approach. Furthermore, the results from teaching a good conventional course may not necessarily differ very much from those that might be obtained from a good functional/notional course.

However, Threshold Level Specifications are certain to give rise to a different kind of framework as a basis for course construction because the starting point stems from an analysis of language needs in communicative rather than grammatical terms. In a conventional course, grammatical items are often taught because they are considered important in themselves. By comparison, the main criterion for choosing and teaching an item in a functional/notional approach can only be its communicative validity. In this discussion it is therefore reasonable to consider (together with their advantages and shortcomings) the following:

> The structural framework
> The situational application of the structural framework

Possible alternative frameworks
The situational application of a functional/notional approach

3.2   The structural framework

With the development of audio-visual and audio-lingual courses from the
mid 1950s onwards, there has been a move away from formal grammar lessons and the presentation of complete paradigms. Courses have been increasingly based on graded sequences of structures, a form of organization which
is known as "structural grading". In such an approach the steps are carefully
ordered in terms of apparent increasing difficulty. Teachers using such
materials have been conditioned to accept (but not altogether unquestion-
ingly) certain prescribed sequences. Although these are arrived at intuitively,
there is sufficient agreement in most language courses to allow us to refer
to "structural grading" as if it were some kind of objective system. For instance, most English courses begin with *be + noun/adjective* combinations,
proceeding to *have/have got + noun/adjective* combinations and then on to
the present continuous, the simple present, the simple past, the present perfect, and so on. In various parts of the world this progression is often reinforced by ministerial syllabuses in which these sequences are outlined fairly
precisely and prescribed textbooks are usually required to conform to the
syllabus. The result (in textbook terms), is a logico-grammatical framework
of interrelated pattern sequences. When one sequence is played out, a new
one is taken up until an extensive area of language has been covered. The
assumption always is that it is easier to teach *I am tired* than *I might have
been able to see you earlier if you had given me a ring*: structural grading can
be simply described as the steps which link these two poles.

The framework described is *linear*. But cyclical variations are also possible.
In a cyclical structural framework, a particular area of difficulty may be de-
liberately re-introduced at different intervals (say, every twenty lessons) so
that a little more information is added each time. Thus, for example, the
present perfect may first be introduced in the form "have been", then later
in conjunction with "just", "already" and "yet", then again in conjunction
with "since" and "for"; at an even later stage the student may be introduced
to the present perfect continuous. The system of structural grading has been
applied with increasing sophistication and it is not unusual to find beginners'
courses which are ordered in a linear fashion, followed by pre-intermediate
and intermediate courses which are ordered in a cyclical fashion.

The system has led to a greater efficiency in the classroom and is a considerable improvement on the formal presentation of paradigms. However, constant application has brought many weaknesses to light and this has provided
some of the impetus for the development of alternative functional/notional
syllabuses. The main weaknesses can be described as follows:

(a) The student cannot always see the practical application of what he is
     learning to real life. While focus on the grammar can produce reasonable
     utterances like *There is a glass on the table*, it can (and frequently does)

give rise to patent absurdities, such as *There is a green book behind your head.* In the case of the adult student, in particular, this can only set up a resistance to learning in the classroom. The learner, who may have been motivated to attend classes for wholly practical reasons, can easily find himself producing utterances which will be far removed from what he really wants to say.

(b) Structural grading attempts to communicate a large part of the grammatical system, often giving as much emphasis to low frequency items as to high frequency ones. Though it is obviously based on a selection of language, it aims at completeness. Consequently, the build-up is slow. The student rarely reaches the past tense by the end of Book One, so that after a year's study he may still be unable to formulate a simple but obviously useful statement like *I went to the cinema last night.* On the other hand, he may have put a good deal of effort into learning and practising the various uses of the impersonal pronoun *its* "for the sake of completeness".

(c) The definition of what is "easy" and "difficult" is usually made wholly in terms of structural progression. Thus a student may be taught to say *I want a cup of coffee* simply because the focus in that particular lesson happens to be on the simple present with stative verbs, but he is denied access to *I'd like a cup of coffee* because the implied use of the "subjunctive" *would* is arbitrarily defined as "too difficult at this stage". As a result, the student is not generally made aware of the stylistic register and the kind of language that is really appropriate to any given situations.

3.3 The situational application of the structural framework

The system of structural grading has been widely applied through the presentation of "situations", an approach that has come to be referred to loosely as "situational teaching". In fact, this term covers a variety of approaches which can be described as follows:

> Classroom situational
> Centre of interest situational
> Structurally controlled situational
> Story-line situational

3.3.1 Classroom situational: This approach takes the classroom situation as the basis for language acquisition and is an extremely common way of beginning a language. It usually takes the form of identifying the objects in the classroom and naming them and makes extensive use of classroom props for a variety of activities. The approach barely merits the term "situational" at all, for it has little to do with ordinary human situations. While the classroom *can* be exploited in positive and useful ways, it is, by definition, an extremely limited environment. It is perhaps inevitable that it often encourages a totally absurd use of language *(Is this a pen? Have you got a nose? Are you a boy? How many ears have you got? Stand up. Go to the door. What are you doing – I am going to the door. Etc.)*. This kind of language is often reflected in textbooks at the beginners' level and is widely taught. More than any other single factor, it probably accounts for loss of motivation to learn a language and for early drop-out (in the case of non-captive student audiences).

3.3.2   Centre of interest situational: In this form of organization the course designer attempts to predict the kinds of situations the student might encounter in real life and seeks to prepare him for them, taking such obvious themes as "the post-office", "the Customs", etc. The situations may or may not be structurally graded depending on the framework the course designer has adopted. Language study is usually derived from each situation. While dialogues based on well-selected centres of interest can obviously have a practical value in that they provide a lot of useful language, they are presented on the demonstrably false assumption that the student will be able to function in the same way when he finds himself in similar circumstances. It is naïve to suppose that we can predict precisely what people will say in such situations; nor is there any way in which the student can learn to cope with the unexpected. Furthermore, although a great many such situations may look different on the surface (e.g. "the restaurant" may seem to be very remote from "buying tickets"), in fact they often give rise to the same kind of language. This suggests we should be looking for communicative features which many such situations share rather than treating each one as if it were linguistically discrete and somehow unique.

3.3.3   Structurally controlled situational: This approach takes a structure or a set of structures out of the graded sequence as its starting point, rather than a "centre of interest". The structure is then "situationalized" or – to use the accepted term – "contextualized". From the course designer's point of view, the situation itself is relatively unimportant: it is the structure that takes precedence over everything else and the main purpose of the situation is to illustrate a grammatical point. Thus, for example, if the course designer wants to illustrate the use of "have been to . . ." he will write a situation round this structure, trying as far as possible to make the use of the form sound inevitable and correct. This approach has the advantage that the student is exposed to only a small amount of new language at any one time. However, the situations tend to be random and inconsequential. Furthermore, in real life, situations never develop within the confines of carefully pre-selected structural items.

3.3.4   Story-line situational: Both the centre of interest approach and the structurally controlled situational approach may have some kind of story-line superimposed on them. A particular unifying theme, involving a character or characters, is set up at the beginning of the course and then developed through a series of episodes, which (in the case of zero beginners' courses) are usually unconnected. The unifying theme may concern a family, or (say) a protagonist who has just arrived in a foreign country and whose subsequent stay is carefully plotted.

Story-lines can be suitable in children's beginners' (up to the age of 12+) or in multi-media courses aimed at adults where thematic continuity is paramount. In the case of children, they provide a useful focal point; in the case of adult multi-media courses, they may have an entertainment value. However, the story-line generally palls in the case of adult zero beginners' textbooks, the antics of the characters becoming increasingly irrelevant to the needs of the learner as the course progresses. The acute linguistic restrictions make it impossible to present anything but the most mundane situations; the development of the story-line is extremely slow and ponderous; few – if any – course designers have the necessary literary skills to create and sustain a story-line which will really appeal to an adult. While the presentation may be attractive in the first book, it merely becomes irritating when the student has got beyond the elementary level.

3.4 Possible alternative frameworks
The behavioural (rather than grammatical) emphasis of Threshold Level Specifications provides us with the means of developing alternative frameworks, but it will be a long time before we have a sufficient variety of such forms of organization to be able to assess their relative efficacy. At the time of writing (January 1977) the models available remain largely theoretical and, particularly in the case of zero beginners' courses, pose a formidable challenge to course designers. Possible forms of organization might be:

> A functional framework
> A structural/functional framework
> A functional/structural framework
> Thematic areas

3.4.1   A functional framework: While it is theoretically possible to conceive of a framework which consists wholly of "language acts", it seems unlikely that such a model could have more than a limited application (in phrase books, for instance). A framework which took functions like identifying, reporting, correcting, asking, expressing agreement and disagreement, etc., as its starting point and consciously ignored the grammatical implications of these acts would be extremely deficient, for the student also needs to operate the grammatical system to communicate adequately. Ultimately, we cannot ignore the need to master grammatical paradigms if fluency is to be achieved. Furthermore, there are dangers implicit in functional labelling; exponents of functions are not necessarily discrete. For example, *It's hot* (with subtle variations in intonation) can be an exponent of describing, complaining, reporting, explaining, correcting, denying, agreeing, disagreeing, and so on. It would be misleading to assume that the student could learn a codified set of exponents for particular functions which would serve in all circumstances.

It should also be noted that the exponents of some functions are merely phrases which can be learnt by heart (e.g. "Cheers!", the exponent of "proposing a toast", is a fixed expression), while other functions relate to total grammatical systems and require an enormous amount of time and effort to master (e.g. the exponents of "Asking"). There are other exponents which are part of the grammatical system but which we may wish to teach early as fixed phrases: for instance, we may wish to teach "I'd like ..." early but not all its paradigms.

3.4.2   A structural/functional framework: The biggest challenge facing course designers is to devise a framework which makes full use of the communicative potential of a functional/notional approach while at the same time enabling the learner to master and operate the grammatical system.

One possible model might involve setting out with grammatical objectives which are interpreted behaviourally: the emphasis being on the *function* the grammar represents, not just the grammar itself. In such an approach it might be possible to retain a structurally graded sequence, but to accrue to it ungraded-but-semantically-related patterns. Thus, if the first lesson were concerned with "personal identification" (in relation to names and jobs) it would be possible to teach *What's your name?* (structurally graded) and *What do you do? (for a living)?* (structurally ungraded) in the same lesson. The low frequency and stylistically clumsy *What are you?* (which strict structural grading would demand) would not be taught at all. *What do you do?* (which would be delayed in a rigidly graded course until the simple present had been reached) would be taught in preference because this is the stylistically acceptable norm when considering an objective of this kind.

A factor any course designer using this model would have to guard against is the possibility that orthodox structural grading might still tend to dominate. A truly communicative approach (implying as it does diversity of utterance) may make such an orderly progression difficult. It could be argued that if the control system is too orderly, the communicative objectives would take second place or get lost altogether.

3.4.3   A functional/structural framework: This might involve setting out with behavioural objectives and deriving language practice from them. Teaching people how to do things would take precedence over the grammar, but the grammatical components of each communicative undertaking would be practised intensively. The student would learn "a bit of everything at the same time". How well course designers, teachers and students will be able to cope with a consciously or apparently unsystematic acquisition of grammar remains to be seen. The approach may, nonetheless, lead to interesting developments.

3.4.4   Thematic areas: Another possible framework might be to deal with a particular "thematic area" over a number of lessons. For example, "Finding the way" might be considered a thematic area of this kind. In this approach the student would be carefully guided through the steps involved in this particular area. Such a sequence would cover the use of a few ordinal numbers; distinguishing between left and right with reference to simple maps *(The first turning on the left, The second turning on the right, etc.)*; giving and understanding simple directions to places *(Where's the nearest bank? It's down the first street on the left)*; handling prepositions *(It's opposite, near, next to, etc.)*; handling the imperative *(Take the first turning ... Go down ...)*; coping with landmarks *(Go down this street until you come to a cinema)*; learning to cope with indoor and outdoor locations; coping with directions as a pedestrian or as a motorist; coping with modes of transport and distances. Thus the student would be actively taught how to, for example, find his way from an analysis of what "finding the way" actively involves. Within such a sequence some of the grammatical components have to be actively assimilated (e.g. prepositional relationship) while others (connectives like *until you come to ...*) would be learnt as fixed phrases. The problem in this approach is to define the thematic areas. There may also be a danger that in isolating particular areas we fail to get continuity in the course as a whole.

The system of grading can still be implemented in a functional/notional framework. For instance, it might be possible to devise a cyclical approach which allows the learner to acquire simple utterances first and more complex ones at a later stage. Thus, for example, when learning how to ask for permission, the learner can set out with a relatively simple and straightforward form like *Can I (borrow your umbrella), please?* and through a process of recycling eventually learns to cope with a really complex request for permission like, for example, *I hope you don't mind my asking, but could I possibly (borrow your umbrella), please?* However, grading, in a functional/notional approach, can be an altogether different kind of undertaking, as will be seen in section 3.5.4.

3.5 The situational application of a functional/notional approach

In the situational application of the structural framework (3.3) such considerations as settings or roles were seen to be of little consequence, the main concern being to present a structure and/or a particular centre of interest. In a functional/notional approach, "situational teaching" cannot be so narrowly defined and takes on an altogether different meaning: it is not merely a presentation device for achieving a limited objective, but describes the sum total of all the aspects of communication which occur within any given context. It is used to cover not only grammar and lexis, but functions, notions and their exponents, settings and topics, social and psychological roles, and style and range of expression. Threshold Level Specifications fully indicate the major factors that come into play in a situation.

3.5.1 Functions, notions and their exponents: Threshold Level concentrates on functions with a wide operational force: that is those which can recur in a large number of different situations. Thus, for example, "expressing preference" can figure in any number of different situational contexts: e.g. shopping, eating out, hotels, travel, etc. This realization emphasizes the undesirability of presenting different centres of interest as if they were linguistically discrete from each other (see 3.3.2). A functional/notional awareness makes it possible for the student to realize that an utterance which applies in one situation can arise equally well in another (see Threshold Level Introduction, 1.1.5). Language functions may apply to a wide variety of topics and events. What varies is the choice of specific notions which is determined by each topic. For example:

Language function and general notion	*Specific notion*	*Topic*
I'd like {	size 14	(shopping)
	a steak	(restaurant)
	a double room	(hotel)
	a return ticket	(travel)

3.5.2   Settings and topics: Two aspects can often be discerned in any setting: the *concrete* and the *general*. The concrete aspect can actually influence and even determine the choice of items the speaker will use. Thus, a ticket office, a restaurant, or a hotel reception desk can be defined as "concrete" in particular circumstances. The general aspect, on the other hand, does not necessarily influence the choice of items the speakers will use: e.g. a beach, a bus stop or a dinner table can provide a background for an open-ended conversation or argument. A single setting may be at one and the same time "concrete" and "general". For example, a restaurant can influence the choice of items the speakers will use when they are ordering food, etc., and at the same time provide a background for the open-ended discussion of a topic. In some settings the "concrete element" tends to predominate and open-ended conversation is unlikely (e.g. a theatre box office); in others the "open-ended element" predominates (e.g. a beach).

This distinction is important because the concrete aspect of a setting can lead to a *transaction*. A transaction can be rapidly identified because the language events that will take place are predictable with reasonable accuracy (excluding, of course, the incidence of the unexpected). For example, a group of people may enter a restaurant; they will be told by, for example, a waiter if the restaurant is full; otherwise they will be asked how many people they want a table for; they will be conducted to a table; then they will be brought a menu; then the waiter will return to take their order, and so on. Much of the language that will be used can be predicted fairly accurately. This kind of *transaction* must be distinguished from the open-ended discussion of a topic:

concrete aspect   →   transaction
general aspect   →   open-ended conversation or argument

The relevance of this distinction to language teaching will be immediately apparent. In teaching "conversation", we have to distinguish between transactions (the steps of which are to some extent foreseeable and therefore relatively easier to teach) and open-ended conversation and argument (the direction of which is not foreseeable). A transaction can be reduced to an algorithmic model indicating the predictable sequence of events. Such a model is known as a "praxeogram". The transactional praxeogram is not only relevant to the general learner but also to the specialized learner who is not concerned with acquiring language but with performing efficiently a well-defined task which involves limited use of language: e.g. operating a machine, serving in a restaurant, etc. A transaction can differ from a centre of interest (described earlier, 3.3.2) because it is concerned only with a narrowly defined sequence of events, not something more general like "the post-office" or "the restaurant".

Settings which act really as a backdrop obviously play a less important role in an open-ended conversation or argument. We should also note that a general conversation can be merely an exchange of information or shift rapidly into argument. For instance, from a straight exchange about, for example, today's weather, we may move directly into an argument involving disagreement about the state of the weather yesterday, last week or last year.

3.5.3   Social, sexual and psychological roles: The relationship between the speakers and their attitudes to each other greatly affects the choice of items and must be clearly established in all situations. It can matter greatly whether the speakers are friends or strangers, male or female, officials or shop assistants, old or young, etc. And this awareness must be built into situations even at the earliest level to prevent the learner from making social blunders and enable him to handle even simple forms with some degree of subtlety.

3.5.4   Style and range: How the speakers will address each other will be a direct by-product of their social and psychological roles. Speakers may adopt formal or informal styles depending on their relationship and they may express themselves in a variety of ways. This "variety of ways" we can think of in terms of a "cline" which can range between extremes like the following: certain/tentative/uncertain or positive/speculative/unpositive. The following three statements will provide an elementary example of what is meant by range:

He's 24 years old (positive).
He may be about 24 years old (tentative).
I'm not sure how old he is (unpositive/uncertain).

Questions of style and range play an important role in distinguishing between lower and higher levels of linguistic ability.

3.5.5   Grading: In a structural framework "grading" is confined narrowly to structures and vocabulary (see 3.2). We have also seen how, in turn, it might be possible to grade functions (see 3.4.4). However, an even broader application of "grading" can be made in the situational realization of a functional/notional approach: complete situations can be. graded in order

The situational application of a functional approach to language teaching: summary

General functional categories	Notions	Setting and topics	Social, sexual and psychological roles	Style and range	Grammar and lexis
Language acts	What?	Where?	Who?	How?	With what means?
1. Factual 2. Intellectual 3. Emotional 4. Moral 5. Suasive 6. Social	General: Often abstract: appropriate to a large variety of topics and situations	Concrete: transaction General: open-ended conversation or argument	Friends, strangers, officials, etc.	Style: formal informal Range: "cline": certain – tentative – uncertain	As they arise in each situation
Two types of exponents: 1. Fixed phrases 2. "Grammatical system"	Specific: Directly determined by the choice of the topic				
Examples					
Inquiring about	the availability of tickets	Concrete: box office	Stranger – official	Formal	As in example
Are there	*any tickets for tonight's performance?*				
Inquiring about	the existence of theatres	General	Friend – friend	–	As in example
Are there	*any good theatres in your area?*				

of increasing difficulty and complexity. Perhaps an example of the way students can learn to handle situations of increasing complexity will make the application of this clear.

Let us suppose that at various stages in a beginners' course, students learn how to describe people in terms of appearance, character, age and skills; suppose they learn to make comparisons and express likes and dislikes. What the students are learning to do can be applied in situations of increasing complexity. For example, early in the course the students may role play an interview situation in which Student A takes the part of the prospective employer and interviews Student B, the prospective employee, by asking him questions. At a later stage in the course the interview situation can develop into a more complex role-play activity consisting of four main situations:

1. Students A and B (prospective employers) interview Student C (prospective employee) and ask him questions.
2. Student C leaves the room and Students A and B talk about his suitability for the job.
3. Student D (the next prospective employee) is interviewed by Students A and B.
4. Student D leaves the room and Students A and B compare the suitability of Students C and D for the job.

Such a situation can be re-introduced a number of times even to a very advanced level with increasing demands being made on the participants. The principle of "grading" can thus be applied in a quite novel way.

The way the components of a situation interact is summarized in the table on p. 160.

4   Method ("How?")

Explicit recommendations about the way language might actually be taught are well beyond the scope of this document. Threshold Level Specifications are sufficiently flexible to allow for the development of many parallel and radically different frameworks and methods. However, there are in the specifications implications which will apply to all kinds of language courses, however diverse the approaches may be. All courses based on functional/notional models must take as their starting point that communication must be taught and is therefore the primary objective, not merely the by-product of other objectives. It is worth considering briefly some of the problems which course designers who are attempting to implement functional/notional principles are likely to have in common. These will include:

Lesson organization
Transfer
Presentation

The teaching of grammar
Receptive and productive skills
Correctness
Testing

4.1 Lesson organization

The structural/lexical syllabus has as its ultimate aim the acquisition of a grammatical system together with a serviceable vocabulary. The structural grading sequence itself dictates the *pace* at which the student will proceed: the course designer is free to speed up or slow down the build-up of structures in accordance with the type of learner he is addressing. Alternative forms of organization, through the application of Threshold Level Specifications, will greatly alter this fairly straightforward approach to *pacing*. Any consideration of pacing is likely to bring with it the need to consider the possibility of individualized study to enable learners to proceed at varying speeds. Some kind of "route planning" may have to be developed which allows the false beginner to skip certain exercises, while at the same time providing the slow learner with additional material.

4.2 Transfer

This can be defined as the ability to use language acquired in the classroom to meet actual needs in real-life situations. It is singly the most important factor in the language learning process, for the learner's success is measured according to the extent he can use language in actual situations. As the emphasis in these specifications is on *communication*, it follows that transfer (often ignored in the structurally based course) will be a key factor in course design. Transfer can take two basic forms: *actual* and *simulated*.

4.2.1   Actual transfer: Questions can be directed at the learner which relate to his own experiences. For example, if the subject of a dialogue is a visit to a cinema, the learner might be asked when he last visited a cinema, how much he paid for his seat, who he went with, where he sat, what he saw, how he enjoyed the film, and so on. This is *actual transfer* because the student is responding truthfully in a conversational context. This kind of transfer carries with it the possibility of student-imposed language: the student should be able to add items as and when he needs them. Thus, if the topic of the lesson is jobs and the student wants to say what he actually does or intends to do for a living, he can ask the teacher for the appropriate English word(s).

4.2.2   Simulated transfer: This involves role playing and improvising in particular situations so that patterns learnt in one context are re-combined to serve the exigencies of another. (The "common core" principle described in the Threshold Level Introduction, section 1.1.5, allows for precisely this kind of possibility.) A student may be asked to *pretend* that he is in a particular situation and he has to respond accordingly. He may be required to act in his own persona or in the persona of someone else. For example, we may set up a situation in which Student A (acting in his own persona) is buying a pair of shoes from Student B (acting in the persona of a shop assistant) and is inquiring about size, price, colour, suitability and so on. Again there is scope for student-imposed language. Such a simulated situation can occur very early in a course so it follows that a good deal of scene setting will be in the student's own language.

4.2.3   *Presentation:* It is reasonable to ask how a functional/notional approach will affect the audio-visual methodology commonly used in structurally based beginners' courses. Audio-visual methodology has the great advantage of enabling teachers and students to operate monolingually for the most part right from the beginning of a course. At a later stage there may be a transition to audio-lingual presentation when students become less dependent on pictures to understand meaning and more dependent on language itself. There is no reason why this principle should not continue in functionally based courses. It will still be possible to present situations audio-visually or audio-lingually according to level. However, as has already been noted (4.2.2) role-playing activities will require the use of the students' own language in the classroom for scene-setting purposes. This means that multilingual classes will become more difficult to conduct. Only different language-editions of a particular course (in which rubrics are in the students' own language) may get round this problem.

4.4   The teaching of grammar

When using structurally based courses, teachers generally debate whether they should drill new language patterns before presenting a situation or after presenting one. This does not alter the fact that patterns are acquired for their own sake, since the ultimate objective of the course is the acquisition of the grammatical system. As we have seen, in Threshold Level Specifications this is only part of the objective. It follows that we do not need to acquire grammatical patterns unless we intend to put them to immediate use. This may well be the criterion for selecting grammatical items and practising them in functionally based material. We must therefore think of grammar teaching within the context of communication. From "grammar-to-communication" might be seen as a three-part activity:

Practice   →   Practice context   →   Role playing/improvisation

4.4.1   *Practice* may involve the acquisition of a paradigm which has been isolated because of its relevance within a communicative framework. When practising *be* and verb forms, students have to learn how to (a) make affirmative statements, (b) make negative statements, and (c) handle question and answer forms. For example, paradigms involving the use of *there is* may be practised in this way *(There is ... There isn't ... Is there ...?)*.

4.4.2   Practice context: Once the student has understood and become
fluent in using a particular form, he can practise it within a context. To pursue
the example of *There is* given in 4.4.1, the student might be presented with
a tourist map in which certain buildings are indicated, and controlled
exchanges may be based on this context (e.g. *Is there a bank near here? Yes,
there's one in West Street*). The raw structure previously acquired is now
being put to use in a controlled way.

4.4.3   Role playing/improvisation: The final phase is to get the student
to role play and improvise a situation which (a) makes use of the structure
that has just been acquired and (b) enables the student to use functions and
structures he has previously learnt. A situation involving, for example, actual
street maps would enable students to put the *There is* structure already practised (see 4.4.1 and 4.4.2) to further (simulated) use in suitably devised situations.

4.5   Receptive and productive skills
An attempt is made at Threshold Level to define the student's receptive command of language by marking certain items "R". But it is clear that while
the learner may control what he wishes to say, he can never have any control
over the language other people will use. This means that he will have to be
trained to understand the gist of what people are saying even at the earliest
stages of learning and this is recognized in these Specifications. This implies
that the student may have to be trained to "get the gist" by being presented
with materials which are beyond his productive command. Such materials
may be devised by the course designer or taken from authentic sources.

4.6   Correctness
The paramount aim in a communicative course is to enable students to communicate effectively. In traditional courses correctness is sometimes over-
emphasized to the extent that errors in pronunciation and/or grammar are
often considered a serious matter whether they interfere with communication
or not. Using a language may be considered to be a performing skill: as with
any other skill, performing ability will vary greatly from individual to individual. It may be a waste of time to demand near-native perfection from per-
formers who will never be able to provide it. Our aim should be to ensure
that the misuse of language is not so serious as to obscure communicative
intentions. While we must always draw the line at wholly unacceptable
utterances, the degree of error we are prepared to tolerate is bound to vary
in accordance with the abilities of individual learners. "Defective but effective
communication" may be a reasonable aim if it means our students are not
to be discouraged and defeated by the demands of perfection.

4.7   Testing
Threshold Level Specifications can be manipulated to yield criteria for testing. Ideally, testing objectives should be the same as teaching objectives, so

there is no conflict between the two activities. Much of the language testing that is conducted in relation to structurally based courses tends to divide language up into separate compartments, from "sound discrimination" to "multiple choice comprehension", and this carries with it the implication that language should be taught in this way. But what has been conveniently evolved for rapid objective marking may not be the ideal tool from a teaching point of view. It is possible that entirely new kinds of tests will have to be developed to accompany functionally based courses, for we are ultimately concerned not with how much the student knows, but how well he performs. Techniques used for teaching may then be very similar to those used for testing. The possibility that continual assessment (to include self-assessment) should be a standard part of course design is something to be considered.

4.8   Conclusion

Perhaps in the past we over-simplified the business of language learning/teaching and were not particularly intimidated by it. If in the present we are swinging the other way, it is right we should be intimidated and possibly rise to the challenge. Books like *The Threshold Level* are intended to be helpful tools for our use. At the same time we should be wary of attaching to them any mystique or regarding them as sacrosanct. Though language may be conveniently codified for reference purposes, it retains that resilient flexibility that made it language in the first place. And this is something we should never lose sight of.